101
Trailblazing
Women of
Air and Space

Aviators and Astronauts

Cover Photograph Credits

Clockwise starting upper left:
Lt. j.g. *La'Shanda R. Holmes*, first Black American female helicopter pilot in the United States Coast Guard, in front of a MH-65 Dolphin helicopter at Air Station Los Angeles, August 17, 2010. (U.S. Coast Guard archive. Photographer Petty Officer 1st Class, Adam Eggers)

Japanese Aerospace Exploration Agency JAXA astronaut, *Naoko Yamazaki*, second Japanese woman to fly in space. (NASA archival photograph)

Captain *Judy Rice* on Epic Flight Academy flight line. (Courtesy Epic Flight Academy)

Dawn sky/cloud background photograph by Penny Rafferty Hamilton. Cover Design by Patricia Shapiro.

Praise for 101 Trailblazing Women of Air and Space

"Hamilton's latest book does an excellent job of recognizing the work of many amazing women throughout the history of aviation. Women whose work has too often gone unrecognized, until now. AOPA appreciates Hamilton's dedication to aviation and to highlighting those who have paved the way for others." - **Mark Baker, Aircraft Owners & Pilots Association (AOPA) President and CEO.**

"Throughout aviation's history women have excelled and made essential contributions to the success and advancement of aviation. The trailblazers shared in Hamilton's book(s) serve as perpetual inspiration for those who come after." **Amy Spowart, President and CEO, National Aviation Hall of Fame.**

"We encourage the next generation of young women, (and men), to explore aviation and space careers. This is the perfect book with worldwide appeal to inspire our future workforce." **Kim Stevens, Vice-President National Coalition of Aviation and Space Education (NCASE).**

"It is always a joy to read about inspiring female pilots and astronauts and Penny Hamilton never fails to deliver." **Jacqueline Boyd, Ph.D., Chair, Amelia Earhart Memorial Fund, The Ninety-Nines, Inc.**

"True stories of aviation and aerospace women with 'the right stuff!' are always inspiring and important to read." – **Ben Sclair, Publisher, General Aviation News.**

"If a girl can see it, she can be it. All it takes is a young girl to see one woman who's a pilot to know it's possible. This inspiring book is chock full of possibilities"- **MayCay Beeler, Certified Flight Instructor, Award-winning author, and record-setting Aviator.**

"What a great look at the International women who blazed trails in sky and space." **Patty Wagstaff, three-time U.S. National Aerobatics Champion and Inductee International Aerospace Hall of Fame.**

"Kudos for this important book promoting the many International women blazing sky trails." **David Morris, CFII and editor of Nebraska PIREPS.**

"Penny Hamilton writes women into aviation history. As she does, she demonstrates that these trailblazers were ordinary people – who inspire us. They did it and you can do it, too!" **Jill Tietjen, award-winning author,** *Her Story* **and** *Hollywood: Her Story***, inductee into the Colorado Women's and Colorado Authors' Halls of Fame.**

"This new book is packed with inspiring stories and photos of fascinating women in history. A fun and easy read!" **Barb Lundy, listed in the** *Directory of Poets and Fiction Writers***, and author of** *The Fiction of Stone.*

"This book is a great contribution to the aviation and aerospace community." **John King, Co-founder of King Schools.**

101 Trailblazing Women of Air and Space

Aviators and Astronauts

Penny Rafferty Hamilton, Ph.D.

Foreword by Captain Judith "Judy" Rice

MOUNTAINTOP
LEGACY PRESS

The author has made every effort to acknowledge sources and individuals, where appropriate. All capitalization, italics, and other emphasis markings appear as in the cited source or as received by the author. If any information is incorrectly attributed or references/citations are incorrect, please inform the author so the information can be updated correctly in future editions.

Trailblazing Women of Air and Space
First Edition
Copyright @ 2021, Penny Rafferty Hamilton, Ph.D.

Published by Mountaintop Legacy Press

ISBN: 978-0-578-30725-1

This book is dedicated to our
World War II Women Airforce Service Pilots (WASP).

FOREWORD

Yesterday is gone. Tomorrow has not yet come. We have only today. Let us begin. ~ Mother Teresa

By Captain Judith "Judy" Rice

The women within these pages accomplished their dream. They did not set out to be trailblazers. Their true stories are testimony of determination, regardless of the obstacles. These women are your models for success.

My personal journey began with hearing these lies. "You are a girl. Good girls do not fly." You may have heard similar words from a parent, teacher, or peer, as I had. I dreamt of flying as long as I can remember. Hearing these devastating words, I kept my dream a secret and my self-doubt grew. Your self-doubt might be growing, as well.

I was a "good girl." As an adult, I had a wonderfully fulfilling career as a special education specialist and enjoyed being a mom with a great son. Though, occasionally, thoughts of my dream would surface again. I quickly pushed them down inside.

It took my son's encouragement and 40 years to gain the courage for a flight lesson. This was the beginning of my journey of discovery. When it came time to solo the airplane, I was terrified, unsure if I could safely command the airplane. After all, those old lies played over again in my mind. "Good girls do not fly." Through this experience of flying the airplane all by myself, I developed self-confidence. And, for the first time, I gained command of my destiny.

My mission and passion quickly became a role model for educators using aviation while teaching science, technology, engineering, arts, and mathematics (now called STEAM). I was also determined to be a mentor for students pursuing their dreams and understanding the determination required for success. This is when I decided to fly around the world as a role model to reach adults and students.

Twenty-eight years after recognizing my purpose, I was finally ready for my flight around the world. The Citation Mustang jet was donated for the global flight. I had earned many certificates and ratings, including the Citation type rating. Through focus, hard work, and determination, I had gained the experience needed with thousands of flight hours.

I established national and international partners, thus growing a large global following. An additional inspirational component to the flight was setting a world speed record from Greenland to Iceland. I flew to over 35 counties, all 50 United States with an outreach of over 10,000 youth and adults. I'd unintentionally earned the title, "Trailblazing Woman."

It was during my tenure as President of the National Coalition for Aviation and Space Education (NCASE) that I first worked on aviation education and outreach with Dr. Penny Rafferty Hamilton. We immediately connected with similar missions and commitment. Penny had also earned her private pilot license later in life, after achieving her advanced academic degrees and business success.

Because only a small percentage of licensed pilots and astronauts are female, Dr. Hamilton took on the personal mission of promoting air and space careers to women and girls worldwide. Her outreach was multi-faceted beginning with pre-school education. She developed the persona of "Penny the Pilot," dressed in vintage flying suit for public appearances. She published aviation and aerospace career articles in many academic and popular periodicals.

Penny was honored with the Federal Aviation Administration Central Region Aviation Education Champion Award and earned numerous other prestigious recognitions. She was featured in a popular documentary series broadcast on Rocky Mountain PBS about *Great Colorado Women* members from the Colorado Women's Hall of Fame.

She is widely recognized for her ground-breaking two-year study, *Teaching Women to Fly Research Project*. One significant finding was the lack of knowledge, even in the aviation community, about the many contributions women make in this field. Penny's earlier award-winning book, *Inspiring Words for Sky and Space Women: Advice from Historic and Contemporary Trailblazers* continued her personal commitment to write women back into aviation and aerospace history.

Enjoy reading our *101 Trailblazing Women of Air and Space* because these female aviators and astronauts already blazed the sky trails for you to follow. We invite you to soar on your own wings as readers discover their journey to the sky and beyond.

Captain Judy Rice, an accomplished pilot, educator, speaker, author, entrepreneur, and award-winning ground instructor at Epic Flight Academy, is dedicated to STEAM education and diversity in aviation and aerospace. Learn more at https://www.captainjudy.com

ACKNOWLEDGEMENTS

Special thanks to Dr. Cindy Lovell, Epic Flight Academy Director of Education, for all her support and for writing the Afterword. Another important Epic Flight Academy team member, Captain Judith Rice, wrote the Foreword and worked hard to promote this project through her extensive aviation and aerospace education network.

Thank you to all the trailblazers for inspiring us to achieve and persevere. I am so grateful to my own book team: Babette Andre, Beth Barela, MayCay Beeler, Liz Booker, Jacque Boyd, Michelle Grant, Cindy Hald, Bill Hamilton, Betty Heid, Gretchen Jahn, John and Martha King, David Morris, Donna Miller, Kelly Murphy, Rol Murrow, Jennifer Non, Margot Plummer, Josh Pruzek, Shanon Searls, Tess Riley, Ben Sclair, Kim Stevens, Ann Stricklin, and Jill Tietjen.

Special thanks to Vernice "FlyGirl": Armour, Sarah Arnold, Captain Beverely Bass, Lane Wallace, Patty Wagstaff, Amy Spowart, and Allison McKay. Thanks to Southwest Airlines for photographs and to the many other donors and archives for access to historic information and photographs.

To our publishing and graphics designer, Patricia Shapiro Book Publishing, I am so grateful for her creative spirit and talent combined with infinite patience for my many and varied projects

INTRODUCTION

Welcome to Our World of Sky Sisters!

*Adopt an explorer's mindset—it's a powerful tool in
building mental strength and resilience.
~ Lane Wallace, Aviator and Author*

And who are the Sky Sisters? They are our pioneering women aviators and astronauts. In *101 Trailblazing Women of Air and Space* we tell the stories of these brave and determined women whose passion to fly above Planet Earth or even into Outer Space earned them a place in the pantheon of aviation history.

For some readers this will be their first introduction to our Sky Stars. We carefully selected 101 women whose accomplishments in the world of aviation will amaze, delight, and inspire everyone who turns these pages. As you read of their exploits be mindful of the era in which our early aviators flew without the benefit of modern technology and equipment. Knowledge of aerodynamics was very limited.

For easy reading, our aviators and astronauts are listed last name first. Wherever possible their stories are illustrated with their photograph or aircraft, ranging from the very early planes that were no more than sticks, canvas, and spruce wood wired together to our modern metal aircraft and space equipment.

In the world of aviation, being the "first" to do something extraordinary merits special attention. So, we offer a growing list of the women who have air and space "firsts" attached to their names forever. To help you on your journey of discovery, the Explore More chapter cites a number of movies and documentary programs. Some of our trailblazers are the subject of books detailing their achievements. Many have written their own stories. We have listed those books for you to enjoy.

For women looking for career opportunities in the world of aviation and aerospace, we list organizations and resources that could be the starting point for your exploration of the wonderful world of air and space.

The number of female aviators and astronauts is very small but growing daily. The door is open wide because the women who are already in aviation and aerospace are eager to welcome others into our Sky Sisterhood. Welcome to our Sky family.

MayCay Beeler, certified flight instructor and record-setting pilot, encourages you to join our World of Sky Sisters! (Courtesy photograph)

TABLE OF CONTENTS

1

A-Alpha to C-Charlie

You'll be surprised at all of the things you can do, if you just keep pushing. You could be flying a fighter one day!
~ USAF Thunderbird pilot, Major Michelle Curran

Armour, Vernice "FlyGirl:" First Black Female Pilot in the U.S. Marine Corps

In 2001, Vernice made aviation history by becoming the first Black female to earn her U.S. Marine Corps Golden Wings. Breaking gender and racial barriers became her hallmark. She flew the Bell AH-1 W SuperCobra. Later, she became the first Black female combat pilot. She completed two combat tours flying the SuperCobra, as the name implies, a sophisticated, twin-engine, attack helicopter capable of land or sea-based flight operations.

Even today twenty years after Vernice flew into aviation history, U.S. Marine aviation remains extremely selective and demanding. In addition to rigorous fitness and visual examinations, future Marine aviators complete a battery of aptitude tests before they even start their flight training. U.S. Marine aviators are already commissioned officers. According to the U.S. Marine Corps, flight training is the "longest and most extensive training" in the Corps.

"In my journey, I have learned that obstacles are opportunities. Acknowledge the obstacles and don't give them power." Vernice "FlyGirl" Armour. (Courtesy photograph)

Armour descended from a family with a military tradition of service. At age 25, she was commissioned as a Marine Corps Second Lieutenant. Her combat flights were completed during the U.S.-led Operation Iraqi Freedom.

In 2007, "FlyGirl" Armour left military service to pursue a business career, founding VAI Consulting and Training, LLC. By 2011, Armour penned the popular book, *Zero to Breakthrough: The 7-Step, Battle-*

Tested Method for Accomplishing Goals that Matter. Vernice is now a very successful author and dynamic public speaker. Vernice received the Bessie Coleman Foundation Award. If ever there was a woman who looked at life as a great adventure, it is "FlyGirl" Armour.

Arnold, Sarah: International Women's Soaring Champion

Sarah is the winner of the 2020 *Fédération Aéronautique Internationale* (FAI) Women's World Gliding Championship in the Standard Class. You may have heard the statement, "An aviator is one with the sky." Well, it is so true with successful glider pilots because a sailplane has no engine. The soaring pilot uses the natural air currents and variable atmospherics of the sky to create lift, rise higher, and glide through the open sky.

Sarah's passion for flight began at age 13. She first explored ultralights. Smaller and very maneuverable, ultralights offer an introduction to the sky experience. A small motor propels these light aircraft. The ultralight pilot learns to understand wind conditions that might not bother the heavier and more traditional airplanes that come from, say, Piper and Cessna.

The air sport of soaring or sky gliding is described as magical because of the silent nature of the soaring experience. Soaring is a highly competitive International sport. Sometimes a sailplane air field is called a gliderport. Learning the principles of flight are important fundamentals to success in this unique air sport.

By age 17, Sarah earned her Canadian private pilot certificate. She continued earning advanced ratings and enrolled in aircraft mechanic (A&P) training. In 2003, Sarah discovered the passion for the world of soaring. At age 24, she bought the Chilhowee Gliderport in Benton, Tennessee. In 2005, Sarah set the U.S. and New Mexico records for gliding distance. In 2008, the altitude record was next. In 2011, she set 11 Tennessee and three U.S. records, and became the Sport Class and Club Class National Champion. The world was next. In 2013, Sarah Arnold earned a bronze at the FAI Women's World Gliding Championship.

International Sky Star, Sarah Arnold, holds her 2020 FAI Women's World Gliding Championship trophy at her home airfield at Chilhowee Gliderport in Benton, Tennessee. (Courtesy Photograph Leigh Hubner)

By 2017, when she was inducted into the Tennessee Aviation Hall of Fame, she had logged around 6,400 flight hours, including 3,700 in sailplanes. She is a Certified Flight Instructor for airplanes and gliders. Sarah is also rated as a Ground Instructor. She was the first woman glider pilot chosen to represent the United States when the 32nd World

Gliding Championship was held in Argentina. In 2017, Sarah earned silver for team USA at the FAI Women's World Gliding Championships held in Czechoslovakia. To Sarah, who loves sharing her passion with students, soaring offers an opportunity to relive the romance of flight.

Auñón-Chancellor, Serena: Record Setting United States Astronaut

After medical school, Dr. Serena Auñón continued her specialized education becoming board certified in Internal and Aerospace Medicine. In 2006, she joined the NASA team as a Flight Surgeon. For nine months, she provided medical care and support to the International Space Station crew members located in Russia's Star City. During this time, she also completed water survival training in the Ukraine

In 2009, Serena joined the 20th U.S. Astronaut class. In 2010/11, now Astronaut Serena spent two months in Antarctica searching for meteorites as part of the ANSMET expedition. (ANSMET stands for Antarctic Search for METeorites.) She explored on the ice fields about 200 nautical miles from the South Pole.

In June 2012, Dr. Auñón-Chancellor was chosen for the NASA Extreme Environment Mission Operations or NEEMO mission. In NEEMO NASA astronauts, engineers, and scientists live in a submersible on the ocean floor off the coast for Florida. This is the world's only undersea research station. The undersea environment acclimates NASA crew members to the space exploration environment.

By 2015, Serena was an aquanaut crew member. Then, in 2018, Astronaut Auñón-Chancellor went back to outer space on the International Space Station clocking 197 days. Always seeking new training and experiences, Serena became certified as an International Space Station CAPCOM which is vital to communications between flight control and the astronauts in space. She served as the lead CAPCOM for the SpaceX-4 and SpaceX-8 cargo resupply missions. Dr. Auñón-Chancellor is one capable and well-travelled female explorer in the sky, sea, and on planet Earth.

In 2018, NASA astronaut, Serena Auñón-Chancellor, posed inside the U.S. Quest Airlock with her spacesuit. Her helmet's visor is coated with a thin layer of gold that filters out the sun's harmful rays during spacewalks. (NASA archival photograph)

Auriol, Jacqueline: French Pilot and World Record Setter

Born in 1917 to a wealthy family, after World War II, nearing her 30th birthday, she wasted no more time pursuing her passion for the sky. She quickly became an accomplished stunt and test pilot. Her fame grew all over Europe.

In 1949, she was badly injured as a passenger in an airplane crash. During three long years of medical care and 33 reconstructive surgeries performed to repair her face and bones, Jacqueline continued to study aerodynamics for advanced ratings. Sure enough, in 1955, Auriol earned a military pilot license which qualified her as one of the world's first female test pilots. She was Whirly Girls member seven.

She was among the first women to break the sound barrier. In the 1950s and 1960s, Auriol set five world speed records. She was awarded the coveted Harmon International Trophy an incredible four times in recognition of her aviation accomplishments and passion for flying. In

1970, she penned her autobiography, *I Live to Fly,* which was published in both French and English.

Famed French aviator, Jacqueline Auriol, was awarded the Harmon International Trophy in 1951, 1952, 1955, and in 1956 for her aviation accomplishments. (Wikicommons photograph)

In 1983, at age 66, Auriol became a founding member of the French *Académie de l'air et de l'espace (AAE).* This important French national air and space non-profit promotes aerospace activities and education. Jacqueline Auriol epitomized the phrase, "To fully live, fly!"

Bailey, Lady Mary: Irish Sky Star of the 1920s

Born into a wealthy and aristocratic Irish family in 1890, her early years were spent on the grounds of the Rossmore Castle. Schooled by governesses, at age 16, adventurous Lady Mary ran away to explore the world outside her castle. Motorbikes and fast cars were the first she tackled. During the First World War, she became a Royal Flying Corps aircraft mechanic, serving in England and France.

In 1927 through 1931, Lady Mary Bailey set many world aviation records. (Wikicommons photograph)

Loving aviation by 1927, Lady Mary earned her pilot's license. She wasted no more time beginning her pursuit of aviation "firsts." She became the first woman to fly across the Irish Sea. Next, on July 5, 1927, she set a women's world's altitude record of 17,283 flying her de Havilland Moth. In 1928, at age 38 and the mother of five children, she successfully flew an epic 8,000 mile flight journey from Croydon in England to Cape Town, South Africa...and back.

On her return flight between September 1928 and 16 January 1929, Lady Mary flew across the Congo, along the southern edge of the Sahara, and up the western coast of Africa. Her flight crossed Spain and France to return to England. This long and complicated flight would challenge today's aviators with fully equipped GPS and advanced aviation technology. Lady Mary Bailey's solo flight, which was the longest accomplished by a woman, earned her the 1929 Royal Aero Club Britannia Trophy which honors aviators accomplishing the most meritorious performance in aviation during the previous year.

Lady Mary Bailey also won the prestigious Harmon Trophy twice in 1927 and in 1928 as the world's outstanding woman pilot. But, wait, there is more! In 1931, Lady Mary became the first woman in the entire United Kingdom to obtain a "Certificate of Blind Flying," which we would know today as an Instrument rating. Until you use your wings, you have no idea how far and wide you can soar.

It doesn't take any more prowess to be a super-flyer than it does to be a super something else.

~ Amelia Earhart

Barnes, Florence "Pancho" Lowe: American Pioneer Aviator
"Pancho" Barnes was a legendary pilot of the 1930s. After only a few hours of flight instruction, she quickly was a proficient flyer. She became a barnstormer. Later, she became a Hollywood stunt pilot. In fact in 1931, under her leadership, the Associated Motion Picture Pilots became a powerful union of film industry stunt pilots promoting flight safety, standardized pay, and insurance benefits. She flew in several

classic aviation films, including the iconic *Hell's Angels* produced by mogul, Howard Hughes.

Pancho Barnes led a very colorful life. In 1929, she was a founding member of the International Ninety-Nines, the women pilots. In August, Pancho set a national speed record of 196.19 miles per hour in the Women's Air Derby in her Wright-powered Travel Air sponsored by Union Oil Company. That bested an earlier record set by Amelia Earhart.

On an earlier adventure in Mexico, Florence adopted the nickname, "Pancho." Married several times, she lost several fortunes but rose like a Phoenix with her legendary aviation accomplishments. Pancho Barnes was an aviation trailblazer who had little use for the societal conventions of her day.

Legendary aviator, Pancho Barnes, flew in Hollywood films in the 1930s. (Wikicommons photograph)

Bass, Beverley: First Female Captain for American Airlines

In 1976, she was hired by American Airlines as their third female pilot. Earlier airline executives told Bass that female airlines pilots would not be accepted by passengers and air crews. Beverley had heard "no" often. Even her own family was hesitant when she wanted to take flying lessons as a young woman. In 1971, as a college student at Texas Christian University, she knew she already had wings, all she had to do was use them to fly. She earned her aviation credentials and built flying hours by spending six hours each afternoon at Fort Worth's Meacham Airport. Her first professional flying position was flying human remains from Texas to Arkansas.

Captain Beverley Bass penned "Me And The Sky" children's book to share her inspiring Sky journey. (Courtesy Captain Beverley Bass)

Beverley kept pursing her ratings, building flying hours toward an airline position. In 1976, at age 24, American Airlines said, "Yes." Having experienced gender discrimination in commercial aviation, Bass knew the importance of a professional organization for women in the airlines. Beverley Bass became one of the founding members of the International Society of Women Airline Pilots.

Ten years later, Bass became the first female American Airlines Captain. Later that year, she made more American Airlines history with their first all-female crew on a flight she captained from Washington, D.C. to Dallas, Texas. In 1999, Beverley Bass became the first woman to Captain for a B-777 in an airline operation.

Then, on September 11, 2001, the world turned upside down. She was piloting an American Airlines Boeing 777 from Paris to Dallas/Fort Worth International Airport when the Islamic terrorists started toppling the World Trade Center. With airspace in the United States shut down due to the terrorist attacks, her flight was diverted to Gander. Newfoundland. Fortunately, Captain Bass, crew, and passengers were greeted warmly and cared for during those tense days by our Canadian neighbors. In 2008, Captain Bass retired from American Airlines.

Recently, her aviation career and experiences were immortalized in a Tony Award-winning Canadian musical titled, *Come from Away*. The Beverley Bass character has an important musical number, "Me and the Sky," which is entirely drawn from the real-life Captain Beverley Bass. Her book is titled after that melodious song.

Bondar, Roberta: Canada's First Woman in Space

In 1992, Dr. Roberta Bondar fulfilled a childhood dream by becoming Canada's first woman in space. In January, she launched into space representing the International scientific community. Dr. Bondar conducted over forty advanced experiments for fourteen nations. As a noted researcher and neurologist, Canada's Roberta Bondar, added to the world's knowledge with her flight on the space shuttle, Discovery. She is a certificated scuba diver, parachutist, private pilot, and a medical doctor.

Her book, *Touching the Earth,* shares her remarkable journey to the stars. Breathtaking photographs taken from space of Earth highlight her powerful message of hope for our environment.

In 1992, Canadian Space Agency's Dr. Roberta Bondar became their first woman in space. (NASA Photograph)

Bragg, Janet Harmon: America's First African American Woman Licensed Commercial Pilot

Born in 1907 in Georgia, Janet Harmon overcame racial discrimination to make aviation history. In 1928, Janet was the first Black woman accepted in the Chicago Curtiss-Wright School of Aeronautics. Later, in 1933, she enrolled in Aeronautical University, a segregated Black aviation school managed by John C. Robinson and Cornelius Coffey.

She was the only woman in the class with 24 Black men. Because the school had no airplane for the Black students to use, Janet provided $600 of her own money to buy the school's first aircraft. In 2021, that is the equivalent of $11,840. But, in 1934, the Great Depression made money even more precious.

Janet Harmon Bragg in her flight suit, circa 1930s. (Smithsonian Institution Archive unidentified photographer)

Because Black pilots were not allowed to fly from airfields reserved for white pilots, she helped build the Aeronautical University's own airfield in Robbins, Illinois. She set up the Challenger Aero Club to purchase land and built an all Black airfield. She grew the airplane fleet to three. Janet continued her aviation training. Finally, she was recognized with her license in 1934.

In the early 1930s, Janet was involved in the nascent National Airmen Association of America. This important group started in the Chicago area to actively pursue and encourage African Americans in aviation and aeronautics

Harmon moved to Tuskegee, Alabama. She completed the Civilian Pilot Training Program and should have earned her commercial pilot's ticket there. But, again, because of her race, the Alabama Federal examiner denied her. Even more determined, she returned to Illinois where she demonstrated her aviation skills.

In 1943, she earned her commercial license. That same year, she applied for the Women's Airforce Service Pilots (WASP) program. However, she was rejected because she was Black. An advocate for aviation and her community, Janet Harman Bragg flew exhibition flights to encourage Black aviation participation in not just flying but the entire field of aeronautics. She tirelessly wrote articles on flying in the *Chicago Defender* newspaper. In 1953, she married Sumner Bragg. A pioneer for women in aviation, Janet Harman Bragg built a sky trail with determination and business acumen. She is enshrined in the Arizona Aviation Hall of Fame.

Brown-Hiltz, Jill Elaine: First Black Female U.S. Airline Pilot

Jill Brown-Hiltz made history as the first Black woman admitted to the U.S. Navy's pilot training program. But her real goal was to fly for the airlines, her girlhood dream that started at age 17 when she soloed in a Piper J-3 Cub. Later, her family purchased a Piper Cherokee and named it "Little Golden Hawk." As a teenager, Jill asked to use the family airplane the way most teenagers ask to use the family car. After her college graduation, she was admitted to the U.S. Naval Aviation Program.

In 1978, trailblazer Jill Brown-Hiltz made airline history as the first Black woman pilot for Texas International Airlines. (Wikicommons)

But she left the Navy to pursue an airline career. Her next big opportunity opened with Black-owned and operated, Wheeler Airlines in North Carolina. She even took on an entry-level ticket clerk position. She was not flying yet. But she was at the airport. She earned her instrument, commercial, and flight instructor ratings. Eventually, she logged 800 flight hours, on top of her original 400 which qualified her to be a commercial airline pilot. Soon, she left the Wheeler ticket counter for the flight deck as copilot.

In 1978, she began flying for Texas International Airlines. But finding Texas International Airlines a little too interested in featuring her ethnicity, she took her talents to Zantop International Airlines, a cargo carrier based in Michigan. She continued her commercial aviation career until the mid-1980s. In retirement Jill Brown-Hiltz continued to advocate for Black aviators.

Embrace today as your perfect opportunity for a new adventure. ~ Unknown

Caputo, Bonnie Tiburzi: First Female Pilot for American Airlines
In 1973, Bonnie Tiburzi made aviation history when American Airlines invited her to join their commercial aviation flight deck. At the same time, she became the first woman in the world to earn a Flight Engineer rating on a turbo jet aircraft.

Bonnie is the daughter of a former airline pilot. "Gus" Tiburzi founded and operated Tiburzi Airways. The Danbury Connecticut Flight School and Charter Company was an early home base for Bonnie. She earned her pilot's license at age 19. It was a natural progression to flight instruct and to be a charter pilot. Her flight hours quickly built. When she landed at American Airlines she continued her pursuit of advanced ratings and responsibilities. She flew as an American Airline Captain on the Boeing 727, Boeing 747, and the Boeing 767.

She married Bruce Caputo and raised her family with him in New York. In 1986, her autobiography, *Takeoff: The Story of America's First Woman Pilot for a Major Airline,* brought renewed attention to her meteoric rise in commercial aviation. After a 26 year airline career, she retired in 1999.

In 1973, Bonnie Tiburzi was the first female commercial pilot hired by American Airlines. (Smithsonian National Air and Space Museum)

She continues to promote women in their careers. In 2018, Bonnie Tiburzi Caputo was inducted into the Women in Aviation International Pioneer Hall of Fame. Her American Airlines uniform is in the Smithsonian Institution Air and Space Museum. She have received numerous awards and honors because of her trailblazing accomplishments in the airline industry.

Chabrian, Peggy Baty: Visionary Founder of Women in Aviation International

An experienced aviator with 2,200+ flight hours and ratings to include commercial, instrument, multi-engine, flight instructor, seaplane, and helicopter, Dr. Chabrian has a strong professional aviation leadership background. In 1990, she dreamed of an all-inclusive International organization which promoted women in all areas of the aviation and aerospace industry. Out of a small conference of industry leaders with a shared vision, Women in Aviation International was incorporated in 1994.

Dr. Peggy Baty Chabrian founded Women in Aviation International (WAI) which encourages young women to explore aviation and aerospace careers worldwide by participating in the annual WAI Girls in Aviation Day. (WAI)

Under Dr. Chabrian's protective wings as CEO/President from 1995 to 2019, WAI experienced worldwide growth and success. As a long-time professional aviation educator, she knows the importance of reaching young minds early. The highly successful annual WAI Girls in Aviation Day is part of her important legacy to the future of aviation and aerospace.

Writing in the 2019 *Women in Aviation International Aviation for Girls* magazine, Peggy Baty Chabrian says, "It is an exciting time to be a young woman in the field of aviation and space. The doors are open and the needs are great. Airlines are looking for qualified pilots, manufacturers are looking for bright engineers, airplane owners are looking for talented mechanics, and companies need passionate individuals to keep it all running." Dr. Chabrian constantly looks toward the future.

Chappell, Willa Brown: A Woman of "Firsts"

Born in 1906, at age 21, Willa graduated from Indiana State Teacher's College with her Bachelor's degree. As an African American woman, during those years this was an astounding feat. Even more amazing is that in 1934, she began taking flying lessons inspired by the pioneering aviator, Bessie Coleman. In 1937, Willa Brown became the first African American woman to earn an aviator's license in the United States. Her story of overcoming adversity continues. She pursued her flight training to earn her commercial pilot license. Brown also became the first Black woman to serve as a Civil Air Patrol officer.

In 1939, she helped establish the Coffey School of Aeronautics at Harlem Airport in Chicago. The school taught qualified Black students under the Civilian Pilot Training Program (CPTP). The school also trained Black pilots in aviation mechanics. It was the first flight school owned and operated by Blacks. As school director, Willa Brown was instrumental in training more than 200 students. Many went on to become the legendary Tuskegee Airmen.

In 1941, at the beginning of World War II, because of Willa's aviation credentials, the United States government named her as the federal coordinator of the Chicago unit of the Civil Air Patrol civilian pilot training program. Willa was ranked an officer in this first integrated unit. In 1943, she became America's first woman to hold both a mechanic's license and a commercial license in aviation.

In 1955, she married the Rev. J.H. Chappell. Willa Brown Chappell became a trailblazer because she had the drive, skills, and passion to change things. She seized every opportunity to share that vision and passion with the Black community.

Willa Brown Chappell was the first Black woman to serve as a Civil Air Patrol officer. (New York Public Library Digital collection)

Chawla, Kalpana: First Female Astronaut of East Indian Heritage

Born in India, Kalpana was always fascinated by aviation. She begged her father to take her to the local airport to see the planes flying. She carefully watched as the aircraft climbed into the sky. As a young Indian woman, Kalpana broke barriers in her home country earning her degree in aeronautical engineering. In 1982, she set off on her own to the United States to seek more education and opportunity to follow her sky dream.

In 1997, NASA Astronaut, Kalpana Chawla, became the first East Indian American woman in space. (NASA photograph)

In 1984, she earned her University of Texas Master's in Aerospace Engineering. In 1988, her doctorate was next from the University of Colorado. Her NASA career began at Ames Research Center. In 1991, Chawla became a naturalized U.S. citizen. Along the way, Kalpana had also earned advanced ratings in airplanes, gliders, seaplanes, with commercial and multi-engine licenses. She was a Certified Flight Instructor for airplanes and gliders. She applied to join our Astronaut Corps. By November 1997, Kalpana became the first East Indian American astronaut and first East Indian woman in space on Columbia flight STS-87.

On this first space flight, Kalpana was a mission specialist with primary responsibility for the robotic arm. Then, in 2001, she was again selected for the Space Shuttle Columbia STS-107 crew. Mechanical and technical problems delayed the mission. Finally, on January 16, 2003, Columbia's 28th mission, Chawla and her crew members lifted off the launch pad. Then, seconds later disaster when the spacecraft burst into flames and disintegrated killing the entire crew.

Astronaut Kalpana Chawla was posthumously awarded the Congressional Space Medal of Honor. In India, she is regarded as a national hero and a symbol of possibilities. She once said, "The path from dreams to success does exist. May you have the vision to find it, the courage to get on to it, and the perseverance to follow it."

Cheung, Katherine: First Female Asian American Pilot

In 1932, Katherine Cheung earned her pilot's license. Born in China in 1904, her family sent her to study at the University of Southern California at age 17. She completed three years of study before marrying her father's business partner and starting a family. Then, in 1932, she took her first airplane ride. She loved the freedom she experienced in the sky. Immediately, she began flight lessons. She soloed after only twelve hours of instruction. She was such a natural flyer she became an aerobatic performer at California air shows. She thrilled the crowd with her loop-de-loops and barrel rolls. She became beloved in her Chinese community. A remarkable accomplishment in itself but particularly because the Chinese community held strict norms on the actions of women.

Katherine Cheung first female Asian American pilot. (Photograph posted by Alexander Davidson on findagrave.com)

In 1934, members of her Los Angeles Chinese community pooled their money to buy Cheung her own plane. In 1935, she joined the Ninety-Nines women pilots. Because of this affiliation, she worked with Amelia Earhart to promote more women in aviation, especially Chinese women. Katherine dreamed of someday returning to China to establish flying schools for women. In 1937, when Japan invaded China, her supporters funded the purchase of a new plane for her to fly to China to teach others how to fly in defense of their homeland. The day of the ceremony to celebrate the new plane and purpose, she witnessed its crash in the distance. Her cousin, who was her original inspiration to fly, had taken it for a test flight. He died in the crash and the airplane was destroyed.

That, and the promise she made to her father on his death bed to give up not only her dream of Chinese aviation schools but flying, grounded Katherine Cheung for a few years. But, soon she did return to the freedom of the sky until retirement in 1942. She was honored in 2000 with induction into the WAI Pioneer Hall of Fame.

Clark, Julie E.: First Female Golden West Airlines Pilot

In her teenage years, Julie Clark experienced a number of obstacles. In 1964, her father, a Pacific Airlines pilot, was killed, in flight, by a deranged passenger. At that time, the doors to the flight deck were unlocked. Captain Ernie Clark was shot and killed at the plane's controls. His death, resulted in a new law requiring airline flight deck doors be locked during flight. Just a year earlier, Julie's mother died. At age 15, Julie was an orphan.

In 1967, Julie took her first flight lesson. She knew she wanted an airline career but she was a woman. Repeatedly, she was told, "We are not hiring women pilots." Julie's first major break came after college in 1976, when Golden West Airlines hired her, their first and only woman pilot. Ironically, in 1977, Hughes AirWest, formerly Pacific Airlines, the same airline her father flew for, hired her. Julie Clark became one of the first women to fly for a major airline. Later, Julie continued her airline career with Northwest Airlines.

Julie Clark retired from Northwest Airlines as an Airbus A320 Captain. She logged almost 33,000 hours in 66 different aircraft types as the pilot over her airline and air show careers. In 1980, Julie Clark also became a beloved air-show performer.

Beloved aerobatic performer, Captain Julie Clark, named her airplane, "Free Spirit."
(Courtesy photo Julie Clark Air Shows)

Captain Clark touches hearts of fans of all ages with her choreographed solo, aerobatic ballet called, "Serenade in Red, White and Blue," which is perfectly choreographed to Lee Greenwood's patriotic song, "God Bless the USA." Julie releases red, white, and blue smoke from her "Smokin' Mentor T-34," called "Free Spirit." What Julie Clark does takes incredible hours of practice and unending passion for flying.

Julie Clark is a popular public speaker. Her book, *Nothing Stood in Her Way*, is a flight plan on how to overcome obstacles and fly. Julie Clark is a Charter Member of the International Society of Women Airline Pilots-ISA+21 which is a strong sisterhood of women pilots in the airline industry worldwide. In 2006, she was named a Living Legend of Aviation. In 2002, Captain Julie Clark joined the other Pioneers in the Women in Aviation Hall of Fame in recognition of her significant contributions to the aviation industry.

Cobb, Geraldyn "Jerrie:" Record Setting American Aviator

Widely known in the aviation industry as Jerrie Cobb, she began her sky journey on Oklahoma airports. Her father was a pilot who encouraged his daughter to fly. In fact, she first flew at age twelve in his 1936 Waco bi-plane. She was a quick study. By age 16, Jerrie Cobb was a full-fledged barnstormer in a Piper J-3 Cub.

By age 17, as a high school student she got around to earning her private pilot license. Her 18th birthday present was earning her commercial license. She flew pipeline patrols and became a crop-duster. Any flying job would pay for fuel and put her in the air.

She kept punching her aviation tickets, Multi-engine, Instrument, Flight and Ground Instructor ratings, and Airline Transport Pilot (ATP). By age 21, she was delivering military planes to foreign Air Forces worldwide. The gal would probably fly the box the airplane came in!

In her 20s, Jerrie Cobb set three aviation records. In 1959, she set the world record for nonstop long-distance flight and the world light-plane speed record. In 1960, she conquered the world altitude record for lightweight aircraft of 37,010 feet. Cobb became the first woman to fly in the famed Paris Air Show which was the world's largest aviation stage. The world indeed noticed with a Life Magazine story, Amelia Earhart Gold Medal of Achievement, and Pilot of the Year award.

At only age 28 in 1959, Jerrie was the pilot and manager for Aero Design and Engineering Company in Oklahoma building the Aero Commander. She used this aircraft in many of her record setting accomplishments. She became one of the very few women aviation executives. By 1960, Jerrie Cobb had logged 7,000 hours in the air.

During the 1958-59 call for astronauts, the NASA requirements to apply were written to exclude women. A select group of American women were recruited for a privately-funded testing program which was modelled after the NASA Mercury 7 testing program. Jerrie Cobb was one of the 13 women who volunteered.

Surprise, Jerrie Cobb was the first woman to complete and pass the rigorous physical and psychological tests. In later years, the secret testing program revealed the women performed as well or even better than some of the male astronauts. This stellar group of sky sisters became known as the Mercury 13.

Jerrie Cobb, one of the Mercury 13, operated the Multi-Axis Space Test Inertia Facility (MASTIF). Jerrie performed at a high standard on the astronaut tests, she was allowed to tackle. (NASA photograph)

In May 1961, NASA Administrator, James Webb, appointed Cobb as a NASA space consultant. Jerrie Cobb testified before Congress for the acceptance of women in our astronaut program. Congress agreed with the NASA decision to exclude women. By June 1963, Soviet Cosmonaut, Valentina Tereshkova, had already completed her record-setting space flight. The first American woman in space would not be until 1983 with NASA astronaut, Sally Ride.

Jerrie Cobb continued in aviation. She began a 30-year humanitarian and missionary flying career in South America. She charted new and safer air routes. Cobb was honored by the Brazilian, Colombian, Ecuadorian, French, and Peruvian governments. In 1973, she was awarded the Harmon Trophy as the Best Woman Aviator in the World. She joins the other Sky Stars in the WAI Pioneer Hall of Fame. In 2012, she was enshrined into the National Aviation Hall of Fame. All her life Jerrie Cobb kept looking up to the sky.

Cochran, Jacqueline "Speed Queen:" First Woman to Break the Sound Barrier

A woman of so many first in aviation, Jacqueline Cochran was legendary with a career spanning important years in aviation history. Along with great executive ability, she was a really good pilot. Born in extreme poverty in 1906, she catered to wealthy clientele through high-end New York and Miami hair salons. In the early 1930s, at a sophisticated dinner party, she found herself seated next to one of the wealthiest men in America at the time, Floyd Odlum. They connected on many levels that night. Jackie shared her dream to leave the salons and build a cosmetics business.

He gave her some sage advice. "There's a depression on, Jackie. If you're going to cover the territory you need to cover in order to make money in this kind of economic climate, you'll need wings. Get your pilot's license." Jackie Cochran immediately grasped the wisdom. Within weeks she earned her private pilot's license. She loved the power of her control of the machine. Aviation became a passion. Cochran quit her hair salon job. With a growing romantic relationship with Floyd, she knew with his resources and connections, her sky had no limits.

Before long, Jackie Cochran became the woman to watch with frequent photographs and press reports about her accomplishments. In 1934, she was one of the first woman to fly in the MacRobertson Air Race from London to Australia. In 1935, she entered the Bendix transcontinental air race which had always been limited to male pilots.

Jacqueline Cochran earned the nickname, "Speed Queen," because of all the world aviation speed records she set in her aviation career. (Wikimedia photograph)

During all these flying adventures, Jackie built a thriving cosmetics empire, using only the best ingredients. Her aviation fame helped promote her beauty line to working women, who saw her as a role model. In fact in 1941, after she became the first woman to fly a bomber across the Atlantic to highlight the importance of supporting England's fight in World War II, hand-written letters poured into her beauty headquarters offices about how proud the women were to wear her make-up. Although Jackie always wanted to be a successful business woman, aviation was her life's passion.

Many readers may know of her leadership during World War II of our WASP which created a corps of American women flyers in non-combat roles to ferry planes from factories to U.S. Air Bases. WASP flew many important missions for the military. She continued her military service by joining the U.S. Air Force Reserve as a Lieutenant Colonel. Before her retirement in 1969, she was promoted to the rank of Colonel.

After the war, Jackie Cochran continued her conquest of the air. In 1947 and 1948, she set four world and U.S. aviation speed records. She moved up to new jet aircraft setting numerous records. On May 18, 1953, she became the first woman to break the sound barrier. Encouraged by her lifelong friend, Chuck Yeager, Cochran flew the Sabre 3 at Rogers Dry Lake in California when her plane went supersonic. Her record-setting continued when in 1961, flying a Northrop Talon supersonic trainer, she set two FAI world altitude records.

Of course, there is more. Jackie was the first woman to land and take off from an aircraft carrier. She became the first woman President of the famed FAI from 1958-1961. She became the first woman to fly above 20,000 feet with an oxygen mask. In the early 1960s, she even flew the Goodyear Blimp.

With little formal education and pockets full of grit, Cochran is a legend in aviation and business in American history. She worked hard for her success. At her death in 1980, Jacqueline Cochran held more aviation records than any other woman. During their later years, she and her husband lived in the Coachella Valley of California. After her death, her home airport was named Jacqueline Cochran Regional Airport in her honor.

Coleman, Elizabeth, "Bessie:" First Licensed African American Pilot

Because she was refused flight instruction, Bessie Coleman had the courage and determination to leave the United States by ship for France to pursue her dream. Born in 1892 to Texas sharecroppers of Native American and African American descent, at a very young age she vowed to leave the cotton fields. With a family of 13 children, she quickly learned to fend for herself.

In 1915, at age 23, she joined her older brother in Chicago. She worked long hours in a local barbershop. Her brother told her "Girls can't fly, especially Black girls." Well, Bessie became determined to prove him wrong. Her first obstacle was she was turned down time and again by flight schools with a "No Blacks" and some "No women" response. Working on Chicago's south side, she met Robert Abbott, the publisher of the *Chicago Defender* newspaper. He encouraged her to pursue flight training in France.

With only an eight grade education, Bessie she did not speak French...yet. Gutsy Bessie enrolled in night school to learn to master this difficult language. She even worked a second job as a restaurant manager to pay for the classes. After enough French proficiency to read and complete the flight school application, she saved every penny to afford the trip to France and the flight school.

Miracle of miracles, she received written acceptance from the Caudron Brothers' School of Aviation in Le Crotoy, France to report for her flight training. Brave Bessie departed for France in November 1919 for her long journey to a foreign country far, far away. After her ocean crossing, Bessie needed to take the train to arrive in Le Crotoy about two hours from Paris in Northern France. She found the town to be a beautiful seaside resort.

Bessie began the flight course learning to fly in a French Nieuport Type 82. She excelled. The schooling included tailspins, banking, and even looping the loop maneuvers. She completed the training. On June 15, 1921, Elizabeth Coleman received her FAI license making her the first African American pilot in the world.

U.S. Postal Service issued the Bessie Coleman commemorative stamp on April 27, 1995. (Smithsonian National Postal Museum image)

Returning to New York in September 1921, she was amazed by a surprising amount of press coverage. Bessie Coleman had become an "Overnight Success." Flying as entertainment had become lucrative. Aviators were highly paid and considered "Super Stars." After watching some of the air show performers, Bessie quickly concluded for safety, she needed additional flight training. Being proficient and comfortable with French flight training, she soon departed for France again for more training.

Returning to America again to even more fanfare, Coleman toured the country barnstorming as "Brave Bessie," raising money for her dream of an African American flying school. She was also called "Queen Bess" because she "ruled" the sky. Bessie would only perform if the crowds were desegregated and entered through the same gates, which was a rarity in some locations. She made speeches about the importance of aviation and the opportunities.

Preparing for one of her many public performances, on April 20, 1926, Coleman was thrown from her Curtiss JN-4 while it was being flown by her mechanic, William D. Wills. At 2,000 feet without her parachute, Bessie died instantly upon impact with the ground. Willis died in the plane crash. It was later discovered that a wrench used to service the engine slid into the gearbox and jammed it. Bessie was 34 years old.

Bessie Coleman said "I refused to take no for an answer." In 1995, Coleman was inducted into the Women in Aviation International Pioneer Hall of Fame. In 2006, the National Aviation Hall of Fame inducted this aviation trailblazer.

Collins, Eileen Marie: America's First Woman Space Shuttle Pilot
Collins always enjoyed challenges. She leaned toward math and science from childhood. In 1978, she graduated from Syracuse University with a degree in Mathematics and Economics. Collins was one of four women chosen for flight training at Vance Air Force Base in Oklahoma. She excelled, earning her wings. As an Air Force officer, Collins was chosen as a T-38 Talon flight instructor. The Talon is a supersonic

twinjet. Next, Collins transitioned to the C-141 Starlifter at Travis Air Force Base in California.

Eileen Collins became America's first woman to pilot the Space Shuttle on February 2, 1995. (NASA photograph)

She managed to earn a Master of Science degree from Stanford University in 1986. She specialized in Space Systems Management for her second Masters in 1989 from Webster University while she was assigned to the U.S. Air Force Academy in Colorado Springs where she was an assistant professor of Mathematics. She also was a T-41 instructor pilot. In 1989, Eileen became only the second female pilot in history to attend the U.S. Air Force Test Pilot School. After graduation, Eileen Collins was selected for the NASA astronaut program.

Collins became an astronaut in July 1991. She was the first woman to pilot the Space Shuttle STS-63 on February 2, 1995. She made more history on July 23, 1999 as America's first woman to command STS-93 Space Shuttle mission. Then, in 2005, Eileen Collins again commanded NASA STS-114 mission. During her NASA career, Colonel Collins logged 38 days, 8 hours, and 20 minutes in space. She retired from NASA on May 1, 2006.

As a trailblazer, Eileen Collins has earned recognition by inclusion in the Women in Aviation International Pioneer Hall of Fame, Irish American Hall of Fame, National Women's Hall of Fame, Astronaut Hall of Fame, and the National Aviation Hall of Fame.

Cristoforetti, Samantha: Italy's First Woman in Space

In 2009, Cristoforetti became an Italian European Space Agency astronaut. Her eyes were opened to the possibilities of space as a Foreign Exchange student in high school. Samantha landed in the United States and was given the opportunity to attend a space camp. That did it for her. She knew space exploration would be her personal mission.

After her short Foreign Exchange experience, Samantha returned home to Northern Italy. She earned advanced degrees in institutions in Italy, France, Germany, and Russia in the fields of Aerospace, Science, and Engineering. She is fluent in Italian, English, German, French, and Russian. As part of her training, she completed the Euro-NATO Joint Jet Pilot training. She has logged over 500 hours and has flown six types of military aircraft. In 2014, the European Space Agency announced that Cristoforetti was set for a long-duration mission to the International Space Station.

As Italy's first woman in space, she made her mark. She logged 119 days and 16 hours in space and held the record for the longest single space flight by a woman until June 2017 when American astronaut, Peggy Whitson, surpassed that milestone.

In 2019, Cristoforetti commanded a NEEMO (NASA Extreme Environment Mission Operations) mission of astronauts, engineers, and scientists to live in the undersea research station called Aquarius. This is the world's only seafloor testing site to mimic deep space conditions and lunar and planetary exploration.

Recently, it was announced that Italy's Samantha Cristoforetti will be the first European woman astronaut to take command of the International Space Station during her mission scheduled for 2022. Space trailblazer, Samantha Cristoforetti, 44, is adding yet another galactic accomplishment in her career in space exploration.

Italian astronaut Samantha Cristoforetti from the European Space Agency (ESA) rests in a chair outside the Soyuz TMA-15M spacecraft just minutes after landing in a remote area near the town of Zhezkazgan, Kazakhstan on Thursday, June 11, 2015. Cristoforetti returned to Earth after more than six months onboard the International Space Station serving as a member of the Expedition 42 and 43 crews. (NASA photograph/Bill Ingalls)

Custodio, Olga Nevarez: First Latina U.S. Military Pilot and First Hispanic Female Airline Pilot

Olga discovered the world of aviation after her graduation from the University of Puerto Rico. She landed a job in the accounting department of Primair (Puerto Rico International Airlines). That is where she met her future husband, Edwin Custodio. Earlier, Olga was turned down by the military because of her gender. With his encouragement in 1980, Olga applied for U.S. Air Force Pilot Officer Training School. She literally passed all the tests with flying colors. As a commissioned Second Lieutenant, her aviation training at Laughlin Air Force Base went just as well. At graduation, Olga Custodio became the first Latina pilot in the U.S. Air Force.

Olga Custodio, became the first Latina pilot in the U.S. Air Force. (U.S. Air Force archival photo)

Her first military assignment was instructor pilot. Olga became the first female at Laughlin to become a Northrop T-38 Talon Undergraduate Pilot Training (UPT) Instructor. She demonstrated superior aviation skill in several emergency situations. Olga Custodio served in our U.S. Air Force for over 20 years. But, there is more to her trailblazing story.

While serving in the U.S. Air Force Reserve, she was hired by American Airlines in June, 1988. During her years on the flight deck, she flew Boeing 727, Fokker 100, Boeing 757 and 767 airplanes all over the world. While at American Airlines, she again made history as their first Hispanic female Captain. She retired in 2008 having logged over 11,000 hours.

Olga Custodio is a Charter member of the Women Military Aviators Association. She is the recipient of the Valor Award that honors Latino and Latina veterans whose sacrifices embody the legacy of American military service. You may have seen the Modelo television commercial, "Fighting for Respect with Pilot Olga Custodio." The opening salvo tells her story well. "Olga Custodio refused to be grounded after being rejected by a military training program because she was a woman. Instead, she fought for her right to become the nation's first Latina military pilot. Modelo believes that it doesn't matter where you come from, but what you're made of and is proud to tell Olga's story."

You have to know what sparks the light in you so that you, in your own way, can illuminate the world.

~ Oprah Winfrey

2

D-Delta to K-Kilo

On being in outer space....
It was hard, it was exciting, it was scary, it was
indescribable. And yes, I'd go back in a heartbeat.
~ Marsha S. Ivins, five-mission veteran NASA astronaut

de Laroche, Raymonde: World's First Woman to Earn a Pilot License

Elsie Raymonde Deroche was born in 1882 to a Parisian family of modest means. At an early age, she developed an appetite for sports, motorcycles, and automobiles. As a young woman, she became an actress, adding the aristocratic "de" to her stage name, Raymonde de Laroche. In 1908, she was inspired by the Wrights Flying Exhibition in France. She met many of the famous pioneer aviators from all over the world. Raymonde said to herself, "I can do that. I will fly."

In October, 1909, using her beauty and social connections, she convinced French aviator and aero-plane builder, Charles Voisin, to give her flying lessons. His Chalons flight school was about 90 miles east of Paris. Raymonde was determined to be a famous flying star. The aero-plane could seat only one person, the pilot. While Raymonde sat at the controls in the pilot seat, Voisin, standing close by, told her how to operate the aircraft. Because she was a gifted athlete and familiar with motorcycles and automobiles, she quickly mastered taxiing. However, supposedly, Voisin forbade her to take off.

Probably on purpose, she taxied too fast and on October 22, 1909, the airplane took flight. Raymonde flew an incredible 300 yards.—about the length of three American football fields. Raymonde controlled the machine well enough that an impressed Voisin agreed to continue her flight training. In fact, the following day, Raymonde circled the airfield twice before landing safely. Raymonde was an apt student. The Aeroclub de France, the world's first organization to issue pilot's licenses, awarded their 36th aero-plane pilot's license to de Laroche on March 8, 1910. This officially made her the first woman in the world to be licensed.

The press went wild with the news about this French female aviation pioneer. In their reporting, the press began calling her "Baroness" Raymonde de Laroche. It did not matter that she made up her stage name and that she was not of noble birth. Even back then, marketing trumped truth and built a big crowd for the Reims Air show. Unfortunately, her faux title did not prevent the "Baroness" from suffering severe injuries in a spectacular crash. In fact, her recovery was in doubt.

But, just like the Phoenix rising from the ashes, the indomitable de Laroche flew not long after in aviation meets in Egypt, Budapest, and France. In Saint Petersburg, after her aviation performance, she was personally congratulated by Tsar Nicholas II, who called her the "Baroness Raymonde de Laroche." On November 25, 1913, de Laroche won the Aero Club of France's Femina Cup for her non-stop, long distance flight of over four hours.

During World War I, flying was considered "too dangerous" for women. A disappointed Raymonde became a sedan driver for senior military officers. Post-war, in June 1919, she set two women's altitude records. She also set a distance record. Her desire was to become a test pilot. On July 18, 1919, she co-piloted an experimental aircraft. It is unknown who was in command of the aircraft when it crashed, killing Raymonde and her colleague. Baroness Raymonde de Laroche, the world's first licensed female pilot, is honored with a statue at Paris-Le Bourget Airport.

Raymonde de Laroche, French Aviator, set many aviation records beginning in 1910. (Library of Congress archive)

Dutrieu, Hélène Marguerite: First Belgian Female Pilot

Born in 1877, Hélène had to leave school at age 14 to support her impoverished family. She became a world champion cyclist. She was so talented that she performed as a stunt cyclist and motorcyclist across Europe. With the fascination of flying sweeping Europe during this era, becoming a pilot was a next logical step for their fearless young woman. In early 1910, Hélène Dutrieu learned to fly a Santos Dumont Demoiselle monoplane. She became the first female pilot in Belgium. Then, on April 19, 1910, she made more aviation history by being the first female pilot to fly with a passenger. Of course, there is more.

On November 25, 1910, Dutrieu became the first Belgian woman to be licensed (license #27) by the Royal Belgian Aero Club. She was a wildly popular aerial performer. Audiences and airshow marketers nicknamed her, "The Girl Hawk." But, there was a minor scandal when it was revealed she did not wear a corset while flying. Responding, Hélène described in great detail the Pairs-designed, high fashion, flying suit made with modesty in mind. That controversy quickly disappeared.

Hélène literally flew her way to more fame. Dutrieu flew non-stop from Ostend to Bruges, Belgium, another first. She won acclaim for her long flights. By watching birds, she learned how to use wind currents for lift. On December 21, 1910, Hélène became the winner of the Femina Cup for her non-stop flight of over two hours and 35 minutes. After being the toast of Europe, the United States would be next. In September 1911, with her Farman III bi-plane, she competed for the women's altitude record, significant prize money, and awards.

Quickly, she returned to Europe to compete in a lucrative air race in Florence, Italy. Hélène and 14 male pilots flew in the King's Cup Air Race. Yes, she won! In 1912, she became the first woman in the world to pilot a seaplane. She competed in several seaplane races in Switzerland and won those, too. In 1913, Dutieu because the first woman aviator awarded membership in the French Legion of Honor. Dutieu wanted to fly in World War I, however, military flying was still considered too dangerous for women. She ended up driving an ambulance, an experience enabling her to see that military hospitals were poorly managed. Seizing the initiative, she took command of a military hospital and made it run properly.

Hélène Dutrieu, a celebrated woman of many firsts in aviation. (Library of Congress)

After the war, in 1922, she married Pierre Mortier and became a French citizen. In later years, Hélène became the Vice-President of the Women's Division of the Aero Club of France. In 1956, she created the Hélène Dutrieu-Mortier Cup for the French or Belgian female pilot who made the longest non-stop flight each year. Hélène Dutrieu Mortier died in Paris on June 26, 1961, at the age of 83.

Earhart, Amelia Mary "A. E:" First Woman to Fly Solo Across the Atlantic

On Friday, May 20, 1932, Amelia Earhart and her red Lockheed Vega were ready for her solo, non-stop Trans-Atlantic attempt. She lifted off from the Harbor Grace airfield in Newfoundland, Canada. Only Charles Lindbergh five years earlier had successfully flown alone over the vast

Atlantic waters. Although, she had prepared well, some fear of failure must have mingled with her desire to do what no other woman had ever done before.

Amelia always said, "Women must try to do things as men have tried. When they fail, their failure must be but a challenge to others." Fifteen hours later, on May 21, Amelia landed safely near Londonderry, Northern Ireland. Although bad weather shortened her flight a bit, Amelia Earhart became the first woman in the world to fly solo across the vast Atlantic Ocean. Moreover, Amelia became only the second person in the world to do so.

This flight was especially important to "A.E." because on June 18, 1928, Amelia had already crossed the Atlantic Ocean non-stop in a Fokker tri-motor named, "Friendship." But, even though Amelia was already a record-setting, licensed pilot, she had to sit in the back while two male pilots did the flying. Even worse, pilot Wilmer Stultz was paid $20,000 and, co-pilot Louis Gordon was paid $5,000, while Amelia was paid nothing. Today, the pilot's pay would be the equivalent of over $300,000. The co-pilot's pay today would be almost $80,000.

Amelia was only "given the opportunity to experience the flight." But, the flight did propel her to fame. She wrote a very successful book about the experience, *20 Hours, 40 Minutes: Our Flight in the Friendship*. Also, that 1928 Friendship flight would change her life forever because she met and worked with her future husband, George Palmer Putman, who turned out to be a public-relations man without peer in the 1930s.

Looking back on Amelia's early life, a kind description would be that her life was unstable financially and, because of her father's alcoholism, somewhat dysfunctional. Amelia had to abandon many opportunities because of lack of money or a family move. Born in 1897, in Atchison, Kansas, at an early age she leaned toward outdoor adventures and sports more than "tea parties." And, she was more interested in science and math. During World War I, she served as a Red Cross nurse's aide in Toronto, Canada, where Amelia spent hours watching pilots in the Royal Flying Corps do their training. If the times had been different for women, she might have flown off to war with them.

In 1920, she moved to California where she experienced her first airplane ride with famed World War I pilot, Frank Hawks, who the media dubbed, "the fastest airman in the world." During one of his appearances at the California State Fair on December 28, 1920, he took 23-year-old Amelia on her first flight. Earhart's father arranged for the flight and paid the $10 fee for a 10-minute "hop." The flight changed her life forever.

Amelia Earhart was a woman of many firsts in aviation. (Library of Congress)

In January 1921, she started flying lessons with female flight instructor, "Neta" Snook. Meanwhile, Earhart worked as a Los Angeles Telephone Company filing clerk to pay for flight lessons. Later that year, "A.E." felt confident enough in her aviation skills to purchase her first airplane, a secondhand Kinner Airster. She named the yellow airplane, "the Canary." In December 1921, Earhart passed her flight test earning a National Aeronautics Association license. Two days later, she participated in her first flight exhibition at the Sierra Airdrome in Pasadena, California.

Earhart set a number of aviation records in her early career. Her first record came in 1922 when she became the first woman to fly solo above 14,000 feet. But, in 1924, after her parent's divorce, Amelia sold her airplane to buy a car. She drove her mother across the United States to Boston. Due to financial hardship, Amelia abandoned her studies because they could not afford the cost. Amelia found employment, first as a teacher. Then, she became a social worker at Boston's Denison House.

During those lean years, A.E. continued as she could with flying. She kept a "dream book" of stories about successful women. Stories to keep her inspired. She joined the Boston chapter of the American Aeronautical Society. She was elected Vice President. In 1927, she flew the first official flight out of Denison Airport in Quincy, Massachusetts, along with the Kinner aircraft sales representative. Earhart penned local newspaper columns extolling aviation for men and women. Consequently, her local profile in aviation circles began to grow.

Then, the promoters of the Friendship flight approached her. They needed an "All-American" girl. Amelia was perfect for what they wanted. That she was a licensed pilot was even better. And, so the legendary aviation career of Amelia Earhart began its meteoric ascent. With all of her records after her 1932 solo across the Atlantic, it is clear she was an accomplished aviator. Flying her Vega on August 24-25, 1932, she made the first solo, nonstop flight by a woman across the United States, from Los Angeles to Newark, New Jersey, in about 19 hours. Earhart is the first person ever to fly solo from Hawaii to the U.S. mainland. She set altitude and aviation speed records.

Over her aviation career, she received the United States Distinguished Flying Cross. On November 2, 1929, she formed The International Ninety-Nines for women pilots. She became a consultant to the airlines in their formative years. She became a visiting Purdue University faculty member and advisor in aeronautical engineering. She was a tireless promotor of women as full participants in the aviation industry. Her tragic 1937 disappearance during her attempt to be the first pilot to circumnavigate the globe continues to fascinate and mystify millions of people, young and old.

Even 84 years after her disappearance somewhere over the Pacific Ocean, Amelia Earhart is still one of the most famous female pilots of all time. She remains an inspiration and role model for women around the world. Amelia was a trailblazer in aviation. She was a successful business woman, author, speaker, and an unceasing advocate for women.

The biggest thing is not to give up. If you stay focused on that goal, you can shape your life in that direction.

~ Anne McClain, NASA Astronaut

Erde, Betty Skelton Frankman: First Lady of Firsts

Born in Pensacola, Florida, in 1926, Betty Skelton was precocious and in love with airplanes. Even as a baby, she watched the sky above her backyard. She smiled when she heard the Naval Air Station airplanes roar overhead. She preferred model airplanes over dolls. At age eight, she devoured books about fast airplanes and cars. Her young teenage parents, David and Myrtle, shared her interest. Family friend, Navy ensign Kenneth Wright, took a special interest in the Skelton family. He flew them in his two-seat Taylorcraft, a popular, single-engine, high-wing monoplane. Sometimes, Betty and her parents would hang around their local airport, watching the airplanes take-off and land. Little Betty took every opportunity to "bum a ride around the patch."

Even in 1938, age rules were in place. It was illegal for a child to fly an airplane. Nevertheless, Betty, the natural aviator, soloed in the Taylorcraft at age 12. Betty was born to fly. By age 16, the U.S. Civil Aviation Authority awarded Betty her pilot's license. Because the WASP were helping America win World War II, she applied to join her much older sisters in the sky. But, the age 18 ½ requirement shut that door tightly against her. Still, Betty flew whenever she could. In 1944, she graduated from high school. To secure an Eastern Airlines clerk position, she fudged her age. She worked at night and flew in the daytime.

She quickly earned single and multi-engine land and sea ratings. At only age 18, Betty earned her commercial pilot license. Certified flight instructor soon followed. She began flight instructing at Tampa's Peter O'Knight Airport. Did I mention she joined the newly formed Civil Air Patrol, too? After her father planned a local Jaycees air show, someone suggested Betty should fly in the air show. Betty was game but, did not know any "showy" aviation maneuvers. Aerobatic pilot, Clem Whittenback, easily taught the gifted aviator a loop and a roll. Two weeks later, Betty flew in her first public air performance in a borrowed Fairchild PT-19. When Betty Skelton discovered the world of aerobatics, a new era began for her. Betty loved the maneuvers and fast pace of this air sport.

Betty bought her own aircraft, a 1929 Great Lakes 2T1A bi-plane. In 1946, Betty Skelton began her professional aerobatic career at the Southeastern Air Exposition in Jacksonville, along with a new U.S. Navy exhibition team, the Blue Angels. The Blues named Betty "Sweetheart of the Blue Angels." Betty proved immensely popular with air show audiences. She was accessible, pretty, and she could fly.

Next, Betty wanted to compete on the International aerobatics stage. On January 1, 1948, she won her first International Feminine Aerobatic Championship with her Great Lakes. A striking, new, little biplane caught her eye. It was the Pitts Special. Betty knew it was destined to be hers. The owner would not allow her to fly it, let alone buy it. Undaunted, Betty turned on her legendary charm. By August, the then experimental single-seat, open-cockpit biplane was hers.

Betty Skelton was a trailblazer in the air and on land. (John "J-Cat" Griffith posted photograph)

Betty designed a unique red and white stripped paint scheme. She painted a little skunk on her renumbered N22E Pitts Special. Her plane was christened, "Little Stinker." She loved the open cockpit. Betty explained she did not just fly the small plane, she wore it. Betty won the

Feminine International Aerobatic Championship in 1949 and, again in 1950. She became the first woman to perform an inverted ribbon cut only ten feet above the ground.

Also, in 1949, Betty set the world light plane altitude record in a Piper Cub at 25,763 feet. In 1951 she beat her own record with a new altitude record for a light plane, again in a Piper Cub, of 29,050 feet. And, because she loved speed, Betty set the World aviation record for piston-engine aircraft, flying 421.6 mph in a P-51 Mustang over a three kilometer course.

In 1959, NASA invited Betty Skelton to undergo astronaut testing. She charmed NASA and the Mercury 7 male astronauts with her vivacious personality and her impressive aviation skills. On February 2, 1960, she graced the cover of *Look* magazine as Mercury "7 ½." Betty Skelton had achieved International acclaim. But, she felt with the gender barriers in those years, she had very little incentive to continue. She sold "Little Stinker." She moved on.

But she didn't stop flying. She worked at her family's Fixed Base Operation (FBO). She flew charter flights out of Raleigh, North Carolina. Then, she met Bill France, the NASCAR Founder, who convinced her he had the cure for her "need for speed." Betty Skelton drove the pace car at Daytona Beach Speed Week. In 1954, she set a stock car record in a new Dodge Ram V8.

What lies behind you and what lies before you are NOT as important as the dream within you.

~ Unknown

All of a sudden, a new passion arose in her. Betty became the first female test driver in the automotive industry. She set new records at Utah's Bonneville Salt Flats. She set multiple land speed records. Betty Skelton was the first female Corvette test driver, first to set many transcontinental automobile speed records, and so much more. For more than half a century, Betty was known as "the First Lady of Firsts." She set 17 aviation and race car records. Thirty five years after her retirement, Betty held more combined aviation and auto records and "firsts" than anyone in modern history.

In 1965, Betty married TV director, producer, and Navy veteran pilot, Donald A. Frankman. They reacquired Betty's Pitts. They donated it to the National Air and Space Museum. It is now displayed in the Steven F. Udvar-Hazy Center at Dulles Airport. Naturally, it is suspended inverted. Don died in 2001. Later, Betty married Allan Erde, a retired Navy doctor. On August, 2011, Betty flew West at 85 years young.

Betty is honored in the International Aerobatic Hall of Fame, the International Council of Air Shows Hall of Fame, National Aviation Hall of Fame, WAI Pioneers Hall of Fame, the Motorsports Hall of Fame, and the Corvette Hall of Fame. Annually, the United States National Aerobatics Championship honors the highest placing female with the *Betty Skelton First Lady of Aerobatics* award. Betty Skelton is probably teaching the angels how to fly faster.

Funk, Mary Wallace "Wally:" First Female FAA Inspector and First NTSB Air Safely Inspector

Wally Funk's important character trait is her dogged determination. Born in 1939, she experienced gender stereotyping in high school. She wanted to enroll in mechanical drawing and auto mechanics. Because she was a mere "girl," she was only permitted to take Home Economics. So, Wally left high school to pursue her passion for aviation. At age 16, she was accepted at Stephens College in Columbia, Missouri. There, Wally joined the "Flying Susies," who were organized in 1941 to meet the growing need for World War II pilots. Wally rated first in her

Stephens College class of 24 women pilots. In 1958, Funk graduated with a pilot's license and an Associate of Arts degree.

Wally Funk is a trailblazer of aviation and space. (NASA archival photograph)

Next, she returned to her home state to continue her education and aviation career. She was drawn to Oklahoma State University (OSU) primarily by their famous "Flying Aggies" program. She thrived at OSU. Wally earned Instrument, Commercial, Multi-engine, Sea, and Flight Instructor ratings. She flew on the OSU International Collegiate Air Meets team. She received the "Outstanding Female Pilot" award, was named the "Flying Aggie Top Pilot," and won the Alfred Alder Memorial Trophy two years in a row.

After graduation, at only age 20, Wally began her professional aviation career as a Civilian Flight Instructor for the U.S. Army at Fort Sill. She taught commissioned and non-commissioned personnel. She was the first woman in this position. In fact, she was the ONLY female instructing. Then, Wally Funk joined the civilian Mercury 13 women being tested in a private program modeled after the NASA Mercury 7 male astronaut program. Wally Funk was the youngest woman in the experimental program at age 23. She already had logged over 3,000 flight hours.

Again, because of gender, Wally and the other twelve stellar women of the Mercury 13 Program were never given the opportunity to join NASA and rocket into outer space. Wally Funk, in her ever determined way, flew on to her next opportunity in aviation. In 1961, Wally accepted a new job as a Certified Flight Instructor, Charter, and Chief Pilot with a California aviation company. By 1968, she earned her Airline Transport Pilot (ATP). She applied to three airlines. All three rejected her because of gender. She was more than qualified. That fact did not matter to the airline executives.

In 1971, resolved to further her professional aviation career, Funk earned her Flight Inspector rating from the Federal Aviation Administration (FAA), becoming the first woman to complete their General Aviation Operations Inspector Academy. Wally Funk was the first female FAA field examiner. In two short years, she was promoted to become the very first woman in the United States to hold a Systems Worthiness Analysis Program Specialist position. In 1974, the National Transportation Safety Board (NTSB) hired Wally as their first female Air Safety Investigator. Concurrent with these important and demanding administrative positions, Wally flew and placed in many air races. Flying her red and white Citabria, Wally won the Pacific Air Race from San Diego to Santa Rosa against a large field of pilots.

In 1985, Funk retired from her position as an Air Safety Inspector. But, professional aviation was still on her horizon. She shared her extensive knowledge of aviation safety as a popular speaker and trainer. She was appointed a FAA Safety Counselor. In 1987, she began a new phase in her aviation education journey. Emery Aviation College appointed Wally as their Chief Pilot, overseeing the entire flight program for students pursuing Private to Multi-engine, and Helicopter ratings. Over the years, Wally Funk provided leadership to five aviation schools across the country. As a professional Flight Instructor, she has soloed more than 700 students and put through 3,000 Private,

Commercial, Multi-engine, Seaplane, Glider, Instrument, Certified Flight Instructor, and Air Transport Pilots. She has accumulated almost 20,000 flight hours.

Since 1960, Wally Funk has harbored the dream of flying in space. In 2020, she penned, *Higher Faster Longer: My Life in Aviation and My Quest for Spaceflight.* Sixty years after she dreamed of flying in space, on July 20, 2021, Wally Funk finally lived her dream. She ascended in Blue Origin's "New Shepard" to reach suborbital flight before returning to earth's terra firma. She became the oldest person to launch into space. With her dogged determination, Wally Funk fulfilled her lifelong mission to go into space.

Gaffaney, Mary Tracy: America's First Female Skywriter

On the ground at her Kendall Flying School and Gliderport in Florida, Mary Gaffaney was surprisingly quiet and unassuming. But, strapped into her black and yellow Pitts Special, Mary Gaffaney became the prima ballerina in the sky. She was America's first female Skywriter. Skywriting is created with a special smoke emitted during flight from the airplane to create readable letters in the sky. It requires exact timing and immense skill to maneuver the airplane in precise patterns in a confined area within a short window of time. To perfect this aerial skill takes hours of intense and focused concentration. The skywriter keeps the airplane flying tight, hairpin turns, and doing quick course reversals. All aerobatic skills honed from years of practice, practice, and more practice.

In 1970, Gaffaney became the first American female to win the World Aerobatic Gold. She repeated that astounding feat in 1972. She won the U.S. National Women's Aerobatic title five times in a row. Mary began her life in the air at only age 16. The freedom she felt in the sky never faded. Mary performed at air shows for years and years. The roar of the airplane engines and the adulation of the crowd propelled her to the sky time and time again.

Mary Gaffaney flew several Pitts in her aerobatic career. This is her N6W. (Photo courtesy of Fred Robbins)

Mary Gaffaney was described as the "Reigning Queen of United States Aerobatics." Mary's aviation ratings included single-engine, multi-engine, helicopter, glider, and seaplane. She was also an instrument instructor, and held Airline Transport Pilot (ATP) rating. ATP was an extremely rare accomplishment, especially for a woman born in 1926. She is Florida's first female helicopter pilot. Mary had a laser focus and single-minded dedication to the artistry of aviation.

In 1950, Mary married Charlie Gaffaney, who shared her passion for aviation. Some joked that Mary married him because he owned a Stearman and a Monocoupe. Gaffaneys strategically placed their gliderport for the best soaring conditions is Southern Florida. At the edge of the Everglades, with constant Atlantic Ocean breezes, gliders could soar and sail in the prevailing winds for hours. For over twenty years, Mary shared this love of the sky with her students.

Charlie actually coached Mary in aerobatics with the idea of featuring her in air shows. Mary enjoyed the Stearman. But, Curtis Pitts was building a plane with aerobatics in mind. Once Mary flew that Pitts, she fell in love with it. Mary explained her immediate attraction this way: "I always had to use both hands to snap the old Stearman. But not the Pitts. So, the first Pitts I flew, Zoom! Zoom! They said it was a beautiful double snap. I had to tell them I only meant one. It's so easy to fly. Point it, it goes; pull it, it snaps! Bang! Bang! Oh, it's fun!"

In 1991, Mary's dedication to the sport was recognized by her peers. Mary Gaffaney was inducted into the International Aerobatic Club Hall of Fame. In 2017, at the age of 91, Mary Gaffaney flew West, probably doing loops, rolls, and spins. Shouting, "What a wild ride!"

Greene, Elizabeth Everts "Betty:" WASP and First Mission Aviation Fellowship Pilot

Born in 1920 in Seattle, Betty was raised in a family of Christian believers. Betty began her flying as a teenager. In 1942, she volunteered to help her country win World War II by joining the Women Airforce Service Pilots (WASP). After WASP graduation at Avenger Field, Betty's significant flight skills quickly became apparent. She was selected to test high altitude equipment at Ohio's Wright Field. This flying experience would serve her well in future years. On December 20, 1944, the military disbanded the WASP. Betty looked to a new challenge.

At only age 25, on May 20, 1945, Betty believed she was "called" to use her aviation skills to provide humanitarian and missionary services around the world. Betty co-founded the Christian Airmen Missionary Fellowship, now known as Mission Aviation Fellowship (MAF). Betty became the first pilot. On February 23, 1946, Betty flew the very first MAF flight in a Waco Cabin Bi-plane. Departing Los Angles for Mexico City, Betty carried two female missionaries. At the time, navigation aids in Mexico were few and far between. Betty used her compass, clock, whatever aviation charts were available, and her experience as a WASP to navigate across Mexico.

But the flight to Mexico City was interrupted by what appeared to be bits of the cowling departing the aircraft. Out of an abundance of caution, Betty diverted to Tuxpan, Mexico. The next day, the missionaries left for Mexico City. Betty stayed with the airplane. After a thorough inspection, Betty found the cowling was intact; however, the cowling was minus much of its paint. On reaching Mexico City, Betty was met by Cameron Townsend, the founder of Wycliffe Bible Translators. Townsend asked Betty to fly him to their Jungle Camp near Tuxtla Gutierriez, a remote village located south of Mexico City. Betty did not hesitate because this was the exact purpose she had for her newly-founded organization.

Missionary pilot, Betty Greene, was also a World War II WASP. (Courtesy of Mission Aviation Fellowship)

To reach Tuxtla, she had to refuel at the village of Minatitlan. After refueling, her Waco ran into a heavy rain storm forcing her to turn back toward Minatitlan. To add to her excitement, the Waco's engine died. Betty, the former WASP, switched gas tanks and attempted a restart. The engine surged back to life and she made it back to Minatitlan safely. Betty discovered the problem, as is so often the case with remote jungle refueling, water in the fuel drum. In later years, her jungle flying experiences helped train future MAF pilots. The next morning, Betty flew Cameron to Tuxtla on a short flight, reaching her destination one week after taking off from Los Angeles on the first MAF flight. She learned many lessons that would serve her and other MAF pilots well in the years to come. Her experiences are shared in the book, *Flying High: The Amazing Story of Betty Greene.*

Betty Greene flew MAF missions for 16 years in many remote locations in Mexico, Peru, Indonesia, Nigeria, Sudan, Ethiopia, Uganda, Kenya, The Congo, and other countries. In 1956, Betty Greene was the first woman to fly in Sudan. The Sudanese Parliament passed special legislation to allow a woman to fly in their county because their own female citizens were not allowed to do so. Betty devoted her aviation skills to delivery of the Gospel, medical care, food, and water distribution to remote and impoverished outposts. Disaster relief was an all-too frequent added mission. Recall, one of Betty Greene's early aviation tasks was testing high-altitude equipment. When Betty became one of the few women to fly solo across the Peruvian Andes Mountains, it must have seemed that she was fulfilling some kind of Divine plan.

As she had done in World War II as a WASP, Betty Greene continued to ferry MAF aircraft and provide important leadership at MAF headquarters. Over her thirty-year MAF career, Betty mentored many pilots and aviation mechanics, sharing her years of "boots on the ground" and "seat of the pants flying." In 1997, Betty flew West. But, in 2017, her significant contributions were recognized with selection into the WAI Pioneer Hall of Fame.

Life is Awesome in the Sky!

~ Unknown

Haizlip, Mary Hays "Mae:*" World Aviation Speed Record Pilot
Born in the early 1900s, Mae grew up in St. Louis. Census records indicate her father was involved with mining. Mae attend the University of Oklahoma and became interested in aviation. Her husband, James, was a World War I veteran and a pilot. He encouraged Mae in her aviation career. In addition to earning her pilot license, Mae became the second woman in the United States to qualify for a Commercial Pilot's license. During the 1920s, she was a test pilot for Spartan Aircraft Company, American Eagle, and Bull Aircraft.

Mae successfully competed in several aviation races and earned prize money. In October, 1929, flying an American Eagle airplane, she joined the National Air Tour, circumnavigating the Eastern states. In 1931, she became the second highest prize winner of all the National Air Race flyers in Cleveland, Ohio. Mae won $5,300 for her efforts, including $1,800 for her second-place in the Transcontinental Derby. That amount of money was much more than most citizens earned for the whole year, especially as the Great Depression deepened. If a woman could find employment during those years, she would expect to earn only a few dollars a day. Mae earned the equivalent of almost $95,000 in today's value.

According to the Aircraft Yearbook, at the 1932 National Air Race, Mae set a new world speed record for women. She flew over 255 mph. Her record stood for seven years. Earlier, on August 29th, her husband, Jimmie, flew that same airplane and won the Bendix cross-country race from Los Angeles, California to Floyd Bennett Airfield, Long Island, New York.

Mae won the 1932 Shell Speed Trophy as the fastest woman flyer. In 1933, Haizlip won first place in both the Los Angeles Aero Trophy Race and the Chicago Walter E. Olsen Trophy Women's Air Race. These wins and the world aviation speed record ensured her place as one of six recipients of the *Outstanding American Flier of the Year Award* from the National Aeronautic Association. Interestingly, her husband, Jimmie, competed in some of the same air races. He also was a recipient of the title that year, along with Amelia Earhart, Frances Marsalis, Louise Thaden, and Major James Doolittle.

In a few years, Mae Haizlip retired from aviation to pursue other business opportunities. In 1982, Mary Haizlip was the first woman pilot inducted in the Oklahoma Aviation and Space Hall of Fame. *Several references cited "May," as the spelling.

World aviation speed record-holder, Mary Haizlip, circa 1930. (San Diego Air and Space Museum archive)

Harmer, Barbara: **First Female Concorde Pilot and Captain**

On March 25, 1993, forty year old, Barbara Harmer became the first woman to qualify to fly the Concorde. Later that year, she became the first female British Airways First Officer to fly the Concorde at the controls of the world's only supersonic passenger jet. Harmer was one of only 40 women pilots with British Airways. But, she made aviation history. As she barreled down the runway, she would fly the Concorde at twice the speed of sound over the Atlantic Ocean to New York's JFK International Airport.

Harmer had a unique journey to this important flight. Born in 1953, she grew up in the seaside British resort of Bognor. She left school at age 15 to become a hairdresser. After a few years, Barbara decided she needed more adventure. At age 21, she became an air traffic controller trainee at London Gatwick Airport. When aviation opened her eyes to a world of possibilities, she focused on advanced courses she had missed when she dropped out of school. At her own expense, she invested thousands of dollars to pay for flight instruction. Barbara really enjoyed the view of the world from her airplanes. She earned her Private Pilot License, then her Commercial Pilot License. She soared on to become a Flight Instructor. She knew her goal was to become an airline pilot. With her advanced ratings and hours of flight building, she completed about 100 applications before she was selected as a pilot with Genair, a small commuter airline. This was just another stepping stone in her aviation flight plan.

In 1984, she joined the private, independent British Caledonian Airline. Barbara flew out of Gatwick airport where she began her aviation journey earlier. Barbara piloted the British Aircraft Corporation One-Eleven, a smaller jet airliner. After about three years of building seniority, Harmer moved to piloting long-haul McDonnell Douglas DC-10s. In 1988, British Airways (BA) took over Barbara's airline. With over 3,500 pilots employed at BA already, finding her place on the British Airways flight deck would be a challenge. Nevertheless, Barbara was selected to fly for British Airways. At that point, Barbara decided that she was destined to fly the Concorde, someday.

World's first female British Airways pilot of the iconic Concorde, supersonic passenger airliner. (Heritage Concorde photograph)

In 1992, British Airways executives hand-selected a few of their pilots to undergo the rigorous six months of training and testing to become Concorde-qualified. Barbara was one of only 37 BA Captains and First Officers out of 3,500, who had the seniority, experience, training, and determination to fly the world's only supersonic commercial passenger jet. The Concorde cruises at a speed of 1,341 mph with seating for 92 to 128 passengers. The Concorde was a fast airliner. For example, on February 7, 1996, the Concorde flew on a Trans-Atlantic New York to London flight in only two hours, 52 minutes, and 59 seconds. Today, the average commercial airline flight time is over seven hours for the same route.

Barbara Harmer went on to her destiny with aviation history when she became the first woman to Captain the Concorde. Barbara flew the Concorde for ten years. In 2003, British Airways retired the Concorde.

Harmer continued to fly for British Airways as Captain of Boeing 777 flights. Over the years, Barbara was a popular speaker about the opportunities in aviation for women. She retired in 2009. At only age 57, Barbara Harmer flew West.

Haydu, Bernice Faulk "Bee:" WASP and Order of Fifinella President

In her book, *Letters Home 1944-1945*, Bernice Falk Haydu chronicles her military experiences in the Women Airforce Service Pilots (WASP) of World War II. Born in 1920, she faced many problems that had to be overcome. She greatly admired her brother, Lloyd, who was serving in the Army Air Corps. So, while working as a secretary, she enrolled in aviation classes on weekends. She discovered a love of flying. Wanting to help America win World War II, she applied and was selected for WASP flight training at Avenger Field in Sweetwater, Texas. Her prior aviation training was key in her success. She was given the nickname, "Bee," short for Bernice. But, some said "Bee" reminded them of a bumble bee in flight!

Her first assignment was Pecos Air Force Base in Texas as an engineering test pilot and general utility pilot for military missions. "If an engine was overhauled and needed to be flown in a certain manner for a certain number of hours before it went into regular service, I would do that. If personnel had to be flown somewhere in the United States, I flew them wherever they had to go." Bee told the *DOD News* in March 9, 2016.

The WASP were promised that if the "women flying military planes experiment worked out," they would receive military benefits and status. Well, the WASP kept their side of the bargain. But, when the military shut down the WASP program in 1944, the U.S. Government did not honor its promises to these brave women. The government even classified the WASP files so their service remained a "secret" for years. Not until 1977 were WASP finally given the military benefits and recognition they had been promised way back in World War II. Unfortunately that was too late for many of these patriotic women. As president of the WASP organization, the Order of Fifinella, from 1975 to 1978, Bee Haydu tirelessly led the effort to get Congress to recognize the WASP as war veterans. During her tenure, the WASP finally received the recognition they so richly deserved and earned.

Bee Faulk Haydu, an outstanding World War II WASP, was truly a proud member of America's Greatest Generation. (U.S. Air Force archival photograph)

In 1951, Bee Falk married fellow aviator, Joe Haydu. They raised a family together. Bee ever busy, ferried aircraft for dealers. In a few years, she opened a Cessna dealership. She owned a flight school. She sold aircraft parts worldwide to stay in the industry she loved. She participated in the air and on the ground at airshows. She flew in two All Women's Transcontinental Air Races, aka Powder Puff Derbies. From 1978 to 1980, she was president of Women Military Aviators.

Bee Haydu continued to donate memorabilia and record oral history for the Library of Congress, National Air and Space Museum, and Texas Woman's University archive about WASP service and contributions to our nation. Bee Haydu is recognized as a member of the Women in Aviation International Pioneer Hall of Fame. She is the winner of The International Ninety-Nines Award of Inspiration. In 2009, she was one of three surviving WASP to accept the Congressional Gold Medal for their World War II service. On December 15, 2020, she turned one hundred. A month later, Bee Faulk Haydu flew West, leaving a legacy of service to her nation and to her sky sisters in the WASP.

Helms, Susan: The First U.S. Military Woman in Space

Born in 1958, Susan Helms was introduced to aviation early. The daughter of a U. S. Air Force officer, she set her sights on the U.S. Air Force Academy, which at the time did not accept women. "I basically decided at a young age - and by young, I mean junior high - that the whole thing of being in the military and, particularly the Air Force, appealed to me. There were a couple of strong points that I wanted. One of them was the opportunity to travel - little did I know how far that would go – and, also the opportunity for a stable career. I like the idea of moving every few years and seeing different places, and it appeared that my dad had had a very rewarding Air Force career. It looked like, as an engineer, I could also have the same," Helms said in a March 1, 2001 NASA Pre-flight interview.

Indeed, in 1976, Susan Helms began her journey at the U.S. Air Force Academy in the first class which accepted women into the cadet corps. Four years later, Lieutenant Helms graduated. Susan was assigned to Eglin Air Force Base, Florida, as a Weapons Engineer for the F-16. Two years later, she became the lead engineer for F-15 weapons separation. Next, came graduate school. Susan earned a Master of Science in Aeronautics/Astronautics at Stanford University. Then, Helms returned to the Air Force Academy as an assistant professor of aeronautics. Just a year later, Susan was selected for the Air Force Test Pilot School at Edwards Air Force Base, California. Excelling in her training, Helms was selected for a U.S. Air Force Exchange to the Aerospace Engineering Test Establishment, Canadian Forces Base in Alberta. Helms worked as a Flight Test Engineer and project officer on the CF-18 aircraft. She was managing the development of a CF-18 Flight Control System Simulation for the Canadian Forces when she was selected for our NASA astronaut program in 1990.

Astronaut Susan Helms in space. (NASA photograph)

Before she began her space training, Susan Helms, as a Flight Test Engineer, flew in 30 different types of U.S. and Canadian military aircraft. Next, would be outer space. In 1991, Major Helms became an astronaut. In 1993, she flew on her first space mission, STS-54. This made her the first military woman in United States history to serve in space. Helms flew on three more shuttle missions, STS-64 (1994), STS-78 (1996), and STS-101 (2000). Helms served aboard the International Space Station (ISS) as a member of the Expedition 2 crew (2001). She is the first woman to serve on the ISS. A veteran of five spaceflights, Helms logged 5,064 hours in space, including a spacewalk of eight hours and 56 minutes, setting a world record. She had a 12-year NASA career that included 211 days in space,

In July 2002, Helms returned to the U.S. Air Force. In 2006, she was promoted to Brigadier General. She became Commander of the 45th Space Wing at Patrick Air Force Base in Florida. Ironically, she was responsible for the processing and launch of U.S. Government and commercial satellites into space from Cape Canaveral Air Force Station, Florida. In 2011, after several other important U.S. Air Force assignments and promotions, she earned the rank of Lieutenant General. In 2014, Lt. General Susan Helms retired from military service. She continues to contribute her knowledge, experience, and enthusiasm for air and space to many important organizations. She has earned many awards throughout her illustrious career, including selection in the Astronauts Hall of Fame.

Howard-Phelan, Jean Ross: Founder of the Whirly Girls

Jean's love affair with flying began innocently enough. At age 11, she listened intently at the Mayflower Hotel in Washington, D.C. to celebrity aviator, Charles Lindbergh, recount the details of his historic Spirit of St. Louis flight. Her fascination with flying continued to grow. One sunny day, Jean skipped her high school classes. She took her Christmas money to the airport. She bought her first airplane ride. The flames only grew hotter in her quest to fly. The next flight was in a Sikorsky Flying Boat or amphibious airplane on a trip in Southern California. In just a few years, another Sikorsky design would play an important role in her life.

In 1941, not long after returning home, Jean's enrolled in the last Civilian Pilot Training class conducted at George Washington

University during World War II. She earned her Private Pilot license. In 1943, the legendary Jackie Cochran recruited female pilots for the new Women Airforce Service Pilots (WASP) training program. Jean was selected. She immediately quit her secure, government job. Then, Jean paid her own expenses to get to Texas WASP training, as did all the other WASP.

Already a licensed pilot, Jean found her way and the Army's way were not a good fit. Jackie Cochran spotted Jean's incredible organizational skills as a huge benefit to the WASP. Cochran personally asked Jean to stay on "to help run the school." Jean was thrilled to help manage this important World War II program. Then, Jean was asked to serve her country as American Red Cross Program Director, until the end of the war. Because Jean had such executive ability, she was invited back to Washington, D.C. to join the staff of the Aeronautical Chamber of Commerce (ACC), which later because the Aerospace Industries Association.

In 1947, Jean was sent as the ACC representative to the world's first helicopter air show. Earlier, famed aeronautical designer, Igor Sikorsky, had perfected the first practical helicopter. His design had been significantly improved for greater utility and reliability. Yes, of course, part of the experience was to take a helicopter flight at the air show. The "flying bug" hit Jean again. Still, it took her six years to convince her boss she would do a much better job for ACC with helicopter training. Larry Bell, President of Bell Helicopter, agreed. After only 18 days of instruction at the Bell Fort Worth factory, Jean became a rated helicopter pilot. Upon landing after her flight check, her helicopter instructor said, "Well, Jean, now you are a real whirly girl." That was in 1953. Jean became the eighth woman in the United States to earn a helicopter rating.

Jean described flying a helicopter like "patting your head and rubbing your stomach simultaneously." Helicopters were fun to fly and utilitarian. It did not take Jean long to identify the twelve other women in the world who held a helicopter rating. By April 28, 1955, Jean had set up the framework for a worldwide organization to support women to become helicopter pilots. She invited the twelve others to join her. All twelve accepted her invitation to be charter members in Whirly-Girls, International Women Helicopter Pilots.

In 1955, Jean Ross Howard-Phelan founded and guided Whirly-Girls. In her retirement photograph, she is wrapped in a quilt made for her by grateful members of the International Women Helicopter Pilots. (American Helicopter Museum)

Jean was one of the 13 founding members, representing women helicopter pilots from France, Germany, and the United States. Early financial support came from Howard Hughes. Hughes made only 150 membership pins for the group, mistakenly believing there would never be the need for more than that. Today, membership is over 2,000 from 49 countries worldwide. Their annual meetings are often called "Hoverings."

From 1969 to 1973, Jean served as the Whirly-Girls first President. During her tenure, Jean encouraged the establishment of hospital heliports and the use of helicopters in emergency medical service worldwide. Jean also remained at the Aerospace Industries Association as Director of Helicopter Activity. In 1986, she retired. In later years, Jean married James D. Phelan, a pilot. Jean Ross Howard-Phelan believed Whirly-Girls would form a worldwide support network to encourage women to pursue missions in the air.

Jemison, Mae Carol: First Black Female NASA Astronaut

Born in 1956, Mae Jemison was the youngest of three children. Her mother was an elementary school teacher and her father was a maintenance supervisor. Mae's family moved to the Chicago area in her early years. Mae was enthralled watching the Apollo space launches on television. But, she was often disappointed because there were no female astronauts. Mae loved school subjects related to math and science. Mae always watched the television show, *Star Trek*. Jemison was inspired by the beautiful, African American actress, Nichelle Nichols, who played the very capable Starship Enterprise Communications Officer, Lieutenant Nyota Uhura. Jemison decided one day she would travel in space.

After high school graduation in 1973, star student, Mae Jemison, was accepted at California's Stanford University. In 1977, Jemison graduated with a Bachelor of Science degree in Chemical Engineering and a Bachelor of Arts degree in African American studies. After graduating from Stanford University, Jemison attended Cornell Medical School.

While in medical school, Jemison volunteered her medical services in Thailand and Cuba. Dr. Jemison graduated in 1981. She interned in Los Angles in general medicine. Fluent in Russian, Japanese, and Swahili, Mae joined the Peace Corps in 1983. She served as a Medical

Officer for two years in Africa. In 1985, Mae Jemison decided to apply to NASA for acceptance in the astronaut corps. Unfortunately, the Space Shuttle Challenger disaster in January, 1986, put a temporary freeze on any acceptance of new candidates. Determined, Mae again applied in 1987. Over 2,000 applications were submitted for only 15 Astronaut Group 12 slots. Dr. Jemison was selected. She trained with NASA. As an engineer, she worked on projects at the Kennedy Space Center and the Shuttle Avionics Integration Laboratory. In September, 1989, she was selected to join the STS-47 crew as a Mission Specialist. On September 12, 1992, Dr. Mae Jemison flew on the space shuttle Endeavor. This voyage made Jemison the first Black American woman in space. On Endeavor, Jemison made 127 orbits around the Earth and returned to the Kennedy Space Center in Florida from the eight-day mission. Just as she had heard over twenty five years earlier as she watched the Starship Enterprise crew, Mae Jemison fulfilled her childhood dream of being in "Space: the final Frontier."

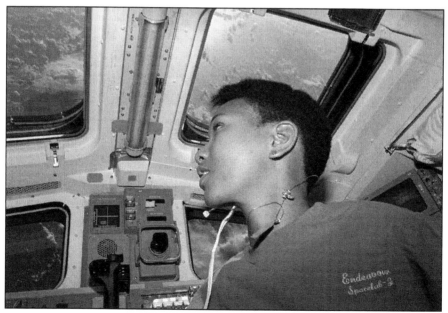

On September 12, 1992, Dr. Mae Jemison became the first Black female to fly into space on the Space Shuttle Endeavor. (NASA photograph)

As a doctor, engineer, and NASA astronaut, Mae Jemison has always reached for the stars. In 1993, Jemison left NASA. She has authored several books, founded a science, technology, and social change consulting firm, and is leading the 100 Year Starship Project to insure human space travel continues. Trailblazer Jemison is in the National Women's Hall of Fame, International Space Hall of Fame, National Medical Association Hall of Fame, and Texas Science Hall of Fame.

Jernigan, Tamara Elizabeth "Tammy:" Astrophysicist NASA Astronaut

Born in 1959, Tammy could not comprehend yet the monumental NASA announcement earlier that year. The world was introduced to America's all male Mercury 7 astronauts. Growing up, Tammy was always inquisitive. She was fascinated with science. At only ten years old, Tammy, along with the rest of the world, watch as Apollo 11 landed on the moon. The memory of watching the astronauts "moon walk," stayed with this bright, young mind during her stellar career.

During high school and her collegiate years, Jernigan enjoyed volleyball, racquetball, softball, and flying. As a Stanford undergraduate, she competed in intercollegiate athletics on the varsity volleyball team. Jernigan earned her Bachelor of Science in Physics (with honors). After graduating from Stanford University with her Master's degree in Engineering Science, in June, 1981, Jernigan served as a research scientist in the Theoretical Studies Branch at NASA Ames Research Center. She also continued studying for her advanced degrees. In 1983, she was awarded a second Master's in Astronomy from the University of California-Berkeley. Then, she completed her doctorate in Space Physics and Astronomy from Rice University.

NASA noticed this brilliant sky star. In 1985, she was selected as an astronaut candidate. In July 1986, Jernigan became a NASA astronaut. She served in a number of roles critical to the NASA mission in flight software development and verification, and spacecraft communications. Tammy Jernigan flew on five Space Shuttle missions.

In 1991, her first was STS-40. As a research scientist, her experiments focused on how humans, animals, and cells respond to microgravity and readapt to Earth's gravity on return.

On May 30, 1999, Astronaut Tamara Jernigan on STS-96 Discovery performed a spacewalk or extra-vehicular activity (EVA) which lasted for seven hours and 55 minutes. (NASA photograph)

Next, she flew on STS-52 (1992), STS-67 (1995), STS-80 (1996), and STS-96 in 1999. On STS-96 Discovery, Astronaut Jernigan performed a spacewalk or EVA (Extravehicular activity). This mission was the first space shuttle docking with the International Space Station (ISS).

In 2001, Dr. Jernigan retired from NASA. During her career, she completed five Space Shuttle program missions (three on Columbia, and one each on Endeavour and Discovery), logging over 1,512 hours in space, including a spacewalk totaling 7 hours and 55 minutes. She provided leadership in several NASA programs. After NASA, Jernigan accepted a position at Lawrence Livermore National Laboratory with a focus on Physics and Advanced Technologies.

Johnson, Amy: Britain's Legendary Aviator

Legendary aviator, Amy Johnson, was born in England in 1903, the same year the Wright Brothers flew at Kitty Hawk, North Carolina. From an early age, Amy was destined to make flying her life. The eldest of four sisters, Amy grew up in a secure, merchant-class family. Amy avidly read the newspaper stories about famous World War I British Aces in the Royal Flying Corps. These stories of heroic pilots stayed with her.

For a short while, Amy studied at Sheffield University. But, adventurous Amy started a new life in London. She secured a typist position with a law firm. In the 1920s, the newspapers were now filled with aviation stories about rich and titled women, such as Lady Heath and Lady Bailey. Amy thought she would try her skills at the aerodrome in North London. On a Sunday afternoon, she boarded the bus to arrive into a world of exciting opportunity. She fell in love with flying.

Johnson described her feelings on flying, "There is nothing more wonderful and thrilling than going up into the spaciousness of the skies in a tiny plane where you are alone, at peace with everyone, and exactly free to do what you want and go where you will." Amy spent all her spare time at the aerodrome. With financial help from her father, Amy pursued flying lessons. She was an excellent student. In 1928, Amy became one of the first British women to gain her pilot's license. Also, she became Britain's first female aircraft ground engineer, which qualified and licensed Amy to certify the airworthiness of an aircraft.

Any was always a big thinker. In May, 1930, she meticulously planned her flight from England to Australia. She knew her de Havilland Gipsy Moth, she named "Jason," inside and out. But, with little knowledge available about the terrain along her route, she just drew a straight line with a ruler on what few aviation charts existed as the most direct route. Remember, in 1930, no radio links existed. There were no reliable weather forecasts. There was no emergency assistance on the ground. Hers was a flight into the unknown, alone, in an open cockpit airplane. All her refueling points were based on the straight line course she had plotted. Amy's longest flight up to this point had been the 145 miles from London to her home town of Hull.

Nevertheless, on May 5, 1930, Amy set off on her solo flight to Darwin; Australia. The British press went wild with their major focus on her gender. As her perilous journey was reported daily, they named her, "British Girl Lindbergh," "Wonderful Miss Johnson," and "The Lone Girl Flyer." Actually, the magnitude of the attempt warranted all the hype. Yes, this gutsy woman made aviation history with this 11,000 mile quest.

> *Cherish your yesterdays. Dream your tomorrows.*
> *Live your todays well.*
> *~ Unknown*

Along the way, a freak sandstorm in Iraq forced a desert landing. In India, she surprised an entire Army garrison when she landed on their parade ground. They had never seen a woman pilot before. They celebrated her landing for an entire day. Newspaper readers were fascinated with the story. Many held their breath as our British heroine flew bravely on. Next challenge was a monsoon in Burma. Then, still in Burma (Myanmar today), a bumpy landing in Rangoon ripped a hole in Jason's wing and damaged its propeller. Miraculously, a local technical institute unpacked World War I surplus shirts for fabric to fix the wing. With rudimentary tools, the propeller was fixed and reinstalled.

The press could not make up all the things that actually happened to this British heroine and her little airplane. Soon, her story took on mythical proportions as a modern version of the Greek Jason and his Argonauts Odyssey. Intrepid Amy Johnson landed in Australia on Saturday, May 24, 1930 to a tumultuous welcome. The worldwide celebrations lasted for six weeks. She was an international Super Sky Star. She was the "it" girl. Women asked that their hair be styled in the

"Amy Johnson wave." At least ten popular songs were written about her. The most famous was "Amy, Wonderful Amy."

Amy Johnson in her Gipsy Moth flew from England to Australia in 1930. (Wikimedia photograph)

Fan mail poured in by the ton…An envelope addressed to "Amy wat flies in England" reached her. Naturally, she was exhausted by the physical and mental strain of her flight, let alone the weeks of celebrations everywhere. Amy did what she had always done, she returned to her peace in the sky. In July, 1931, Johnson flew with her mentor and mechanic, Jack Humphreys, to Tokyo, Japan. They set world record times to both Moscow and Japan. Then, another love entered Amy's life.

In 1932, after a short courtship, Amy married record-setting, Scottish pilot, Jim Mollison. The world now fell head over heels in love with the "flying sweethearts." Also, in 1932, Amy set another record for her solo flight from London to Cape Town, South Africa. The next year, Amy and Jim flew together across the Atlantic Ocean. A dangerous flight given the storms and few navigation and communications instruments that were available. Because of the long distance, they had to carry a large amount of fuel. On August 1, 1933, they reached the United States making them the first married couple to fly the Atlantic east to west. They had planned on a New York landing but due to weather, a navigation error, and running out of fuel, they crash landed in Bridgeport, Connecticut. This "minor detail" was overlooked by the over 50,000 adoring fans attending their New York City ticker tape parade.

Wait, there is more: The intrepid aviator couple flew a new de Havilland DH 88 Comet in the famed MacRobertson Air Race. Aviators were to fly from London to South Africa with winners announced for various legs of the course. Early on, the world's flying sweethearts set another record-breaking time. However, in India, engine trouble grounded their hopes of winning significant prize money. In May, 1936, Amy Johnson flew from England to South Africa alone, regaining her previous record. Although the couple remained friends, they divorced in 1938. Then, the winds of War blew into Europe again. In 1940, Amy joined the Air Transport Auxiliary. Her job was to ferry airplanes around the county for delivery to the Royal Air Force (RAF).

Tragically, in 1941, on a cold Sunday, January 5 morning, Amy Johnson left Blackpool flying an Airspeed Oxford twin-engine monoplane for delivery to the RAF. Get ready, this does not end well. Either mechanical failure, poor navigation in snowy conditions, fuel starvation, or all these contributing factors ended the life of one of Britain's brightest sky stars. Her body was never recovered. Although, later, some personal items, her logbook, and a travelling bag washed up nearby on the shores of the Thames Estuary. Johnson was declared missing and dead from drowning.

Of course, some rumors started immediately about a "secret mission." Newspapers even picked up the idea that a second person, a "Mr. "X," was in the plane when it crashed into the water. Some reported that Amy parachuted out but landed in the water where rescuers could not reach her in time. The mystery of her disappearance only adds to the mystique of her legacy in aviation history. Her story is one of soaring above adversity. In 2016, Johnson was celebrated with induction into the Women in Aviation International Pioneer Hall of Fame.

Johnson, Evelyn Stone Bryan "Mama Bird:" Celebrated American Flight Instructor

Born in 1909, Johnson was living with her first husband, Wyatt Jennings Bryan, in Florida. Right after Pearl Harbor, he enlisted in the Army Air Corps. His example inspired Evelyn. When Evelyn saw a "Learn to Fly" sign, she knew that message was meant for her. At age 35, she learned to fly and never stopped loving aviation from that point on. Flying became her passion. With every take-off and landing her hours and ratings climbed.

By 1947, Evelyn became a Certified Flight Instructor. Over the years, she sold Cessna airplanes, flew in U.S. air races, wrote about aviation, joined the Civil Air Patrol, and became Whirly Girl member #20. At age 92, Evelyn became the world's oldest flight instructor. She continued until ill-health grounded her at age 95. She earned the nickname, "Mama Bird." Over her aviation career, she logged over 57,000 hours in airplanes. The *Guinness Book of World Records* listed her as having the most flying hours of any woman in the world. Mama Bird said, "I don't care how many problems you have down on the ground, you forget about them while flying."

In 1953, Evelyn became the Morristown Regional Airport manager in Tennessee. Even after a 2006 automobile accident required the amputation of her leg, until age 100, Evelyn faithfully visited the airport to check on operations. After the death of Evelyn's first husband in 1963, a few years later, Mama Bird married Morgan Johnson, who loved her passion for all things aviation. Her husband always knew he could find her at the airport.

Evelyn Bryan Johnson, nicknamed, "Mama Bird," logged over 57,000 hours in the sky. (Wikicommons)

Along the way, Evelyn was named Flight Instructor of the Year by the Federal Aviation Administration (FAA) and the Whirly Girls honored her with their Livingston Award. In 2007, at only 98 years young, she became a proud member of our National Aviation Hall of Fame. She is in WAI Pioneer Hall of Fame and the Tennessee Aviation Hall of Fame, all, because she knew she needed to learn to fly and share the gift of flight. Evelyn Johnson trained more pilots and gave more FAA exams than any other Flight Instructor in recent history. She flew West in 2012, at age 102. She is probably giving the angels flying tips and keeping them current.

Kimbrell, Shawna Rochelle: First U.S. Air Force Black Female Fighter Pilot

Shawna's Guyanese family migrated to Indiana for educational opportunity and to seek the American dream of a better life. Soon, they became naturalized citizens. Then, Shawna was born as their youngest of four children. Eventually, her family moved to Colorado. In fourth grade, Shawna declared she would become a fighter pilot. Her first flight lesson was at age 14. Next, Shawna became a Civil Air Patrol cadet. Her pathway to the sky continued.

Shawna loved aviation. She volunteered at air shows. The joy of watching the airplanes soar across the sky propelled Shawna to earn her Private Pilot license. An excellent student, she was accepted at the United States Air Force Academy. Her whole family celebrated achieving her American Dream. In 1988, she graduated with a Bachelor of Science in General Engineering. Flight school soon followed at Laughlin AFB. In August, 1999, she earned her U.S. Air Force Flight Silver Wings. Shawna now served her county in the sky.

Next, would be advanced aviation training at Randolph AFB. She flew on to Luke AFB for her initial F-16 training. The F-16 or Fighting Falcon is a highly-sophisticated, single-engine, multi-million dollar, jet fighter aircraft. In August 2000, Shawna graduated from her initial F-16 training becoming the first Black American female fighter pilot in the United States Air Force to do so. Wait, her story gets even better.

Fighter pilot Shawna Kimbrell's first operational assignment was with the 13th Fighter Squadron, in Misawa, Japan. During this duty tour, her Squadron was deployed to Turkey and Saudi Arabia in support of both Operation Northern and Southern Watch. During Operation Northern Watch, Shawna became the first U.S. Air Force Black female pilot to engage the enemy in actual combat.

U.S. Air Force Fighter pilot, Shawna Kimbrell. (U.S. Air Force photograph by Airman 1st class Ashley Wood)

Shawna Kimbrell continued her Air Force career in several flight squadrons around the world. In 2013, she transferred from the active duty Air Force to the Air Force Reserves. Over her stellar career, she earned a Master's in Business Administration from Touro University in California. After her retirement in 2019, at the rank of Lt. Colonel, Kimbrell returned to the U.S. Air Force Academy to guide a new generation of Air Force leaders as the director of culture, climate, and diversity.

The advice she offered in a February 23, 2012, *U.S. Air Force News* interview still is valid today. "It's really hard to build a road, if you don't know where you're going. A lot of people have goals, but don't really put them into context. If a goal is really your end state, you have to look at the terrain you have to go through to get there, how you're going to build that road and what you're going to do. Nothing's easy. Expect road blocks, expect that there are going to be people out there who don't want you to succeed, expect people are going to tell you 'no.' But the desire that comes from within -- if it's something that you really want -- will carry you through."

King, Martha Rockwood: Award Winning Flight Instructor

If you asked "Siri" or "Alexa" to tell you the name of America's most recognized female flight instructor, odds are Siri and Alexa would shout: "Martha King." In 1975, Martha, with her business partner and husband, John, founded the highly successful King Schools. As Certified Flight Instructors, they travelled from state-to-state, providing a jam-packed two-day ground-school for wannabe pilots. Then, in the early 1960s, with Video Cassette Recording (VCR) sales booming, the Kings became the "kings" of easy-to-understand flight instruction delivery via the "magic" of video recordings. They produced scores of videos, covering every aspect of learning to fly and to fly safely. Flight schools across America gobbled up the King's videos and sat thousands of their students down in front of video screens. Flight schools found it was like having Martha and John King on their staff.

It was not long before the reach of the King team became worldwide. When the personal computer craze hit, the Kings adapted and went online. The King team became the industry leader in personal aviation education. By 1994, John and Martha King were the first and only couple in aviation history to hold every FAA instructor certificate for every type of General Aviation aircraft and for every type of flying: Private, Commercial, Instrument, you name it.

Martha King is the first and only woman to achieve this complete ratings sweep. Martha King, not only holds the Airline Transport Pilot (the Ph.D. of flying), she is rated to fly: fixed-wing, rotary-wing, glider, seaplanes, balloon, drones, powered parachutes, and even blimps. If it flies, Martha has the FAA rating for it. Somehow, Martha finds time to write for a variety of aviation magazines and is often the headliner at aviation conferences across America.

In 1994, Martha King became the first woman to achieve ratings in every FAA category and class for pilot certificates. (Courtesy King Schools, Inc.)

The array and diversity of the King Schools courses is breathtaking. Some free on-line courses encourage exploration of aviation. Safety and having fun flying have been a hallmark of King Schools. For almost half a century, Martha and John King have become the personal mentors to a whole generation of aviators, flight instructors, and aviation mechanics. They have been honored by the National Association of Flight Instructors and the National Aviation Hall of Fame. Martha said when she established the Martha King Scholarship for Female Flight Instructors through Women in Aviation International, "As a flight instructor today, when the aviation industry needs pilots more than ever before, I want nothing more than to pass along the same knowledge, enthusiasm, and scholarships that I've been graciously given to tomorrow's aviators."

Koch, Christina Hammock: Record Setting NASA Astronaut

On October 18, 2019, Astronauts, Christina Koch and Jessica Meir, completed the first-ever spacewalk with an all-female NASA team. In their history-making spacewalk, the women replaced a broken battery charger on the International Space Station. This momentous step in space history was actually Koch's fourth spacewalk. Their historic extravehicular activity (EVA) began officially once both female astronauts switched to battery power in their spacesuits. They were guided by veteran NASA astronaut and capsule communicator (CAPCOM), Stephanie Wilson, back on earth and, fellow astronauts, Luca Parmitano and Andrew Morgan, located on the International Space Station (ISS).

Astronaut Christina Koch works on space botany using the Veggie PONDS research gear to cultivate and harvest lettuce and mizuna greens for consumption on the International Space Station. (NASA photograph)

Christina was born in 1979. Growing up in North Carolina, Christina dreamed of being an explorer or astronaut. "We always had *National Geographic* and *Astronomy* magazines, and *Popular Mechanics* lying around the house. I got interested in exploration and different parts of the world and different parts of the Universe just from seeing those things around the house," Koch explained. During her early years, all eyes were on space exploration. Because Sally Ride already flew in space, Christina often saw images of women astronauts in magazines and on television.

In 1997, Christina graduated with an Electrical Engineering and Physics degree from North Carolina School of Science and Mathematics. Soon, she earned advanced degrees in her field of engineering. An opportunity at the National Oceanic and Atmospheric Administration (NOAA) American Samoa station opened for a Station Chief. She took it. Then, NASA invited the brilliant engineer to additional training at the Goddard Space Flight Center. While there, Koch concentrated on electrical engineering at Goddard Laboratory for High Energy Astrophysics. She contributed to scientific instruments on several NASA missions.

From 2004 to 2007, Koch was a scientist in the United States Antarctic Program, researching the Arctic and Antarctic regions. She spent a winter season at the Amundsen-Scott South Pole Station where extreme cold temperatures were the norm. Christina experienced a season at Antarctica Palmer Station. She described her time there as challenging, mentally and physically. Researchers there experience months without sun, isolated with the same crew members, extreme cold, little fresh food, and lack of sensory stimulation. Koch learned to focus on inner strength.

In 2007, Koch landed at the Johns Hopkins University Applied Physics Laboratory focusing on space science instrument development. She again spent multiple seasons back in Antarctica, Greenland, and Alaska for NOAA. In 2013, Christina was selected for NASA space exploration. Her primary areas of expertise are space science instrument development and remote scientific field engineering. In 2015, Christina Koch became a mission-ready astronaut.

On March 14, 2019, Koch finally launched into outer space to the International Space Station. During her ISS mission, Koch performed six spacewalks. Because of scheduling, Koch's ISS mission was extended. On February 6, 2020, Christina Koch made space history again when she returned to Mother Earth after 328 days – the longest single continuous stay in space for a woman. Ever the research scientist, Koch's extended mission is being used to study the physical, biological, and mental effects of long-term space travel on women. Recently, it was announced that Christina Koch was selected as one of the Artemis space flight crew scheduled for 2024.

Korchuganova, Galina Gavrilovna: Russian Aerobatic Champion and Test Pilot

Born in 1935 in the Soviet Socialist Republics, Galina was always adventurous and inquisitive. She was a top student with honors in high school. As a young, thrill-seeker, Galina discovered her passion for aviation when she joined a sport parachute club. The adrenaline rush as she flew through the sky after her jump from the airplane kept her returning. But, she also was interested in the airplane which allowed her to climb high in the sky. Galina was accepted at the prestigious Moscow Aviation Institute to study aviation technology. In 1959, she graduated with a strong knowledge of aeronautical design and advanced aviation ratings. She began her engineering career at Ramensk Avionics Construction Bureau.

She entered aerobatic competitions and quickly began winning important titles. In 1965 she set her first world record on a 100 km closed circuit flying the Yak-32 jet. Next, Galina became the first Russian absolute world women's aerobatic champion, winning gold and silver medals at the World Championship in Moscow. This world recognition was very important to Soviet leadership. Only after winning championships and flying more than 1,000 hours did Galina finally receive a reply to her request to attend test pilot school from the Ministry of Aviation.

In 1965, Galina Korchuganova set a world aviation record in a Yak-32 jet aircraft on a 100km closed circuit course. (Wikimedia photograph)

They responded, "If you can find a brave man, who is willing to take you as a test pilot, we won't object, as an exception to the rules." There was no brave man found; however, there was a talented woman. Hero of the Soviet Union, Valentina Stepanova Grizodubova, was head of the Science Research Center of Flight Test. She agreed to sponsor Galina, already one of the Soviet Union's most outstanding aerobatic pilots. Galina graduated from the flight school in Kirovograd with flying colors.

Over Galina Korchuganova's test pilot career, she set 42 world-flight records flying more than 20 types of aircraft. In 1980, flying a Yak-40 Galina set two world records. Through hard work and skill, Galina advanced in rank from test pilot of the 5th class to 2nd class. In 1984, at her retirement, she had flown 1,500 hours as a test pilot. Over her entire career, she had flown over 4,000 hours logged in the extremely challenging areas of aerobatics and test pilot without one significant incident.

Galina continued to promote aviation to future Soviet generations through the Museum of Aviation and Astronautics in Moscow.

Concerned that talented young women were being directed to other careers, in 1992, Galina founded Aviatrissa, the first Russian aviation club for women. She served as its President. Tirelessly, Galina organized conferences which provided support and guidance to women in aviation fields. In 2004, after a long illness, Soviet Aerobatic Champion and Test Pilot, Galina Korchuganova, died. But, she was not forgotten. In 2006, she was posthumously inducted into the Women in Aviation Pioneer Hall of Fame.

If offered a seat on a rocket ship, don't ask what seat.
Just get on.

~ Christa McAuliffe, U.S. Teacher and Astronaut

3
L-Lima to P-Papa

We say "Godspeed" or, we say "ad astra" -- to the stars.
~ NASA Astronaut Megan McArthur,
message to departing space crews

Law, Ruth Bancroft (Oliver): U.S. Pioneer Aviator-First Woman to Fly at Night

Ruth Law was born in 1887, back when America only had 38 states. It was a time for expansion and new ideas. Ruth always worked hard to keep up with her older brother, Rodman. He patiently taught Ruth all he could about sports, mechanical things, and being fearless. It was natural that Ruth would follow his lead into the air. Overtime, Rodman became a well-known parachutist, movie stuntman, and flyer.

Ruth knew she would be a great pilot. At age 21, she asked Orville Wright to teach her to fly. He refused because she was a woman. He felt women were not mechanically inclined and his planes were too valuable. Ruth took this as a challenge. In 1912, she actually bought a Wright Model B for the incredible sum of $5,000. That would be a little over $140,000 today. Ruth Law was determined to prove Orville wrong. And, she did.

On August 12, 1912, Ruth soloed. She was instructed by Harry Atwood and Arch Freeman at Atwood Park in Saugus, Massachusetts. Her early training was perfected on the 500 feet of the homestretch at the Saugus racetrack. In September, 1912, Ruth Bancroft Law became the first woman to fly in Rhode Island. Newspaper reports from the Providence Air Meet indicated, "Miss Law went up in a biplane and for ten minutes entertained the 100,000 spectators" In November, 1912, Ruth Law was awarded her pilot's license. She said, "There is the world-old controversy that crops up again whenever women attempt to enter a new field. Is a woman fit for this or that work? It would seem that a woman's success in any particular line would prove her fitness for that work, without regard to theories to the contrary."

Pioneer aviator, Ruth Law, arriving at Governor's Island, New York, after her record-setting flight from Chicago in 1916. (Library of Congress)

Ruth Law was a first-rate pilot and mechanic. She fashioned a black satin flying ensemble to wear during her air show performances. In 1915, as part of a large air demonstration at Daytona Beach, Florida,

Ruth announced to a huge crowd that she was going to loop-de-loop for the first time. Yes, of course, she did it. Not once, but twice. She is credited as the first American woman to do so. Her new husband, Charles Oliver, almost fainted.

Ruth became enormously popular as a stunt pilot. After Law had dropped golf balls from the air at a nearby golf course to kick off a big tournament, Ruth was approached by Brooklyn Dodgers' management to do the same with baseballs. In 1915, on a sunny March afternoon, Ruth flew over the baseball field where then Dodgers' outfielder, Casey Stengel, was supposed to throw baseballs down to his players looking up from the stadium grass. Well, the story gets a bit fuzzy at this point as to who did what. Apparently, instead of a baseball, "someone" heaved out a ripe grapefruit. The soft grapefruit splattered on impact, covering the Dodgers' manager with wet goo. The shock caused him to think he had been injured and was covered in blood. Thankfully, he just needed to shower. However, this is supposedly one theory of how the "Grapefruit League" nickname began.

Later, Ruth bought a fast, Curtiss 110-horsepower bi-plane. On November 19, 1916, Ruth Law broke the existing distance record flying non-stop from Chicago to Hornell, New York. With the help from a strong tailwind, she flew the 590-mile distance in record-setting time. Her feat made her even more famous. President Woodrow Wilson attended a dinner in her honor.

Eventually, Ruth Law was called "Queen of the Air," because of her many aviation records and her dazzling airshow performances. She would change planes in mid-air. Ruth would wing-walk, while a pilot looped the airplane. She was fearless. Her husband continued to fret over the danger. He feared for her safety with each new stunt. On a quiet morning in 1922, Law woke up to read with surprise that she had retired from stunt flying. Her husband had tired of her dangerous job and had taken that drastic step to end her flying career.

Ruth Law was one of only a handful of female aviators invited to join the "Early Birds of Aviation," an organization celebrating pioneers who flew before December 17, 1916. She was the first woman to fly at night. She set numerous aviation records and, was a fearless aerial performer. After her "retirement," she never took to the sky again. But, in her time, Ruth Law's sky star shined brilliantly. In 1970, Ruth Law died at age 83.

Leavitt, Jean Marie Flynn "Jeannie:" U.S. Air Force First Female F-15E Fighter Pilot

Born into an Air Force family in 1967, Jeannie grew comfortable around aviation and military protocols. She always leaned toward technical subjects. In 1990, she graduated from the University of Texas with a bachelor's in Aerospace Engineering. In 1991, she completed her master's from Stanford in aeronautics and astronautics. Already a commissioner officer as a distinguished graduate of the U.S. Air Force ROTC program, Jeannie was accepted into U.S. Air Force pilot training.

In 1992, her Undergraduate Pilot Training began in a T-38 or Talon. This Northrup two-seat, twin jet is the world's first supersonic trainer. She excelled as she was being trained as a T-38 instructor pilot. Then, in April 1993, Congressional mandate dropped restrictions on women flying military combat missions. Immediately, Jeannie began formal combat training in the McDonnell Douglas F-15E Strike Eagle at Randolph AFB in San Antonio, Texas. The F-15E is a multi-role, high performance, jet fighter aircraft, designed for long-range, high-speed interdiction, without relying on escort or electronic-warfare aircraft.

By the end of 1993, Jeannie Flynn, call sign, "Tally," was the first female F-15E fighter pilot in the U.S. Air Force. Later in her career, she became the first U.S.A.F. female to command a fighter wing. Her flight hours include 300 combat hours, mostly in Operations Southern and Northern Watch, Iraqi Freedom, and Enduring Freedom.

From 2002 to 2010, in addition to important U.S. Air Force assignments, Jeannie Leavitt, earned three more master's degrees, a Master of Business Administration from Auburn University, Master of Military Operational Art and Science from Air Command and Staff College, and a Master of National Security Strategy from the National War College. She is the mother of two, and married to a retired Air

Force Colonel. She currently holds the rank of Major General. In 2009, she was honored as the recipient of the National Aeronautical Association Katherine and Marjorie Stinson Award. In 2020, she joined the WAI Pioneer Hall of Fame.

In 1993, Jeannie Flynn, the first Air Force F-15E female pilot, sits in the cockpit with the 555th Fighter Squadron patch visible on her right shoulder. (United States Air Force photograph)

In her 2018, TED "Women Spotlight" talk, General Leavitt said, "I truly see diversity as a competitive advantage. What we really want to get at is that diversity of thought. If I have people around the table who think differently, who have different backgrounds, then we're going to come to a better solution–it's going to take longer; there will be vastly different opinions, but we're going to get to a better solution in the end." Still on active duty, Jeannie Leavitt is leading our nation in the United States Air Force

Lee, Hazel Ying: World War II Chinese American WASP

Born in 1912 into a large Chinese American family, living in Portland, Oregon, Hazel was always strong-willed. Growing up, she knew she would not be the stereotype of the passive Chinese woman. She enjoyed risk and adventurous activity. In 1930, after high school graduation, instead of working in her parents' Chinese restaurant, Hazel became a department store elevator operator. Then, Hazel took her first plane ride at an airshow. From that point on, she knew exactly what she wanted to do. She had to fly. Despite her mother's opposition, Hazel began her flight training at the Chinese Flying Club of Portland (CFCP). This was also the location of the Al Greenwood Flying School at the main airport on Swan Island.

Greenwood coached Hazel in the finer art of flying the small bi-plane through graceful loops, rolls, and spins. Hazel was a natural aviator and loved the command of her plane. In October, 1932, Hazel Ying Lee became one of the few licensed Chinese American woman pilots. Then, Hazel met her future husband, Clifford Louie Yim-qun, who was also a CFCP pilot. When Japan invaded Manchuria, Hazel, Louie, and scores of other Chinese Americans responded to provide aid to the Chinese Air Force. Louie joined a flying squadron and taught Chinese flyers to fight in the air. Even with the enormous need for pilots, the Republic of China Air Force would not accept a woman. Hazel was forced to "fly a desk." Disappointed and frustrated, she moved to Canton, where she was able to fly for a private airline. With few women aviators in the entire country, she was "allowed" to fly because her aviation skill was desperately needed. In 1938, Hazel again offered her aviation talent to the Chinese military. She was again rejected because she was a woman.

As Japanese bombs continued to fall on her friends and neighbors in Canton, Hazel knew, as a non-citizen, she needed to return to the United States. She escaped through Hong Kong to New York City. She became a buyer of war materials for besieged China. After the Japanese attack on Pearl Harbor, Hazel was vigilant for another opportunity to contribute her talent to help win World War II. In 1943, when the Women Airforce Service Pilot program was created, Hazel was accepted into the 4th class or 43-W-4 at Avenger Field for the flight training. At graduation, she became the first Chinese-American woman to fly for the United States military

Next, Lee was assigned to the Third Ferrying Group at Romulus, Michigan. The WASP mission was to fly recently manufactured aircraft from the converted automobile factories to various locations across America. Those new airplanes were shipped to the European and Pacific theaters of operations. Flying newly manufactured airplanes over long distances is extremely dangerous. Other WASP describe Hazel as always calm and fearless, even in frequent air emergencies, or "off-field landings," aka crashes.

Hazel was always fun and high-spirited. She would often use red lipstick to print Chinese good luck characters on the tails of the airplanes she had to fly. One time, Hazel had a forced landing in a Kansas wheat field. The farmer, armed with a pitchfork, chased her around her plane while he called to his neighbors, "The Japanese have invaded Kansas." Fighter that she was, Hazel jumped on him shouting in English that she was an American and her plane had official United States military markings on it. Maybe the red lipstick with Chinese characters threw him off. Eventually, they believed Hazel and the Kansas farmer and neighbors pitched in to help her.

In September, 1944, Lee was chosen for intensive flight training for Pursuit School at Brownsville, Texas. Only 134 WASP were selected to fly the faster, high-powered P-63, P-51, and P-39 fighter airplanes. Lee and the other WASP were the first women to pilot fighter aircraft for the United States military. Hazel loved the P-51 Mustang, as do many pilots today. During World War II, over 15,000 P-51s were manufactured.

Chinese American, Hazel Ying Lee, was an accomplished pilot and strong leader in the Women Airforce Service Pilots. She was killed on a World War II aviation mission. (U.S. Air Force archival photograph)

In November 1944, Lee received orders to pick up a P-63 Kingcobra from the Niagara Falls Bell Aircraft factory for delivery to Great Falls. During WWII, Hazel and other WASP delivered over 5,000 of these fast airplanes to Montana, which was a Lend-Lease program supply link for airplanes to the Soviet Union. From Great Falls, male pilots flew the fighter aircraft to Alaska. Then, Soviet pilots flew them back to Russia to fight the Nazi forces. Bad weather often delayed the process, jamming the Great Falls airspace.

But, on November 23, weather had cleared, allowing Hazel to approach the Great Falls airport. Tragically, due to air traffic controller confusion, Hazel's Kingcobra collided with another P-63. Hazel was able to get her flaming aircraft back on the ground where rescuers pulled her from the burning wreckage. Burned too badly, Hazel died a horrible death two days later. Because WASP were considered civilians by the military, when killed on a mission or in aviation training, the military would not pay for the shipment of their remains to their homes for burial. The grieving family or other WASP paid the expenses for shipment of the bodies. The WASP were not allowed to be buried with an American flag and other military honors. Families were not even authorized to display a Gold Star in their windows.

When the Lee Family prepared to bury Hazel's remains, they were informed by the Portland cemetery that the location chosen was in a 'White only section," where Asians could not be buried. Only after a legal battle was Hazel allowed to be buried where the family had planned. But, not with military honors. Incredibly, not until 1977, were World War II WASP given Veteran status. In 2015, citing limited space at Arlington National Cemetery, the Secretary of the Army denied WASP burials at Arlington. Martha McSally, former U.S. Air Force Fighter Pilot and, then U.S. Congresswoman, introduced bi-partisan legislation to reverse the Obama Administration policy. Thanks to McSally and Congress, the WASP may have their remains interred at Arlington National Cemetery. The WASP fought nearly 75 years to be recognized for their bravery and for their contributions in defeating the Axis Powers. Their stories need to be told often.

With brave wings, she soars.
~ Unknown

Lindbergh, Anne Spencer Morrow: First U.S. Woman to Earn a Glider Pilot's License

After quiet, reserved, Anne Morrow married the world-famous aviator, Charles Lindbergh; her life was never the same. Born in 1906, Anne's wealthy father was a partner in J.P. Morgan and Company. Later, he was appointed as the United States ambassador to Mexico. Eventually, he was elected to the U.S. Senate. Anne's mother was a poet and teacher with a degree from Smith College. All of the Morrow children were encouraged to study hard, to prepare for a life of service to others.

Anne attended the private, all-girls Chapin School, dedicated to the intellectual growth of its students. Anne, a reserved but natural leader, served as president of the student body. Next, she followed in her mother's path to Smith College. Then, in December, 1927, while visiting her parents in Mexico City, Anne met their world-famous house guest, Charles Lindbergh. But their initial shyness did not last long. Soon, they were chatting like life-long friends.

Christmas break over, Anne returned to Smith College. In 1928, she graduated with a Bachelor of Arts degree. Then, in May, 1929, Anne and Charles were married in a private ceremony at her parents' home. To be more helpful to Charles, Anne took flying lessons. But when it came to powered flight versus gliders, the quietly spiritual Anne much preferred flying through the sky without the sound of a motor. The quiet solitude of soaring was a welcome balance to the frenetic life of being married to the famous aviator. Anne Morrow Lindbergh became the first American woman to earn a glider pilot's license. She also earned a private pilot license.

In the 1930s, Anne and Charles explored and charted air routes between the continents. They were the first to fly from Africa to South America. They explored polar air routes from North America to Asia and Europe. As a result, Anne received numerous honors and awards in recognition of her contributions to exploration and aviation. In 1933, she received the U.S. Flag Association Cross of Honor for her charting of transatlantic air routes. In aid of the Lindbergh's need for long-distance communications, Anne learned Morse code, earning a radio operator's license. In 1934, the National Geographic Society honored Anne with their Hubbard Medal, for completing a 40,000 mile exploratory flight over five continents.

Anne Morrow Lindbergh was a talented aviator, explorer, and writer. (Lindbergh Collection Yale University Archive)

In 1979, Anne's contributions to aviation history were recognized by induction into the National Aviation Hall of Fame. In 1982, Anne Morrow Lindbergh was selected for the National Aeronautic Association (NAA) Katharine Wright Award. This NAA award is named in honor of Orville and Wilbur Wright's sister, Katharine, whose behind-the-scenes business acumen played a key role in financing and promoting the Wright Flyer and her brothers.

Anne did the same for Charles Lindbergh's aviation accomplishments. She was literally the wind beneath his wings, allowing him to soar to ever greater heights. In 1993, Anne Morrow Lindbergh was honored by Women in Aerospace with an Aerospace Explorer Award in recognition of her achievements in and contributions to the aerospace field. In 1996, she was inducted into the National Women's Hall of Fame. In 1999, Anne was named to the WAI Pioneer Hall of Fame. Anne Morrow Lindbergh was also a gifted author whose books: *North to the Orient, Listen to the Wind, Gift from the Sea*, and *The Steep Ascent,* made her famous in another field. In 2001, she died quietly in her Vermont home. She left us with these words: "It takes as much courage to have tried and failed as it does to have tried and succeeded."

Lockness, Doris Estella Rhoads: WWII WASP and Whirly Girl

Born in 1910, Doris grew up in Pennsylvania. During the Great Depression, she moved with Paul, her first husband, and their four small children to California. They settled next to a small airport in Wilmington. Doris was fascinated with the small planes and with famous lady pilots as Amelia Earhart. Doris knew that she could be a lady pilot one day, too. In 1939, when Doris began learning how to fly, her husband did not share her enthusiasm. In fact, they divorced.

Of that time in her life, Doris is quoted in *Encyclopedia of Women in Aviation and Space* saying, "I really didn't have that good a support background when I was twenty-nine that a lot of pilots have, but I just made up my mind that was something that I wanted to do. There wasn't anything that could stop me, not even an angry husband and four youngsters."

A few years later, Doris met and married, Robert Lockness, who did share her passion for flying. He encouraged her aviation dreams. By then, America had entered World War II. Doris worked close to home for Douglas Aircraft. She was a Liaison Engineer on the military conversion of the DC-4, which was a four-engine, propeller airliner before the war. Already a pilot, she was recruited by Jackie Cochran for the WASP. Doris was off to Sweetwater, Texas, to help America win the war. When the WASP were disbanded by the military, Doris returned to California.

WASP Doris Lockness loved her World War II warbird named Swamp Angel.
(Wikicommons photograph)

Her love for flying grew even stronger. She "adopted" a World War II single-engine Stinson that served in New Guinea during the war years. She named it, "Swamp Angel." Doris flew her "warbird' to hundreds of airshows across the United States. By April, 1963, after 22 years as a fixed-wing pilot, Doris discovered helicopters. In fact, she became Whirly Girl member #55. Next, she earned her commercial gyroplane rating. Doris was only the second woman to hold that rating in a constant speed prop gyroplane. In 1995, she was honored with the Whirly Girls Livingston Award.

In all, Lockness had an aviation career which spanned almost 80 years. She was rated to fly airplanes, seaplanes, helicopters, gyroplanes, gliders, and hot-air balloons. She also was a Certified Flight Instructor. Ultimately, Doris owned nine planes, including her beloved, "Swamp Angel." At only age 87, Doris became the 100th pilot to fly into Amelia Earhart Memorial Airport in Atchison, for the "Wings over Kansas," celebration of the 100th anniversary of the Wright Brothers historic flight. Doris flew as a member of the United Flying Octogenarians (Yes, UFO). She was also a member of the OX-5 Aviation Pioneers, whose purpose is to honor those who built the aviation industry. Doris earned the OX-5 Legion of Merit Award and, also their Pioneer Women's Award.

In 1991, and again in 1995, The National Aeronautic Association awarded their Elder Statesman of Aviation Award to Doris Lockness. In 1997, NAA gave its Katharine Wright Memorial Award to Doris for her "aeronautical achievements which inspired many to set higher goals and stretch to reach them, encouraging countless women over more than seven decades to put on their wings and fly." Women in Aviation International listed Doris as one the 100 Most Influential Women in Aviation. In 2002, WAI inducted her into their Pioneer Hall of Fame. In 2017, at almost 107 years young, Doris Lockness flew West at her California home to join her pilot husband, Robert.

Lucid, Shannon Matilda Wells: International Space Record Setting Astronaut

Born in 1943 to Baptist missionary parents in Shanghai, China, Shannon was destined to live an adventurous life. During World War II, the Japanese imprisoned Shannon and her family. Blessedly, the three of them were released in a prisoner exchange negotiated with the United States. After the war ended, her family returned briefly to China. However, with the rising power of the communist regime, at age six, Shannon, and her parents resettled in Bethany, Oklahoma. In 1950, the

Aero Design and Engineering Company put Bethany on the aviation map. They built the highly successful Aero Commander. This twin-engine corporate aircraft became so popular that Dwight Eisenhower added two of them to his presidential aircraft fleet.

In her aviation-minded town, Shannon excelled in high school. She earned her private pilot license shortly after graduation. She bought a plane to fly her preacher father to revival meetings. The University of Oklahoma was her next step, earning her bachelor's in chemistry in record time. Then, her master's in biochemistry. Finally, by 1973, Shannon earned her doctorate in biochemistry.

In March, 1996, Dr. Shannon Lucid works out on a treadmill in space on Mir, the Russian Space Station. (NASA photograph)

In 1978, NASA advertised for female astronaut candidates. She was accepted into the NASA Astronaut training program. Only five other women were selected into this important astronaut class. Shannon was the only one who was already a mother at the time of her selection. Another first for NASA and Shannon.

In June, 1985, Astronaut Lucid's first NASA space flight was on Space Shuttle Discovery. This seven-day mission deployed international communication satellites, completing 112 orbits around the earth. Discovery astronauts flew in space over 169 hours and travelled 2.5 million miles. In 1989, Dr. Lucid was a crew member on Atlantis (STS-34). This was another important five-day mission with a myriad of experiments and system tests. They flew 1.8 million miles, completing 79 orbits in 119+ hours.

The 1991 Atlantis flight (STS-43) was 9 days with deployment of satellites and multiple experiments. This flight accomplished 142 Earth orbits, covering 3.7 million miles. In 1993, Astronaut Lucid again returned to space on Columbia. On this record-setting 14-day mission, the STS-58 crew performed medical experiments on themselves, expanding knowledge of the impact of the space environment on humans. This mission travelled 5.8 million miles in 225 Earth orbits. With these flights, Lucid logged over 838 hours in space. Much more was in her future.

Following a year of training at Star City in Russia, she was ready for her fifth spaceflight. Shannon became the first American woman to serve onboard the Russian Space Station, Mir. During this mission, Lucid became the first non-Russian woman to hold an international record for the most flight hours in orbit. She spent 188 days in space, from March 22 to September 26, 1996, including 179 days aboard Mir. Her return was delayed twice, extending her stay on Mir by about six weeks. During the mission, she performed numerous life science and physical science experiments. In all, Shannon Lucid traveled over 75,000,000 miles. In 1996, Dr. Lucid became the first woman to be awarded the Congressional Space Medal of Honor. No wonder, in 2002,

Discover Magazine listed Dr. Lucid as one of the 50 most important women in science.

Shannon Lucid continued her NASA service as Chief Scientist. Later, she served as CAPCOM, lead communicator, for Mission Control for multiple missions. In 2012, she retired from NASA. She once said, "Basically, all my life I'd been told you can't do that because you're female. So I guess I just didn't pay any attention. I just went ahead and did what I could and then, when the stars aligned, I was ready." Dr. Shannon Lucid is in the International Space Hall of Fame, National Women's Hall of Fame, and the United States Astronaut Hall of Fame.

It is never too late in fiction or in life to revise.
~ Nancy Thayer

Malachowski, Nicole Margaret Ellingwood: First Female U.S. Air Force Thunderbird Pilot

Born in 1974, Nicole's interest in aviation began at a central California air show in 1979. She was only five years old. Growing up, Nicole saw women military pilots in magazines and newspapers because in 1974 the Army and the Navy accepted women into military aviation training. In 1976, the U.S. Air Force soon followed. During her teen years, Nicole, as the daughter of a retired U.S. A.F. officer, was encouraged to become a Civil Air Patrol cadet. Nicole was a good communicator and leader. She earned the highest rank a cadet could earn, Cadet Colonel. She began flight training before she graduated from high school. In 1992, she entered the cadet corps at the U.S. Air Force Academy. In 1996, as a newly-commissioned 2nd Lieutenant with a Bachelor of Science in Management and minor in French, Nicole looked forward to flight training. While at the Academy, she was a cadet instructor pilot in their TG-4 two-place, tandem basic training sailplane program.

In Air Force Undergraduate Pilot training, Nicole flew well. Next, she was selected for the only F-15E Strike Eagle slot in her entire class. She barely met the height and weight requirements for Air Force fighter pilot. She trained at Seymour Johnson AFB in North Carolina. After her graduation as a fighter pilot, she was assigned to overseas operational tours in England and South Korea. Explaining her call sign, she says, "Fifi," is "a small person with a big attitude." Also, the Disney-inspired mascot, Fifinella or Fifi, was often painted on WASP airplanes and flight jackets. Early in 2005, during her second deployment, her Fighter Wing joined in support of Operation Iraqi Freedom, flying 26 combat missions.

In 2005, Nicole Malachowski became the first female U.S.A.F. Thunderbird pilot. She flew the Right Wing Slot 3 position in the iconic diamond formation. (U.S. Air Force photograph)

In 2005, Nicole was accepted as a U.S.A.F. Thunderbird pilot. She completed extensive training in the F-16 Fighting Falcon, single-engine fighter, used by the precision aviation team. In addition to superior aviation skills, members of the Thunderbirds flight team become the liaison to the public for the United States Air Force across the nation. Nicole was a natural crowd pleaser. An excellent pilot in the wing position, airshow fans were often surprised to see and talk to this vivacious, female pilot. Even during the years of 2006-2007 air show season, on the flight line after the airshow performance, children and adults would show surprise that Nicole was a "Lady" pilot. She completed 140 performances during her Thunderbird year.

In 2009, Malachowski was named to the White House Fellow Program. In 2010, after a difficult pregnancy, Nicole and her husband, Paul, a retired Air Force Lieutenant Colonel, welcomed twins, daughter, Norah, and son, Garrick. In 2011, Nicole commanded the 333d Fighter Squadron at Seymour Johnson Air Force Base, where her fighter pilot training started years earlier.

During her Air Force career, Nicole completed additional graduate degrees and served on the staff of the United States Air Force Warfare Center. As a student at the Naval War College in Newport, Rhode Island, Nicole graduated with distinction. Malachowski became the first Air Force officer to earn the Admiral Stephen B. Luce Award. Unfortunately, in 2017, an earlier incorrect diagnosis of a tick-borne illness, ended her stellar 21 years of Air Force service. Today, Colonel Nicole Malachowski is a speaker and advocate on behalf of patients suffering from tick-borne illness. Just as she had advocated earlier for recognition of the WASP and their valued service to our nation. In 2008, Nicole Malachowski was inducted into the Women in Aviation International Pioneer Hall of Fame. In 2019, she was recognized by the National Women's Hall of Fame. She is a popular public speaker on leadership and overcoming obstacles.

Mariner, Rosemary Ann Bryant Merims (Conaster): U.S. Navy First Female Tactical Jet Pilot

Rosemary wanted to be a pilot since childhood. Born in 1953, just a few years later, her Air Force father, was killed in an aviation accident. He served in the U.S. Army Air Corps in World War II and, in the U.S. Air Force during the Korean War as a fighter pilot. Rosemary's mother, a World War II nurse, encouraged Rosemary's interest in aviation. Rosemary enjoyed watching the Miramar Naval Air Station airplanes fly over their house. Rosemary worked odd jobs, even washing airplanes at the local airport, to earn money for flight lessons and flight time toward her pilot license.

Extremely bright and a good student, Rosemary was accepted at Purdue University. In 1972, at only age 19, she graduated with a degree in aviation technology. She was the first woman to graduate from their aeronautical program. Rosemary also earned her Federal Aviation Administration private pilot license and, also, Flight Engineer rating, before she joined the U.S. Navy. Rosemary was selected as one of the women in the first class of naval aviators. She completed Office Candidate School in Newport, Rhode Island, before heading to Pensacola, Florida, for basic flight training.

In 1974, Rosemary earned her Gold Naval Aviator Wings. She became one of only six women to do so. The next year, she became the Navy's first female tactical jet pilot, flying the A-4C (Skyhawk), a single-seat, carrier-capable, light attack bomber aircraft. In 1976, she transitioned to fly the A-7E (Corsair II), making her the first woman to fly a Naval front-line tactical strike aircraft. Next, she went back to California for Naval Weapons Center training. By 1982, she had sea duty on the USS Lexington, which made her the Navy's first female aviator assigned to an aircraft carrier. In 1984, Rosemary qualified as a Surface Warfare Office (SWO). SWOs are involved in every aspect of the Navy's mission and operations. In 1987, Mariner became the first woman screened for command for an aviation unit in the U.S. Navy.

Commander Rosemary Mariner was the first woman in United States history to command a Naval Aviation Squadron. (U.S. Navy photograph)

In 1990, she became the first woman to command a Naval aviation squadron, VAQ-34, based in California at the Pacific Missile Test Center at Pt. Mugu. Later, she attended the National War College in Washington, DC, earning a Master's in National Security Strategy, and served on the Staff of the Joint Chiefs in the Pentagon. Her final military assignment was as the Chairman of the Joint Chief's Chair in Military Strategy at the National War College, before retiring in 1997. During her 24 years of service, Mariner logged more than 3,500 flight hours in 15 types of aircraft with seventeen carrier landings. Throughout her career, Captain Mariner willingly served as a mentor to others. She was instrumental in the repeal of restrictions on women serving in combat. Mariner authored several books, including *Crossed Currents: Navy Women from World War I to Tailhook, Women in the Military: An Unfinished Revolution, Tailspin: Women at War in the Wake of Tailhook*, and *Ground Zero: The Gender Wars in the Military*. Mariner provided leadership as president of the Women Military Aviators from 1991 to 1993.

After her military service, Captain Rosemary Mariner was a resident scholar at the University of Tennessee Center for the Study of War and Society. She continued to serve as an advisor on national defense policy and women's integration into the military for ABC News, PBS, and the Department of the Navy. In 2019, after a courageous five-year battle against ovarian cancer, at only age 65, Rosemary Mariner slipped the surly bonds of Earth. Her wingman of 40 years, husband, retired Navy Commander Tommy Mariner, and their daughter, Emmalee, mourned the loss. At her funeral, the United States Navy conducted an all-female pilot flyover. The Naval women aviators flew a Super Hornet (F/A-18F) "Missing Woman" Flyover in her honor.

Markham, Beryl Clutterbuck: First Person to Fly Across the Atlantic Ocean East to West, Solo, Non-Stop

Born in 1902 in England, Beryl moved with her father to the wilds of the African continent at only age four. Her father, Charles, was a well-known horse trainer. In colonial British East Africa, which later became Kenya, he built a successful horse racing farm. Beryl lived an adventurous childhood there. She learned to hunt, ride, and became a respected horse trainer. In 1919, her father left Africa for Peru, seeking other business opportunities. Beryl stayed in Africa training horses. At age 18, she became the first woman in Africa licensed as a race horse trainer. Adventurous, free-spirited, and beautiful, Beryl was a noted non-conformist, even in the Roaring Twenties. She gave new meaning to the term "free spirit." She married three times, taking the name Markham from her wealthy second husband.

In her late 20s, Beryl was taught to fly by former RAF World War I pilot, Tom Campbell Black, who resettled in British East Africa in 1922. Tom Campbell farmed a coffee plantation and was an avid rider, who bred award-winning horses. Later, he was instrumental in the founding of Wilson Airways, which provided airline service across Kenya. He had a long friendship and love affair with Beryl Markham.

Beryl earned a good living as a bush pilot, spotting big game herds from the air for wealthy hunters on safari. She also became East Africa's "go-to" person when settlers and natives with serious medical problems needed to be evacuated from deep within the jungle. Markham developed an uncanny ability to fly at night without the benefit of navigation aids, guided mostly by village fires to deliver medicine, food, and medical personnel. Consequently, she became an extremely competent aviator.

Competent to the point that Markham starting planning a flight that no one, man or woman, had survived. In 1935, Beryl decided to fly against the prevailing winds from Europe to North America. Knowing that several pilots died in the attempt, Beryl was meticulous in her planning. She chose the Percival Vega Gull, known for its powerful engine, good speed, and its long-range capability. She named her plane, "The Messenger."

In the 1930s, tobacco companies would insert beautiful art cards of sports figures, films stars, and famous aviators of the day with biographical information printed on the back. Beryl Markham was #21 in the Carreras Cigarettes Famous Airmen and Airwomen series. (New York Public Library)

On September 4, 1936, Beryl, took off alone from Abington in southern England on her quest to fly solo, non-stop across the vast Atlantic Ocean. After flying all night, she was relieved the next morning to see the rocky shoreline of Nova Scotia. "The Messenger" performed well against seemingly endless hours of head winds in icy, dark skies.

Beryl was almost out of fuel. Ice was building up on the fuel tank vents. She knew she had to put "The Messenger" on the ground and soon...

She found what appeared to be an open field on Cape Breton Island, Nova Scotia, Canada. But the open field turned out to be a soggy peat bog. When she touched down, her landing gear sank into the wet goo, causing her craft to nose over, thrusting Beryl forward into the instrument panel. Ignoring the cut on her forehead, she climbed out, exhausted from over 21 hours of flying. Although hungry and dehydrated, Beryl Markham became the first person to fly non-stop from Europe to North America.

Using another plane, Beryl flew to New York City. She was greeted with a ticker tape parade and much acclaim. She became world famous for being the first person to fly east to west. In 1942, her memoir, *West with the Night*, was published. It was well received. But, with World War II raging, it quietly went out of print. Only to be reprinted in later years when Ernest Hemingway had high praise for Beryl Markham's book and writing. After surviving many press conferences and interviews, almost more tiring than her epic flight, Beryl eventually returned to Africa. Markham became one of Kenya's most successful race-horse trainers. She trained six of the winners in the Kenya Derby.

In 1982, her memoir was republished, a few years before the release of the movie, *Out of Africa*. Felicity, a character in that movie, is eerily similar to the real Beryl Markham. Shortly after her death in 1986, PBS broadcast *World without Walls, Beryl Markham's African Memoir*. In 1988, Stephanie Powers starred in a television film, *Shadow of the Sun*, about this remarkable adventurer and aviator. In 2014, she was inducted into the Women in Aviation International Pioneer Hall of Fame.

Marvingt, Marie: Balloonist, Aviator, Most Decorated Woman in French History

If you wrote a movie script about Marie Marvingt, Hollywood producers would throw you out of their office saying, "No woman could do all this in one lifetime." Well, Marie did. Born in 1875, she loved sports and adventure. She became a world class athlete. She was a swimmer and cyclist. She won gold medals in skiing, bobsledding, skating, rifle shooting, fencing. Did I mention, she was the first woman to climb many of the peaks in the French and Swiss Alps? She was such a "Wonder Woman," that she was described as displaying "unlady like characteristic" in that "she competes fervently" and "really tries to win." She was the only person in history to earn the gold medal of the French National Sports Federation "For All Sports."

Marie Marvingt was a French balloonist, aviator, athlete, mountaineer, and more. The press called her "Fiancée of Danger." (Library of Congress)

Marie took this same laser focus to the air. In 1901, Marie experienced flight in a balloon. She was the first French woman to obtain a balloon pilot's license. She won numerous competitions and set records. In 1903, she was described as "the fiancée of danger," which newspapers used to describe her for the rest of her life. In 1909, she became the first woman to pilot a balloon from the Continent to England over the English Channel. Then, she set her eyes on becoming an airplane pilot.

During 1910, she studied fixed wing piloting in an Antoinette aeroplane, an early French high-wing, monoplane. That same year, the Aero Club of France awarded Marie Marvingt airplane license #281. She was the third French woman to do so. In her first 900 flights, she never "broke wood," aka crashed, which was a record unequaled at that time. On November 27, 1910, she became the holder of the first formally recognized women's flying record, with a flight of 53 minutes, during which she flew 42 kilometers. Early on, Marie could see the airplane as an integral part of medical transport with civilian and military applications. As early as 1910, she recommended the creation of airplane ambulances. Remarkably, by 1912, she had designed a medical air ambulance. She collected public donations to order it from the French Deperdussin Factory, which was building a high-wing monoplane. The medical airplane would be given to the Red Cross. Well, long story short, the Deperdussin Factory went bankrupt and the winds of World War I changed those plans.

As a qualified surgical nurse, Marie became the first trained and certified flight nurse. During World War I missions, she tended the wounded on the planes as they flew to the military hospitals. There is evidence in official Legion of Honor French records that Marie piloted a bomber on at least two occasions during attacks on German-occupied Frescaty (near Metz) in 1915. She may have been the first woman to pilot an aircraft in combat. After the war, Marie devoted her enormous talents and energy to promoting the air delivery of medical care and medivac missions. She organized about 6,000 public conferences on five continents, directed and acted in two films, and established civil air ambulances in French Colonies in North Africa. She recognized the need for Flight Nurses, and was instrumental in creating the first training program for this category of medical specialty. When formal training was established in France, she became their first certified Flight Nurse. She founded the Friends of Medical Aviation to promote this life-saving program.

In 1931 she created a prize for the best civil aircraft transformable into an air ambulance. In 1934, Morocco had her establish their civil air ambulance service. That country awarded Marie the Medal of Peace of Morocco. She built a corps of trained medical staff to provide battlefield care, which was vital during World War II. During that war, she resumed work as a Red Cross nurse. She fought in the French resistance. After the war, she founded and maintained a home for wounded aviators. In 1955, she was recognized by the French National Federation of Aeronautics for her work in aviation medicine.

Sick and injured people of every nation have benefited from the tireless and pioneering work of Marie Marvingt to create professional medivac services worldwide. In 1963, Marie died as the holder of four aviation ratings: fixed-wing airplane, balloon, hydroplane, and helicopter. She was the most decorated woman in French history with more than 34 medals and decorations in sports, aviation, and public service. In 2007, she joined the Women in Aviation International Pioneer Hall of Fame. Marie lived what the French describe as *joie de vivre*-joy of life.

Meir, Jessica Ulrika: NASA Astronaut, Aquanaut, First All-Women Spacewalk

October 18, 2019, NASA Astronauts Jessica Meir and Christina Koch completed the first spacewalk outside of the International Space Station with an all-women team. A history-making event which lasted over seven hours in outer space. This was the first spacewalk for Meir. Jessica joined the NASA Astronaut program with extensive academic and scientific credentials. She was born in 1977 in Caribou, Maine, near the Canadian border, to immigrant parents. Her mother was Swedish.

Her physician father was Iraqi-Israeli. In an interview before her launch, she attributes her abiding dream of personally participating in space exploration to the love of nature, which she learned from her parents. "And, it might have had something to do with the fact that the stars shone so brightly in rural Maine," Meir explained.

Meir earned a Bachelor of Arts in Biology from Brown University, a Master of Science in Space Studies from the International Space University in France, and a Doctorate in Marine Biology from Scripps Institution of Oceanography in California. Before joining NASA, Meir worked at Lockheed Martin Space Operations as a scientist, Harvard Medical School, and the University of British Columbia. In 2002, Jessica joined the NASA Extreme Environment Mission Operations (NEEMO) on an aquanaut crew, serving on Aquarius, an undersea research laboratory four miles off shore from Key Largo in Florida. She spent five days saturation diving from the laboratory as a simulation of space conditions.

Meir applied in 2009 to NASA for the Astronaut program. She was a semi-finalist. For the next few years, she continued in NASA-related projects and research. In 2013, Jessica joined the NASA astronaut program. She completed that extensive training in 2015. Then, in 2016, Meir was selected for the European Space Agency Cooperative Adventure for Valuing and Exercising (ESA CAVES) human behavior and performance skills training. A three-week course to prepare astronauts to work safely and effectively in multicultural teams. This is experienced in caves. So, Jessica Meir had experience in the sea, in the earth, now she was ready for outer space.

On September 25, 2019, Meir launched into outer space aboard the Russian Soyuz MS-15 for the International Space Station. She served as the Flight Engineer. She spent 205 days in space, orbited the Earth 3,280 times on a trip of 86.9 million miles. In 2020, *Time* magazine included Jessica Meir on their list of the 100 Most Influential People in the World. She continues to work on space missions and projects. She is a member of the science advisory board of Adventurers and Scientists for Conservation. On explaining her journey to the stars, Jessica Meir said,

"There's no one path to becoming an astronaut. I think that's one of the great things about the job these days. You know, originally, all of the astronauts were white male military test pilots. And now the program is much more diverse."

NASA Astronaut Jessica Meir in a high altitude flight suit. (NASA photograph)

Mock, Geraldine Fredritz "Jerrie:" First Woman to Fly Solo around the World

Born in Ohio in 1925, Jerrie enjoyed outdoor games and sports. Her lifelong interest in flying began at age seven. Her father took her on a Ford Trimotor flight. Sometimes called "Tin Goose," this airplane was popular for passenger transportation. Just as Henry Ford's cars and tractors were well made, the Trimotor had a combination of metal structure and simple systems which contributed to its safety and ruggedness. Jerrie's father even got her a ride in the cockpit so she saw all the dials and controls, and the big view of the sky. She was hooked. At age 11, Amelia Earhart was her idol. She rushed home from school to listen to the radio for reports on Earhart's attempt to fly around the world. Jerrie continued to listen for updates, even after all hope was lost.

In high school, Jerrie was the only girl in the engineering class. Aviation was still her passion. She headed to Ohio State University to study aeronautical engineering. She was the only female in that program. In 1945, before she graduated, Jerrie left OSU to marry, Russell Mock. They built their family with an eye toward the sky. By 1958, both Jerrie and Russ earned their private pilot rating. They enjoyed flying with their three children, using aviation to take them where they had never been before.

Jerrie always yearned to "see the world." What better way than to fly around the world. No woman had yet done it since Amelia's ill-fated attempt. From her Ohio suburban home, Jerrie began carefully planning for her flight. She enlisted the help of U.S. Air Force pilots about how best to plan her stops, giving special thought to cultural norms, wars, natural disasters, and weather. She contacted foreign embassies for their paperwork and requirements for fuel, food, and a multitude of logistical details. She even planned on wearing a skirt with a modest sweater and sensible shoes for the entire trip to be culturally sensitive to travel in other countries.

Her airplane was her single engine Cessna 180 Skywagon, which was now christened the "Spirit of Columbus" for Columbus, Ohio. No, not for Christopher Columbus. She also wanted to pay homage to

Charles Lindbergh and his 1927 "Spirit of St. Louis," solo flight. Jerrie nicknamed her plane "Charlie." This unassuming, 38-year-old house wife and mother of three left the runway of the Port Columbus airport on the chilly morning of March 19, 1964. Her epic quest began. The world held its breath. Because of the media focus on this important flight, often a very tired Jerrie would be greeted at airports with great fanfare. For example, the president of the Aero Club of Morocco hosted Jerrie in his beautiful home with a huge celebration dinner party. During her travels in Saudi Arabia, where women were not even allowed to drive cars, it was considered very strange that her government allowed her to fly, anywhere.

Jerrie Mock's Cessna 180, Spirit of Columbus, hangs in the National Air and Space Museum. (WikiCommons)

In all, Jerrie Mock flew for 29 days, 11 hours, and 59 minutes, flying over 23,000 miles, alone in a single-engine Cessna 180 Skywagon. Her odyssey certainly gave her an opportunity to see the world. She flew East from Columbus, Ohio to Bermuda in the Bahamas, Santa Marie in the Azores, Casablanca in Morocco, Bone in Algeria, Tripoli in Libya, Cairo in Egypt, Saudi Arabia, Karachi in Pakistan, Delhi and Calcutta in India, Bangkok in Thailand, Manila in the Philippines, Guam, Wake Island, Honolulu, Oakland, Tucson, El Paso,

Bowling Green, landing back home at Port Columbus Ohio Airport at 9:36 p.m., April 17, 1964.

This astonishing accomplishment included so many firsts for Jerrie Mock: first woman to fly solo around the word, first woman to fly around the world in a single-engine airplane, first woman to fly from the United State to Africa via the North Atlantic, first woman to fly the Pacific Ocean in a single engine airplane, first woman to fly both the Atlantic and the Pacific Oceans, first woman to fly the Pacific Ocean in both directions. She also established a women's world aviation speed record with this successful around the world flight. To say, Jerrie Mock made the world notice is an understatement.

The awards and recognitions for her stunning achievement came from all over the world. The Fédération Aéronautique Internationale, American Institute of Aeronautics and Astronautics, National Aviation Trades Association Pilot of the Year, Amelia Earhart Memorial Award, and Federal Aviation Administration Gold Medal presented at the White House by the President of the United States, not to mention all the Ohio awards. Her flight was widely recognized, not only as an important aviation accomplishment, but also for the American "can do" attitude of a woman born and raised in what the media sometime describe as "fly over America."

In 1970, Jerrie published the story of her epic around-the-world flight, *Three-Eight Charlie*. The Skywagon was registered as N1538C. So, Three-Eight-Charlie would be her radio call sign in the air and on the ground. Three-Eight Charlie hangs in the Smithsonian Air and Space Museum. In 2008, Women in Aviation International added this incredible woman to the Pioneer Hall of Fame. In 2014, Jerrie Mock quietly flew West.

Moisant, Matilde Josephine: Pioneer Aviator Women's World Altitude Record Setter

Born in the late 1870s to French-Canadian immigrants, Matilde was the younger sister of the famous aviator, John. The whole family embraced new opportunities with sugar plantations in El Salvador, aviation businesses, and a New York flight school to feed the growing appetite for lucrative air shows. Brothers, John and Alfred, formed the Moisant International Aviators, a flying circus of barnstorming aviators that toured around the United States, Mexico, and Cuba. Originally, John was one of the performers. His death in 1910 during the Michelin Cup aviation competition in New Orleans did not deter Matilde from pursing aviation. Her best friend, Harriet Quimby, was taking flight training at the Moisant Aviation School on Long Island, New York. Matilde continued on, as well.

In August, 1911, Matilde became the second woman in the United States to earn her pilot's license. Harriet Quimby was the first. Matilde loved to reach high altitudes in the sky with her plane. A report in her entry on the Early Birds of Aviation site said, "On September 24, 1911, Matilde Moisant flew her Bleriot monoplane to an altitude of 1,200 feet over Nassau Boulevard flying field at Garden City, Long Island. Nassau County police officials tried to arrest her for flying on a Sunday over Garden City, after warning her not to fly; however, she disregarded their warning and jumped the gun, taking-off regardless. Eventually the sheriff caught up with her but when he attempted to arrest her, 300 of Miss Moisant's fans came to her rescue and beat back the police in a riot that lasted more than half an hour. A later attempt by the sheriff to serve Miss Moisant with a warrant failed when the Justice of the Peace said he could see nothing wrong with flying on Sunday."

I am not sure of the veracity of this story. Other sources report Matilde did set an altitude record that September, launching her aviation career at the Nassau Boulevard Aviation Meet in New York. She won the coveted Rodman-Wanamaker altitude trophy by flying her 50 HP Moisant monoplane to an incredible height, which bested both Quimby and, the International Belgian sky star, Hélène Dutrieu. Press reports of the day varied on the altitude up to a reported 4,000-feet. Whatever the altitude, it was very high for a woman in 1911. Matilde was lauded with glowing press reviews about her bravery. One reporter wrote, "This is the greatest altitude ever reached by a woman aviator. The flight was made in a puffy wind and Miss Moisant displayed remarkable skill in handling her machine."

In 1911, Matilde Moisant, Early Bird Aviator, became the second woman in the United States licensed to fly an airplane. (Smithsonian National Air and Space Museum archive)

Together, Matilde and Harriet joined the famous Moisant International Aviators air show as featured performers. Matilde and Harriet flew in air meets throughout the United States and Mexico, garnering a growing legion of fans. They achieved what would later be known as: rock star status. Moisant continued to soar to higher altitudes than most of the male pilots at the air shows. In the spring of 1912, Harriet left for Europe to attempt the first flight by a woman across the English Channel. With Harriet gone, Matilde's family pressured her to leave this dangerous aviation business. Matilde scheduled her last flying performance for April 14, 1912, in Wichita Falls, Texas. It was almost her final act of any kind as her aircraft burst into flames upon landing, due to a leak in the fuel tank. Moisant was pulled from the mangled wreckage with her clothes on fire. Fortunately, because she flew at such high altitudes where the air was colder in the open cockpit of her airplane, she always wore a heavy wool flying costume. The layers protected her from serious burns.

Just a few months later, her friend, Harriet Quimby, died in another aviation air meet near Boston, Massachusetts. Although, Matilde eventually recovered physically from her injuries and burns, she gave up flying. During World War I, she performed Red Cross duties on the ground. However, she worked for the Red Cross in France until the armistice so she was still living dangerously. She managed her family sugar cane plantation in El Salvador for several years, before returning to live in California. She died in 1964.

Mukai, Chiaki: First Japanese Woman Astronaut

Chiaki was born in 1952 in Japan. The country was rebuilding from the destruction of World War II. Japan placed high value on education. Chiaki was a top student. In 1971, she graduated from the Keio Girls Senior High School. She was immediately accepted into the Keio University for medical training. In 1977, she graduated with a doctorate in medicine. Dr. Mukai worked as a resident in General Surgery at Keio University. She gained emergency surgery experience at several hospitals. In 1980, she became a resident in Cardiovascular Surgery at

Keio University Hospital. Eventually, she became an assistant professor in the Department of Cardiovascular Surgery. In 1985, Dr. Mukai was selected by the National Space Development Agency of Japan for their astronaut program. During her astronaut training, she also earned another Doctorate in Physiology in 1988 from Keio University School of Medicine. The next year, Mukai became a board-certified cardiovascular surgeon in the Japan Surgical Society.

Dr. Chiaki Mukai, astronaut with Japan Aerospace Exploration Agency (JAXA), smiles as she gets a final fitting of her flight suit prior to walkout and transport to Launch Pad 39B for STS-95. (NASA photograph)

As a science astronaut, Dr. Mukai joined the Division of Cardiovascular Physiology at the NASA Johnson Space Center. In addition to preparing for space flight, she became a surgery research professor at Baylor College of Houston. During multiple space launches, Dr. Mukai served as a Spacelab communicator for crew science operations. In 1994, her opportunity to travel in space came. On STS-65 aboard Space Shuttle Columbia, she became the first Asian woman and first Japanese woman in do so. The crew conducted 82 life science experiments in human physiology and space biology. Dr. Mukai would make more space history.

In 1998, aboard Space Shuttle Discovery (STS-95), she became the first Japanese citizen in history to serve on two space missions. During this flight, Dr. Mukai was able to carefully study the effect of space travel on the human body. In particular, former Mercury astronaut, U.S. Senator John Glenn, the first American to orbit the Earth, was also on his second space mission on STS-95. On both flights, Chiaki spent a total of 23 days in space. In August, 2000, Dr. Mukai was assigned as a deputy mission scientist for the STS-107 mission to coordinate science operations for the mission, which was launched in January 2003.

From 2004-2007, Dr. Mukai moved to France. She became a visiting professor at the International Space University (ISU). She provided her specialized knowledge on space medicine and human space exploration health management for the ISU Master Program students. In 2007, she returned home to Japan where she served as Director of the Space Biomedical Research Office, Human Space Technology and Astronaut Department, Human Space System and Utilization Mission Directorate of the Japan Aerospace Exploration Agency (JAXA). In 2011, Dr. Mukai served as Senior Advisor to the JAXA Executive Director. The next year, she became the Director of JAXA Center for Applied Space Medicine and Human Research. In 2015, she became Vice President of the Tokyo University of Science. In addition, she became JAXA Technical Counselor. Her long journey to serve her nation reminds me of the Japanese proverb, "Beginning is easy. Continuing is hard."

Nichols, Ruth Rowland: American Pioneer Aviator

Born in 1901 to a wealthy family, her father gave Ruth an airplane ride in 1919 as her high school graduation present. This was not an ordinary airplane flight. Her father hired Eddie Stinson, Jr. to be her pilot. Stinson was an Early Bird of Aviation. He founded the Stinson Aircraft Company. This one flight changed the direction of her life. Her parents sent Ruth to the Masters School in New York in preparation for a life as a socialite. At Wellesley College, Ruth began studies in pre-medical.

Ruth Nichols simultaneously held women's aviation world records for speed, altitude, and distance. (Library of Congress)

However, Ruth began to secretly take flying lessons. In 1924, she graduated from Wellesley. Shortly thereafter, Ruth earned her pilot's license. But, she did not stop there. Next, she obtained a hydroplane licensed. She became the first woman in the world to do so. Believing if it worth doing, it is worth overdoing, Ruth continued her record-setting aviation life. In January, 1928, as a co-pilot with her flight instructor, Harry Rogers, they set a record for their non-stop flight from New York to Miami, Florida. Due to the family background, the press reported that she was the "Flying Debutante." Ruth continued to set records and gain aviation experience. By 1927, she became one of the few women licensed to fly transport planes. Nichols held simultaneously women's aviation world records for speed, altitude, and distance.

In 1929, Ruth became a founding member of The Ninety-Nines (women pilots). She flew in the 1929 Women's Air Derby, known at the "Powder Puff Derby." During the 1930s, Nichols made several record-setting flights, most of them in a Lockheed Electra. In March, 1931, she set the women's world altitude record of 28,743 feet. In April 1931 in Detroit, she set the women's world speed record of 210.7 miles per hour. In June, 1931, Ruth attempted to become the first woman to fly solo across the Atlantic Ocean. However, she crashed and was severely injured. (In May, 1932, Amelia Earhart became the first woman to fly the Atlantic Ocean.) Undaunted, after her injuries healed in October, Ruth set yet another women's distance record with a flight from Oakland, California to Louisville Kentucky, 1,977 miles.

In February, 1932, Nichols set another new world altitude record of 19,928 feet flying a Lockheed Vega at Floyd Bennett Field in New York. Despite several aviation accidents resulting in severe injuries, Nichols continued with her commitment to flying. Over her aviation career Ruth Nichols held more than 35 women's aviation records. During the course of her career, Nichols flew every type of aircraft developed, including the dirigible, glider, autogyro, fixed wing, seaplane, transport, and even a supersonic jet. In 1958, at age 57, as co-pilot, she set new women's world records for altitude of 51,000 feet, and a speed record of 1,000 miles per hour in a TF-102A Delta Dagger.

In her own words, writing in her autobiography, *Wings for Life*, Ruth Nichols explained her passion. "To the public I suppose I have often seemed to be the original 'flying fool.' While flying over one hundred and forty different models of aircraft, I have piloted a plane in a plaster cast and a steel corset, too impatient to wait for bones to knit from the last crash. I have frozen my tongue sucking oxygen at sixty below zero, six miles up. I have escaped twice from burning planes. I have clung to a life raft in cold, mountainous seas. I have had most of the bones in my body broken... Maybe it doesn't make sense. I have been told that so often that it has become a kind of background drumbeat to my life. Family and friends have urged me to keep my feet on the ground... The only people who haven't tried to change me are flyers. They comprehend."

Later in her life, Ruth worked with several humanitarian and relief organizations using her aviation celebrity to call attention to the needs for funds. She organized Save the Children, UNICEF, and several other important charity projects. Nichols knew aviation could provide relief flights during natural disasters in worldwide efforts. In 1960, Nichols died. In 1992, she was posthumously inducted into the National Aviation Hall of Fame. In 2009, Ruth Nichols was induced into the Women in Aviation International Pioneer Hall of fame.

Noyes, Blanche Wilcox: Pioneer Aviator First Female Licensed Pilot in Ohio

Born in 1900 in Cleveland, Blanche was both bright and beautiful. She interrupted a promising movie and theater career to marry a handsome, young airmail pilot named Dewey Noyes. In 1929, Dewey bought an airplane and taught her to fly. A natural aviator, Blanche soloed after only four hours of training. By June, she earned her pilot's license, making her the first licensed female pilot in Ohio.

Pioneering Aviator, Blanche Noyes, is photographed with her airplane, "Miss Cleveland," departing for the Women's Air Derby in 1929. (Cleveland State University Special Collections)

Just a few months later, Noyes entered the first Women's Air Derby from Santa Monica to Cleveland. She was one of twenty historic women aviators to compete. Along the way, she narrowly escaped death when her plane caught fire in mid-air near Pecos, Texas. Blanche noticed smoke seeping in from her baggage compartment, rapidly filling her plane. Only 3,000 feet above the rough plains of West Texas, she had no time to search for a good landing spot. She brought the plane down quickly, crashing through bushes. The hard landing slightly damaged her landing gear. Blanche jumped out and frantically threw sand on the fire, scorching her fingers. With the fire finally out, she assessed the damage and decided the plane was still fit to fly. She climbed back on board and finished fourth in the Women's Air Derby "heavy" class, just behind Amelia Earhart who came in third. In the 1929, National Women's Air Derby, fourteen of the original twenty women completed the air race, a higher percentage than for any of the men's cross-country air races at that time.

Noyes' forced landing increased her concerns about aviation safety. Her first-hand experience would be important to her later life-long contributions to air safety and aviation navigation. On November 2, 1929, she joined her good friend, Amelia Earhart, in the founding of the International Ninety-Nines (women pilots). In 1931, she was hired by Standard Oil as a demonstration pilot. During those lean years of the Great Depression, Blanche and Dewey Noyes continued in various aviation roles. In early December of 1935, Dewey Noyes was flying over Nunda, New York, in a Beechcraft Staggerwing when a sudden ice storm enveloped his plane, sending Dewey to an icy death. Grief stricken, Noyes looked for a way to improve safety for other pilots. Within a year after her husband's death, Noyes took a pilot's job with the Federal Bureau of Air Commerce's National Air Marking Program.

That same year, she joined Louise Thaden as co-pilot, to compete in the Bendix Trophy Air race from New York City to Los Angeles, California. Ironically, they flew a Beechcraft Staggerwing, setting, a new world aviation speed record of 14 hours and 55 minutes. They won the coveted 1936 Bendix Trophy. Upon landing, Blanche told reporters, "The credit should go to my husband." Louise and Blanche earned a prize of $4,500, which would be almost $90,000 today. The Bendix National Transcontinental Air Race began in 1931. Funded by industrialist, Vincent Bendix, the purpose was to interest engineers in building faster, more reliable, and durable aircraft.

Upon her return home, Noyes joined a handful of leading women aviators in the Federal Bureau of Air Commerce. Funded by the Work Progress Administration (WPA), their mission was to map out a ground-based aerial navigation system across America. Phoebe Omlie, Louise Thaden, Nancy Harkness, Helen MacCloskey, and later, Helen Richey, laid out an innovative air marking program of painting town names on water towers, airports, roof tops, and train stations. They even laid out huge directional arrows to point the way to the next airport. And, sometimes, the mileage, as well. To get the air marking done, they enlisted the aid of Boy Scout troops, civic clubs, and federal agencies such as the U.S. Forest Service. With over 3,500 air markings completed, Blanche and her colleagues were probably congratulating themselves when disaster struck.

After Japan's air attacks on Pearl Harbor, on December 7, 1941, the Civil Aeronautics Administration (CAA) feared air makings could potentially aid enemy pilots. The CAA mandated the obliteration of almost all of the air markings. In about one month, their many months of intensive labor could no longer be seen from the air. Undeterred, Blanche wrote countless articles on aviation safety and navigation. She also continued to do inspections of the few remaining air markings. And, for many years, she was the only female pilot allowed to fly U.S. government aircraft.

After World War II, Noyes continued as CAA head of the air marking program. Noyes told *Flying Magazine* in January 1948, "The skyway has taken hold of the public imagination and the need for air marking at last is becoming apparent to everyone." From 1948 to 1950, she also served as President of the Ninety-Nines, which had been involved in air marking from the beginning. To this day, the 99s paint easily read airport names on airport parking ramps and even paint colorful compasses on the tarmac, indicating the Cardinal Directions: north, south, east and west.

By 1962, more than 45,000 air markings could be seen by pilots. In 1970, Blanche Noyes was inducted into the National Aviation Hall of Fame. In 1972, she retired from Federal service but continued to fly.

She died in 1981. Her legacy is summed up in the quote from William James, "The great use of life is to spend it for something that will outlast it. " Blanche Noyes did that.

Ochoa, Ellen: First Hispanic Woman in Space

Born in 1958 in Los Angeles, Ellen enjoyed learning about new things. Science and how things work were often on her mind. After her 1975 high school graduation, she attended San Diego State University with a focus on physics. She was a very good student, earning her Bachelor's degree there. Soon, she entered Stanford University, where she pursued her master's and doctoral degrees in electric engineering. She became a research engineer at Sandia National Laboratories and NASA Ames Research Center. Ochoa studied optical systems for performing information processing. She is a co-inventor of three patents, and the author of several technical papers on the topic.

NASA Astronaut, Ellen Ochoa, works at the Space Shuttle Atlantis Remote Manipulator System controls during the orbiter's 2002 International Space Station space rendezvous. (NASA photograph)

In 1990, she moved to the Johnson Space Center when she was selected for the NASA astronaut program. As a mission specialist astronaut in 1993, Ellen Ochoa served on STS-56 aboard Space Shuttle Discovery. She because the first Hispanic woman to go into space. On their nine-day mission, Discovery crew members travelled 3.9 million miles and orbited the earth 148 times. She returned to space on STS-66 (1994), STS-96 (1999), and again on STS-100 (2002). She logged over 1,000 hours in orbit. In 2013, she became the Johnson Space Center Director, again making history as the first Hispanic director of NASA.

In 2018, Dr. Ellen Ochoa left NASA to become vice chair of the National Science Board. She has earned numerous awards, including NASA highest, Distinguished Service Medal. She is a Fellow of the American Association for the Advancement of Science. She is in the U.S. Astronaut Hall of Fame. As part of her aerospace legacy, six schools honor her in their name, Pasco, Washington Middle School, Cudahy, California Elementary School, East Los Angeles Charter Middle School, Grand Prairie, Texas STEM Academy, Pico Rivera, California Prep Academy, and Union Public School elementary school in Tulsa, Oklahoma.

Married to Coe Miles, an intellectual property attorney, Dr. Ochoa is the mother of two sons. On reflecting on her important place in aerospace history, she said, "What everyone in the astronaut corps shares in common is not gender or ethnic background, but motivation, perseverance, and desire — the desire to participate in a voyage of discovery."

Omlie, Phoebe Fairgrave: First U.S. Female Licensed Aircraft Mechanic

Phoebe was born in Des Moines, Iowa, in1902, to parents Harry and Madge Park. But the Park marriage did not last. Madge went on to marry Andrew Fairgrave who adopted Phoebe and her brother, Paul.

When Phoebe was 12, the family relocated to St. Paul, Minnesota where Phoebe was able to attend Madison School and Mechanic Arts High School, setting the stage for Phoebe to later become America's first licensed female aircraft mechanic in a few years. On the day before Phoebe graduated, President Woodrow Wilson visited Minneapolis. Phoebe was in the crowed when President Wilson was honored with a fly over and an air show. From that moment, Phoebe was captivated by aviation.

In the early 1920s, aviation was largely unregulated and considered quite dangerous. Nevertheless, Phoebe got her local airport manager to arrange for her first flight lesson. Hoping to scare Phoebe away from flying, the manager directed that her first flight consist of violent aerobatic maneuvers. But the scheme backfired when Phoebe demanded more flights just like the first one. A natural pilot, within four hours of instruction, Phoebe was flying solo.

When Phoebe inherited some money, she bought a Curtiss Jenny. But piloting was not daring enough for Phoebe. She got another pilot to fly while Phoebe practiced wing walking. At the time, the Charleston was the dance rage of the 1920s. The media-savvy Phoebe danced the Charleston while high in the air. Soon, the media called Phoebe a "daring angel of the skies."

Next on Phoebe's agenda was a record setting parachute jump. For this dangerous stunt, she asked experienced pilot, Vernon C. Omlie, to fly her up over 15,000 feet in the sky. On July 10, 1921, nineteen year-old Phoebe and Omlie took off. Thousands of people lined the fence around the airfield, holding their breath and praying for her safe return to the ground. The next morning, the front page of The *Minneapolis Sunday Tribune* told the world about Phoebe and her record-setting 15,200 feet parachute jump.

The world and Hollywood took notice. Phoebe landed a movie deal to perform flying and aerobatic stunts in the popular movie serial, *The Perils of Pauline*. The pilot during the filming was her future husband, Vernon C. Omlie. He was a lean and lanky aviator, who served in the Army Air Corps in World War I. His pilot's license was signed by Orville Wright. He was skillful, careful, and very steady. Married in 1922, they barnstormed the nation as the Phoebe Fairgrave Omlie Flying Circus.

Barnstorming proved to be highly successful with the press. Large and small town newspapers printed front page stories and photographs of the darling and daring Phoebe. She even became the first woman to be issued a commercial pilot certificate. On June 30, 1927, the National Aeronautics Board issued Phoebe Transport License #199. She was also a successful air racer, winning large cash prizes.

On August 31, 1931, Phoebe Omlie won the National Air Race Transcontinental Sweepstakes Handicap Derby. She powders her nose to accept the prize and meet the press. (Library of Congress)

The Omlies moved to Memphis, Tennessee, offering flying lessons and mechanical services to the growing number of aviation enthusiasts. In 1927, Phoebe became the first woman to earn an airplane mechanic license. Vernon provided flight instruction and ran the thriving aviation business. Phoebe also worked for the Mono Aircraft Company, flying their popular Monocoupe 90. A small, light airplane with an enclosed cabin and two-seats. This sporty and relatively inexpensive aircraft became popular in American air races of the 1920s and 1930s.

In 1928, Phoebe set a world altitude record for women when she reached 25,400 feet. That same year, she flew in the Edsel Ford Air Tour. She became the first woman to cross the Rocky Mountains in a light aircraft. On her way to compete in the 1929 "Powder Puff Derby," Phoebe could not find the Santa Monica airport in the dark. Low on fuel, she landed in a farmer's field. The farmer and his son tied down her airplane and put her up for the night.

But, with the dawn, came the local Sheriff who accused poor Phoebe of "running dope." Fortunately, the other women pilots signed for the air race learned of Phoebe's plight. The Sheriff was about to cuff Phoebe when Amelia Earhart arrived, leading a phalanx of angry women. Earhart vouched for Phoebe and the sheriff gave up his prisoner and Phoebe was released in time to take part in the prestigious air race.

Well, of course, the rest is aviation history. This race was an important first for women. The nine-day, 2,759 mile race was covered by all the media. At stake was $8,000 in prize money (around $130,000 today), plus generous prizes for each leg of the race. Each racer had to fly with a gallon of water, a three-day supply of food, and a parachute. The race was divided to two divisions: a smaller, lighter, sport planes, called the CW class. The second division covered up to 800-cubic inch displacement engines, which was for the heavier, working aircraft, or the DW class. On August 26, 1929, landing in Cleveland, Phoebe Omlie won the CW class. Louise Thaden won the DW class. In 1929, when the International Ninety Nines were formed, both of them joined their "Sisters of the Sky" as founding members.

Phoebe's aviation fame became known in Washington D.C. political circles when, in the 1932 presidential campaign, she was asked to fly a "female speaker" around. Eleanor Roosevelt and Phoebe had similar views about how women could contribute. Soon after FDR's inauguration, Phoebe was appointed "Special Adviser" for Air Intelligence to the new National Advisory Committee for Aeronautics. This was another first for women. Phoebe became the first woman to be appointed to a federal aviation position. Then, on August 5, 1936, Vernon Omlie and seven passengers were killed on a commercial flight near St. Louis when it crashed in foggy weather.

Devastated Phoebe immediately resigned her new federal position in Washington and returned to Memphis. She continued the successful aviation business. Later, she sold the flying service. In 1941, she did return to D.C. She accepted a Civil Aeronautics Authority position as Senior Private Flying Specialist. Phoebe felt she could address the severe need for pilots for World War II service. She established a network of 66 flight schools across 46 states, including the school in Tuskegee Alabama that later trained the famous Tuskegee Airmen. With the Tennessee Bureau of Aeronautics, she began an experimental program to train women pilots as flight instructors. In September, 1943, the first class of ten women began. Phoebe explained, "If women can teach men to walk, they can teach them to fly." These women went on to instruct both men and women pilots both in military and civilian flight training programs, including the Navy's V-5 program.

In 1952, unhappy about the increasing regulation of the aviation industry by the United States Government, Phoebe resigned. She died of lung cancer in 1975. A few years later, in 1982, a new air traffic control tower at the Memphis International Airport was dedicated to both Phoebe and Vernon Omlie. In 2015, Phoebe Omlie joined the other sky stars in the Women in Aviation International Pioneer Hall of Fame.

O'Neill, Norah: First Female Flying Tiger Pilot

Born in 1949, in the Seattle area to Jack and Bertha O'Neill, Norah was a strikingly beautiful child with reddish-blonde curls. She was very precocious. Because of her high IQ, Norah soon became a member of Mensa. Although she had no idea of what she wanted to do in life, she earned a degree in journalism. She took a job as a model for ski clothes. The photo shoot was on the side of Alaska's rugged Mount McKinley. As fate would have it, Norah was given the right seat in the bush plane that flew the crew to Mt. McKinley. Entranced by the scenery and intrigued by the airplane, Norah decided she needed to find a job in Alaska and become a pilot.

Airline pilot, Norah O'Neill, was the first woman jet freighter pilot for the Flying Tiger Line. (Wikicommons)

So, at age 23, Norah found a job in the most popular bar on Kodiak Island. In order to have daylight hours for her flight lessons, she worked from 9:00 p.m. to 5:00 a.m. In just a few months, Norah took her Private Pilot check ride. The FAA Examiner told her it was the best check ride he had given in his thirty years. Norah also scored 100% on the written exam. Within another nine months, Norah earned her commercial, instrument, flight instructor, and ground instructor ratings. To say Norah was a natural aviator is not an exaggeration. She quickly went from modeling ski clothes to teaching others how to fly.

But being accepted as a flight instructor by some of Alaska's backwoodsmen was not always easy. In a 2013 You Tube interview, Norah reflected on her thirty-five year aviation career, "While working as a 23-year-old flight instructor in Alaska, the boys, I call them boys because they were immature, told the company owner, 'We don't want to work for a company with a woman. It is embarrassing to us.' I felt horrible and wanted to quit. But, if I quit, they would win."

In 1974, Norah became the first woman pilot hired for Alaska Central Air. In 1976, the historic Flying Tiger Line hired her, making Norah their first woman pilot. During her long flying career with Flying Tiger and Federal Express, Norah amassed 22,000 hours. In 1977, she became the first woman in the world to pilot the Douglas DC-8. In August, 1980, Norah became the first woman to fly passengers on the Boeing 747. Piloting larger Flying Tiger cargo planes on trans-pacific routes resulted in many interviews by Asian publications. Norah was the first woman airline pilot to land in Korea, Japan, Malaysia, Saudi Arabia, Hong Kong, and the Philippines.

Having experienced gender discrimination first hand, Norah mentored other women to join her on the airline flight deck all over the world. In 1978, she became one of the founders of the International Society of Women Airline Pilots (ISA+21). For twenty years, she served as their historian.

In 2005, Norah penned her autobiography, *Flying Tigress,* a no-holds barred look at the aviation industry in the 1970s. A believer in the importance of mentors, O'Neill was an active member of the Airline Pilots Association (ALPA), International Ninety-Nines, Women in Aviation International (WAI), and The Flying Tiger Pilots Association. After a courageous battle against colon cancer, Norah O'Neill passed in 2017 with her children by her side. Her life story reminds me of the words from East Indian Film Director, Mandeep Benipal, "Never mess with a Courageous woman. She is not just a woman. She is a tigress. She knows how to rise above the odds, even if the world seems against her."

Orr, Marion Alice Powell: Pioneering Canadian and WWII Air Transport Auxiliary Pilot

Marion Powell was born in 1918 in Toronto, Ontario. When she was a little girl, Marion would gaze at the sky, knowing someday she would be a pilot. Money was always scarce in her home growing up. After completing eighth grade, the teenage Marion, with her sister Marge, left home. To support themselves, the young girls found work at a factory. Still dreaming of flying, Marion would often walk the ten kilometers to the nearby Barker Airfield. Flying lessons cost $6 an hour. Marion only earned $10 a week. She figured, if she skipped some meals, and was very careful with her pennies, she might be able to begin flight lessons.

Canadian Pioneer Aviator, Marion Orr, began flying in 1939. (Canadian Hall of Fame)

Showing her determination, she worked odd jobs at the airport to earn even more toward flying lessons. In December, 1939, Marion reached her goal of earning her private pilot license. She was one of very few Canadian women to do so. She immediately put her aviation experience to work with de Havilland Aircraft of Canada as an aircraft inspector. Marion was still on the ground but she was gaining aviation knowledge and industry contacts. She knew she needed to take the next step. She began commercial pilot training. Her flying instructor was Doug Orr. Over time, they grew close. In December, 1941, Marion earned her commercial pilot license. Shortly, thereafter, Marion and Doug married. The marriage was brief. But, Marion kept Orr as her last name.

With World War II raging in Europe, new opportunities for women pilots were opening up. Marion has hired as the manager and flight instructor at the St. Catharine's Flying Club in Ontario. She became the first Canadian woman to run a flying school. Unfortunately, a fire destroyed the business. Needing a job, Marion moved nearby to Goderich Municipal Airport. She became Canada's second woman qualified as a control tower operator. But flying is what Marion wanted to be doing. A friend told Marion about the Air Transport Auxiliary (ATA) in England. Women pilots flew airplanes in support of the Royal Air Force (RAF). Marion applied. After testing in Montreal, Marion was immediately accepted to the ATA. Marion moved to England with her aviation friend, Violet Milstead. In June, 1943, Marion flew her first ATA mission. She loved the Spitfire, which she considered the most beautiful plane ever built! She always tried to be on the flying roster for the Spitfire. She would even give up a day off for the chance to fly it.

Marion's ATA records show she ferried about 15 aircraft types, including the Airspeed Oxford, the only twin-engine aircraft. Marion flew aircraft to and from the factories, squadrons, and airfields. In September, 1944, Marion was honorably discharged from the ATA with the rank of Second Officer with 700 logged flying hours. Marion dreamed of flying and she lived her dream.

Marion returned to Ontario, Canada. She gave flight instruction and looked for a new aviation opportunity. In 1947, she assumed the manager responsibilities at Barker Airfield. In two years, Marion acquired the flight school. But, developers forced the airfield to close. Undaunted, in 1954, Marion got permission to open her own airfield with two grass strips, named Maple Aerodrome near Maple, Ontario. She moved her Aero Activities Limited flight school there. After several years, Marion sold the airport and flight school to join her sister, living in Florida.

Now, Marion was ready to try helicopters. In a matter of weeks Marion earned a U.S. Helicopter Instructor rating. She was with a new student at the controls when the engine failed. They both survived the crash. After Marion's broken back healed, she headed back to Canada. Almost immediately, she was hired as a Flight Instructor by the new owners at Buttonville airport. Marion loved being in the air and sharing that love with her students. Records reveal Marion taught over 5,000 students to fly or increase their aviation skills.

In 1981 Orr was made a member of Canada's Aviation Hall of Fame. During her long aviation career, Marion Orr flew over 21,000 hours, 17,000 of that as an instructor in single or twin-engine airplanes on wheels, skis, floats, and, for a short time, in helicopters. She was honored with the Order of Canada presented to citizens who have made extraordinary contributions to their nation. In 1994, ill-health grounded her. She was killed the next year in an automobile accident.

Paterson, Daphne: Canadian Pioneer Aviator
Born in 1905, in St. John, Newfoundland, Daphne and her brother, Pierce, were encouraged by their parents to strive for a good education. In fact, in the 1930s, Daphne's father became First Minister of Education. Daphne earned a University degree in science from McGill, one of Canada's top schools. Founded in 1821 in Quebec by Royal Charter, this legacy University had rigorous standards. Daphne loved engines and raced cars. She held an automobile speed record. In the 1920, aviation was growing across Canada. Because airplanes would be

faster than cars on many of the winding roads in Canada, Daphne turned her eyes toward the sky.

Until 1920, Canada did not have an Air Force, although many Canadians flew in World War I. Canadian civil aviation was largely built by pioneer aviators. Daphne experienced her first flight at the Montreal Light Aeroplane Club. The Chief Flying Instructor tried to scare her off by flying aerobatic maneuvers. He was shocked and dismayed the next day when she returned to begin flight lessons. Her assigned Flight Instructor was Tony Spooner, who was not threatened by the idea of a woman pilot. In fact, within a few lessons, he found Daphne a natural and quite good at "tinkering with the engine."

Daphne soloed after only about seven hours of dual flight instruction. On May 29, 1929, she passed her flying tests, receiving her Private Pilot's Certificate. Daphne actually fell in love with flying. She continued flight training. Her reputation as a first-rate aviator spread "to all those Chaps who doubted her." Later, she became the first Canadian woman to qualify for her Commercial Pilot's License. Initially, the Canadian Department of National Defense, which issued all aviation licenses, rejected Daphne's because she was female!

Flight Instructor Spooner and several of the male Aeroplane Club members challenged the decision. They countered the government bureaucrat that "Pilot," as defined in the Regulation, did not specify the pilot had to be male. In a panic and for fear the media might find out, the Canadian Government Aviation Regulations were hastily rewritten to indicate that if the "pilot" was female, they would be required to take a medical physical every three months, instead of the six months required of male Commercial Pilots. Daphne was awarded her license.

Daphne was an aviation industry leader in eastern Canada. An active member of Flying Clubs in Montreal, St. John's, the Fredericton Flying Club, and the Toronto Flying Club. She was always a very strong promoter of general aviation. This was key in building aviation in Canada because the Canadian government was so slow developing a nationwide program. Daphne was involved in many flying activities to reach the public. Her presence as an aviator spoke to the fact women could be aviators. She generated a lot of press, but the airlines were not considering hiring females under any circumstances, no matter how qualified they were.

Webster Trophy medal awarded to Daphne Paterson for runner-up position, 1937
Amelia Earhart Medal presented to Daphne Paterson by the 99's in 1978.

In 1937, Canadian Aviation Pioneer, Daphne Paterson, was awarded the Webster Trophy runner-up medallion. In 1978, the Canadian Chapter of the Ninety-Nines presented her with an Amelia Earhart Medallion for her stellar accomplishments. (Canadian Aviation History image)

Daphne won several important air racing awards, including the Canadian Flying Clubs' de Havilland Trophy, and was runner-up twice for the prestigious Canadian Webster Trophy. Daphne met and married aviator, Tony Shelfoon, who eventually became a Squadron Leader in the Royal Canadian Air Force. As a qualified aviator, Daphne believed when war was declared, even the Canadian government would see the need to employee every aviator no matter their gender. She began training for her Flight Instructor rating. In May, 1940, she achieved that goal.

Again, even with the shortage of flight instructors, she was told that it was "improper for women to teach men to fly!" By then, she was considered too old to join the Air Transport Auxiliary in England. In desperation, she contacted Jacqueline Cochran and the newly formed WASP. But, Daphne did not qualify because she was not an American citizen. Of course, during the war, all flying club activity was grounded so flight instruction in the civilian sector was not needed. Grounded, Daphne moved to the lake area of Trenton.

In 1978, the First Canadian Chapter of the Ninety-Nines honored Daphne with the presentation of an Amelia Earhart Medallion. Maya Angelou said, "How important it is for us to recognize and celebrate our heroes and she-roes!" This is so true of our Pioneer Women in Aviation, who had the skill, determination, and courage to become Sky Stars.

Pfister, Elizabeth Haas "Betty:" WWII WASP and Whirly Girl
Born in 1921 on Long Island, Betty grew up surrounded by airfields and aviation manufacturing, and even women pilots in the news. Her first flight with a barnstormer in an open biplane, opened her eyes to the joy of flying. She made a deal with her father, if he paid for flying lessons, she would stay in college. In 1941, she became a pilot and graduated from Bennington College in Vermont. Betty joined WASP class 43-W-5. In September, 1943, she joined other WASP in the ferry command. Betty flew a variety of military airplanes. Because of her prior flying experience and aviation skills, Betty was most often assigned to fly larger, complicated airplanes for delivery to U.S. Military bases.

Betty flew the Douglas C-47 military transport, which was originally a civilian DC-3 airliner design. Ironically, if it had been a passenger airliner, back in 1943, the airline executives would not have hired Betty because of her gender. Betty also flew the Boeing B-17 Flying Fortress, a four-engine bomber. Betty also flew the Boeing B-24 Liberator, which was a long-range heavy bomber. These were not easy planes to fly. The B-17 could fly higher than the B-24, which was faster. Crews often complained that the B-24 was difficult to fly with stiff and heavy controls. And, yet, Betty safely flew them.

Betty Pfister was a World War II WASP and a Whirly Girl. (Colorado Aviation Hall of Fame archive)

After the WASP were disbanded, Betty continued to ferry military planes under contract as a civilian pilot. Betty became a Flight Instructor in California. In October, 1946, Betty was able to purchase an Army surplus Bell P-39 Aircobra fighter airplane. She bought it for less than $1,000. That would be about $10,000 in 2021 dollars. That was a whole lot of airplane at a bargain basement price. She named her plane, "Galloping Gertie." Being surplus and Army drab green, Betty prevailed on family friend, famous artist, Norman Rockwell, to get creative with her new paint scheme. The stunning result was a red and white racing design that emphasized the lines of the P-39.

Betty flew *Galloping Gertie* at airshows and races for the next three and a half years, averaging over 100 hours each year in her P-39. In 1950, and again in 1952, she won the International Air Race, as well as many other smaller races around the country. As fate would have it, a WASP friend invited Betty to her wedding in Carbondale, Colorado. While skiing on Ajax Mountain in Aspen, Betty spied a fellow standing in the lift line with a cardboard sign hanging around his neck that read, "If you think I'm handsome, I'm available" followed by his four-digit phone number. Betty called him. In 1954, Art Pfister and Betty married.

Art flew the "Hump," over Burma, China, and India during World War II. They both loved flying and skiing. They bought the Lazy Chair Ranch on Buttermilk Mountain. They lived there the rest of their lives. Art encouraged Betty to give up air racing. Betty sold Galloping Gertie. But, by no means was Betty done with the freedom she felt in the air. Even as the mother of three daughters and a civic leader in the Aspen community, Betty became a glider pilot. She flew hot air balloons, competing in races in the Swiss Alps. In 1968, Betty and Art founded the Pitkin County Air Rescue, in partnership with the Civil Air Patrol. Betty tirelessly worked with the Aspen Valley Hospital building a heliport.

That opened a new world to Betty, Helicopters. In 1964, Betty learned to fly helicopters and fell in love all over again. She was the 52nd woman in the world to obtain a helicopter license. She became an esteemed member of the Whirly Girls, the international organization of women's helicopter pilots. In the early 1970s, Betty became a member of the United States Helicopter Team. Her team represented the U.S. in the World Helicopter Championship in both England, and in Russia. Upon her return home, Betty bought her own Bell-46-G. She painted it to resemble a pink, yellow, and orange butterfly. She named her, Tinker Bell. Betty told a friend, owning and flying that helicopter was one of the highlights of her life.

Betty was a proud 40-year member of the Ninety-Nines. In 1981, she organized the Aspen Chapter. In 1984, Betty was inducted into the Colorado Aviation Hall of Fame. In 1985-87, Betty became President of the Whirly Girls. In 1992, Betty received the National Aeronautic Association (NAA) Katharine Wright Memorial Award. In 1994, she was given the NAA Elder Statesman of Aviation Award. In 2001, Betty was inducted into the Women in Aviation International Pioneer Hall of Fame. Finally, in 2010, Betty and the other living WASP of World War II were given the long overdue Congressional Gold Medal. As she said at that time, "Better late than never!" In 2011, Betty Pfister flew West from Aspen, Colorado.

Passion is energy. Feel the power that comes from focusing on what excites you.

~ Oprah Winfrey

4
Q-Quebec to S-Sierra

All adventures, especially into new territory, are scary.
~ NASA Astronaut, Sally Ride.

Quimby, Harriet: America's First Female Licensed Pilot
Born in Michigan in 1875, Harriet's family moved to San Francisco in the early 1900s. In those days, San Francisco was California's largest city. Harriet was smart, beautiful, and inquisitive. In 1902, Harriet was hired by the San Francisco Dramatic Review and, wrote drama critiques for the Sunday editions of both the San Francisco Chronicle, and San Francisco Call. Through her contacts in the budding California entertainment industry, the seven screen plays Harriet wrote were produced. Several featured popular silent film stars. Clearly, Harriet knew a lot about drama and entertainment because this is a remarkable feat for a woman in 1902.

In 1903, Harriet moved across the country to New York City. The important Leslie's Illustrated Weekly hired Quimby as their theater critic. At that time, Leslie's was a powerful literary and news magazine. Over her nine-year career at the magazine, Harriet had 250 bylined articles, and contributed to many others. In fact, the editors sent Harriet to cover the October 22-30, 1910 International Aviation Tournament at the Long Island Belmont racetrack. It was a huge event with over 150,000 spectators.

The prize money offered for flyers and their new airplanes was $75,000. That would be around $5,000,000 today. The average American income was only $200 to $400 for the entire year. The Belmont Park International Aviation Tournament week was filled with galas, awards, and big names in the budding aviation industry. Harriet met the legendary airplane designer and flyer, John Moisant. More importantly, his sister, Matilde, attended. Harriet struck up a close friendship with her. The Moisants had opened a new flight school on Long Island. Harriet approached her editors with an exciting idea. They could pay for her flying lessons. In return, she would write all about it.

On April 16, 1912, Harriet Quimby became the first woman to fly across the English Channel from England to France. (Library of Congress)

Her editors agreed. Harriet joined her new friend, Matilde, at the Moisant Aviation School in Hempstead. The school had six Blériot aeroplanes equipped with 50 horse power motors. Through her magazine articles, readership increased each week. Readers wanted to find out what Harriet was doing now in the sky. Harriet encouraged the magazine's women readers about the new and wonderful opportunities in aviation. She said, "There is no reason why the aeroplane should not open up a fruitful occupation for women."

On August 1, 1911, Harriet became America's first woman to earn an AeroClub of America aviator's certificate. Her friend, Matilde Moisant, soon earned hers. Immediately, they joined the famed, Moisant International Aviators as featured performers. The media hype soon followed. Harriet was called the "Dresden China Aviatrix" or "China Doll," because of her petite stature and fair skin. New sky star, Harriet Quimby, made her professional debut, earning $1,500, in an air demonstration flight over Staten Island before a crowd of almost 20,000 spectators. In 2021, that one performance would pay over $40,000.

As one of the country's few female pilots, Harriet capitalized on her femininity by wearing a purple satin flying suit with trousers tucked into high lace-up boots with a matching beautiful purple satin blouse with a darling hood. She always wore a necklace and antique bracelet. She continued to write for Leslie's readers. Harriet fully explained her departure from the normally expected long skirt for a lady of her stature. "If a woman wants to fly, first of all she must, of course, abandon skirts and don a knickerbockers uniform … There must be no flapping ends to catch in the multitudinous wires surrounding the driver's seat." Well, that explanation made such perfect sense to everyone. When she performed at the flying circus, the crowd knew immediately who the beautiful woman in the purple flying suit was.

Quimby drew huge crowds when she competed in cross-country air meets and races. As part of the Moisant Exhibition team, she showcased her talents around the United States. She continued writing exciting stories about her barnstorming which kept Leslie's readers coming back. Harriet even wowed a large crowd in Mexico City at the celebration for Mexico's President Francisco Madero. Because no woman in the world had yet flown the English Channel, Harriet prepared for a trip to Europe to be the first.

Harriet ordered a new Blériot plane for her April 1912 flight. When she arrived in England, it was not ready. Louis Blériot, the airplane designer, loaned Harriet his personal airplane for her historic attempt.

On the chilly morning of April 16, Harriet received last minute instruction from Louis before she lifted off from Dover. In less than an hour, a cold and tired Harriet Quimby landed on a beach in France. She was about 25 miles away from Calais where she intended to land. But, she did it. She became the first woman to successfully fly across the English Channel from England to France. Harriet said, "I was annoyed from the start by the attitude of doubt by the spectators that I would never really make the flight. This attitude made me more determined than ever to succeed." Early reporting called Harriet "America's First Lady of the Air."

News of her amazing accomplishment was largely buried inside most major newspapers because just the day before the luxury steamship, RMS Titanic, sank to the bottom of the Atlantic Ocean, which was heart-breaking news felt around the world. After her new plane was ready, Harriet sailed by ship with it back to America. Upon her return, she was contacted by the marketing executive of Vin Fiz, sparkling grape soda. Her sparkling personality and signature purple satin flying suit caught their attention. They recruited Harriet to be their spokesperson. Her image in her distinctive purple satin flying suit soon graced the label on the Vin Fiz soda bottles and advertising.

But, just a few months later, tragedy struck. On July 1, Harriet flew in the Third Annual Boston Aviation Meet in her new, two-seat Blériot monoplane. Her passenger was the organizer of this important aviation event, William A.P. Willard. At about 1,000 feet over the harbor, the aircraft unexpectedly pitched forward, ejecting Harriet and her passenger from their seats. They fell to their deaths. In 1991, Harriet Quimby was honored with a commemorative stamp from the U.S. Postal Service. She was featured in her signature purple flying suit. In 1998, Women in Aviation International inducted Quimby into their Pioneer Hall of Fame. In 2004, Harriet Quimby was enshrined in the National Aviation Hall of Fame.

Raiche, Bessica Faith Medlar: First U.S. Woman to Solo in an Airplane she Built

Bessica was born in Wisconsin in 1875. America had only 37 states. Ulysses Grant was President. Bessica was always creative and fearless about life. After she graduated from high school, she convinced her parents to allow her to study music in France. As a young adult, she embraced French society. She became fluent in French. France was an early leader in aviation and airplane designs. Bessica was always inquisitive. Aviation was another interest she cultivated there.

Bessica Raiche was awarded a gold medal as the "First Woman Aviator in America" by The Aeronautical Society of America. (Wikicommons)

Bessica met a dashing, young Frenchman, Francois C. Raiche. They shared a love of adventure and interest in aviation. In 1903, they quickly married. They decided to return to the United States to be part of the growing aviation industry on Long Island, New York. Bessica learned dentistry. She earned a Doctor of Medicine degree from Tufts University. She was accomplished in so many fields. Bessica Raiche was a Renaissance woman. She was an artist, musician, scholar, and linguist,

Now, aviation became their focus. Together, Bessica and Francois built their own airplane in their living room. It was similar to the Wright biplane. They used much lighter materials of bamboo, silk, and piano wire. This made their aeroplane very fragile. They assembled the larger airplane parts in their yard. They had learned from many of the early French aeroplane designers. They studied drawing of the early Wright models. They named their new aviation engineering and manufacturing enterprise, the French-American Aeroplane Company. They partnered with C.M. Crout for a 30-horsepower engine for their new creation. It was decided Bessica would fly because she was lighter.

On the early morning of September 19, 1910, Bessica flew her plane without much instruction. After all, she helped design and build it. Bessica Raiche became the first American woman to fly solo in the plane she built. Some historians credit Blanche Scott a few weeks earlier as being the first American woman to solo. However, National Air and Space Museum Historian, Dorothy Cochrane, explained, "While Scott beat Bessica by a couple of weeks, Scott's flight isn't considered 'official' because Scott only reached an altitude of 40 feet. Scott's flight is considered more of an accident than intentional because she was simply practicing taxiing on her own when 'something happened' and she went airborne. So to be totally accurate, Scott is the first American woman to fly solo in an airplane, but Bessica is the first one to do it intentionally."

The Aeronautical Society of America credits Bessica Raiche with the first intentional solo flight. The society awarded Bessica a gold medal, studded with diamonds, and inscribed The First Woman Aviator in America. Bessica and Francois built and sold two more aeroplanes. But, Bessica began to have health problems. That prompted a move to a better climate. Bessica was told to give up flying because it was not good for her lungs and health. In 1912, Bessica and François moved to California.

By 1920, Bessica was one of a handful of qualified women physicians. She was one of the first Obstetrics and Gynecology specialists in the entire United States. Francois was now Frank with a thriving law practice. Because Bessica did not continue barnstorming or setting aviation records, her aviation accomplishment was largely overlooked. By 1925, Bessica and Frank divorced. Relatives of Bessica report Frank burned many of their early aeroplane drawings and records in the fireplace. Bessica Raiche moved on in her medical practice in Newport Beach. In 1932, Bessica died in her sleep at her California home. She blazed a trail in the air and in medicine for American women.

Rasche, Thea Doku: Germany's Flying Fraulein
Born in Westphalia in 1899, Thea's father was the director of a popular brewery. They encouraged Thea to excel in outdoor pursuits. Tennis, hockey, and riding were high on her list of accomplishments. Her family planned for her to attend the Agriculture Institute for Women. They believed their daughter would need domestic skills for a "good marriage." Her father chose a suitable husband for Thea. However, Thea broke off the engagement. She left home. She became an agricultural inspector for a farm in Frankfurt.

That summer of 1924 changed the direction of her life. Thea registered as a flight student in Muenster. But, friends introduced her to the Wasserkuppe, Germany's center for glider flying. Thea's first lesson was with World War I Ace and glider instructor, Paul Bäumle. It was exhilarating. In only four days, 25-year-old Thea obtained her glider pilot license.

Thea cancelled her flight training in Muenster. She moved to Hamburg where Paul had an aviation business and flight training. Under Paul's expert tutelage, Thea, a natural aviator, excelled. Because her parents cut off any support, Thea worked in several clerical positions to fund her new passion. She trained in Paul's Udet Flamingo. When Thea earned her airplane license, she became the first German woman after World War I to do so. In another five months, Thea secured her aerobatic license. She became Germany's first female stunt pilot. Thea loved the precision and focus aerobatic flying required. She soon became known as one of Germany's best female aerobatic pilots.

Famed German World War I Ace, Ernst Udet, said of Thea's ability, "This woman can really fly - nobody can touch her." Thea was called "The Flying Fraulein," as she performed at air shows and in competitions. In 1929, Thea flew aerobatics at several high profile American aviation events and exhibitions. When the important "Women's Air Derby," the first official women-only air race, was announced, Thea was contacted by the Moth Aircraft Corporation of Lowell, Massachusetts. They asked Thea to fly a de Havilland Gipsy Moth for them in this first ever women's air race. Thea immediately said, "Yes!" She was promised a new plane. But, it was not ready in time for the race.

Thea Rasche was a beloved German aerobatic pilot. (San Diego Air & Space Museum archive)

Thea flew an older Gipsy Moth which was in Los Angeles. Thea had to fly the borrowed plane from Santa Monica on race day without testing it. She was able to complete the race. In Cleveland, she finished in the Light class, which was won by Phoebe Omlie. Later in 1929, Thea joined with many of the women air racers in the founding of the International Ninety-Nines. Obviously, Thea was the first German member of this now long-standing International organization.

In 1932, Thea became the first woman in Germany to be awarded a seaplane license. During World War II, she trained as a nurse in Berlin. For several years after the War, Thea moved to the United States. In 1953, she returned to Germany. She continued to mentor young women in aviation. In 1971, she died in Essen. Part of her aviation legacy is remembered with three German streets named in her honor in Frankfurt, Freudenstadt, and in Berlin near the Gatow Airport.

Raskova, Marina Mikhaylovna: Legendary Russian Aviator of World War II

Marina was born in Moscow in 1912 when the Romanov Dynasty was in power. Marina's father was a music teacher. Growing up, Marina wanted to sing opera. In 1917, the Russian Revolution changed the social order drastically. Then, Marina's father died in an accident. Marina was forced to focus on surviving during all the turmoil of her family and country. Through study and determination, Marina trained as a chemist. She married an engineer, Sergei Raskova. They had a daughter named Tanya. Their marriage ended in divorce.

In October, 1931, Marina now worked in the drafting department of the Nikolai Zhukovsky Air Force Engineering Academy. Her talent was recognized quickly. She was recommended to join the Soviet Army Air Force. She became their first female navigator. After only a year, Marina was promoted to navigation instructor. She was invited to train as a pilot at the Moscow Air Club. She joined two other women pilots, Polina Osipenko and Valentina Grizodubova. They formed a close bond. In fact, in September, 1938, these three women military pilots set a new distance record for non-stop flight from Moscow to the Sea of

Okhotsk. They flew across almost the entire width of the Soviet Union. This brought them celebrity status in the entire Soviet Union. Their story was even printed in The New York Times. They flew a modified Tupolev-ANT-37, a twin-engine experimental bomber.

In 2012, a Russian postage stamp honored the legendary World War II Aviator, Marina Raskova. (Wikicommons)

They named their airplane, "Rodina," roughly translated to English means "Motherland." This instantly endeared these intrepid female flyers to the Soviet people. On the cool morning of September 24, dignitaries, media, and military leaders assembled to watch the fuel tanks being sealed to insure the integrity of the flight. However, in the media hype, the fact that the tanks had not been topped off before sealing was overlooked. Marina took her place in the Navigator position in the glass nose. Marina knew that the maps of the far eastern Soviet Union were not adequate for aerial navigation. But, she had total confidence in her own abilities to navigate with a compass and sextant. All that celestial navigation skill depends upon seeing the sky. The marginal weather conditions with thick cloud banks and ice building up on their wings challenged Marina.

In the early hours of September 25, Rodina reached the Komsomolsk area in far eastern Russia. But, their landing field was hidden with low clouds and poor visibility. When they asked Marina for an alternate landing area, the three women heard the sickening sound of a sputtering, fuel starved engine…then quiet. This was a dire situation with the runway obscured and Marina in the nose, in a crash, she would be killed. Marina grabbed her parachute. Right before Rodina crashed in a marsh, Marina jumped. It took eight days before rescue teams reached Osipenko and Grizodubova. Badly injured in the parachute jump, Marina had to wait another three days before she was located in the vast wilderness. But, they were all alive and completed the mission. Stalin himself presented all three women with the Hero of the Soviet Union Medal. They were the first Soviet women to receive this highest award.

With this new status, Marina now had access to the Soviet top brass and, especially, Joseph Stalin. She was ideally placed to promote women in military aviation. In 1941, when Germany invaded Russia, Marina convinced Stalin to allow her to recruit and train Soviet women to fly and fight against the German invaders for the good of "Mother Russia." Stalin reluctantly agreed. Marina announced on Radio Moscow about the formation of Russia's first all-female Air Regiments. Literally, thousands of Soviet women applied. Marina and her team interviewed potential pilots for three new Air Regiments. Also, all the ground crews and support positions had to be filled with women. Aircraft mechanics to cooks were needed to support the three new all-women units.

The rock that is an obstacle in the path of one person becomes a stepping stone in the path of another.

Tirelessly, Marina trained and organized the women of the 586th Fighter Aviation Regiment, flying the combat equipped Yak-1 fighter. From the 586th, Lydia Litvyak and Katia Budanova became the two highest scoring female fighter aces in world history. The 587th Bomber Aviation Regiment was equipped with Pe-2 planes. Marina took leadership of the Regiment. On missions, Marina took her familiar navigator position. The third Air Regiment was poorly equipped with outdated and underpowered Po-2, open cockpit biplanes. The 588th Night Bomber Regiment's mission was to harass the German forces on the ground. The cover of darkness supposedly made up for the poor equipment.

The 588th became known by the Germans as the "Nachthexen" or "Night Witches," because of the whooshing sound their airplanes made as they swooped from the sky to drop bombs. One crew of the 588th supposedly flew 17 operational sorties in a single night. The Night Witches were relentless in their attacks. Twenty two Night Witches earned their country's highest award, Hero of the Soviet Union. Marina Raskova proved that Russian women would fly and defend the Motherland effectively.

Sadly, in January 1943, after a year on the front line commanding the 587th and flying many combat missions, Marina was leading a detachment of three Pe-2 bombers back to base after a successful mission when winter weather hit them. Thirty-three year old Marina and her entire crew were killed in the crash. Major Marina Raskova was mourned by her nation. Her ashes were placed in the Kremlin Wall. She was given the first state funeral in Red Square since the German World War II invasion.

Resnik, Judith Arlene: Astronaut and Second American Woman in Space

Born in 1949 to Ukrainian immigrants, Sarah and Marvin Resnik, Judith grew up in an observant Jewish family. Judith studied at Hebrew school every weekend. Her father, fluent in eight languages, had served in World War II in U.S. Army aerial reconnaissance. He was a respected optometrist in their Akron, Ohio, home town. While still in kindergarten, Judith was precocious. By elementary school, Judith was noticed for "intellectual brilliance." By high school, she excelled in math, languages, and classical piano. During these formative years, her parents divorced. Judith asked the court to switch her custody from her mother to her father because she was particularly close to him. The judge agreed.

Astronaut, Judith Resnik, was one of the Space Shuttle Challenger crew members tragically killed seconds after liftoff in 1986. (NASA photograph)

Her senior year of high school, she was Homecoming Queen Runner-up. At graduation, Judith was class valedictorian. She earned a perfect score on her SAT college admission exam. She was the only female in the country to do so that year. In fact, at that time, she was one of only 16 women in United States history to have done so. At age 17, she entered Carnegie Mellon University. She joined only two other female electrical engineering students. In 1970, Judith graduated with a Bachelor of Science of Electrical Engineering. By 1977, Dr. Judith Resnik earned a Ph.D. in electrical engineering with honors from the University of Maryland. She was recruited by RCA as an engineer on naval missile and radar projects. Later, she was a senior systems engineer for Xerox Corporation.

At age 28, NASA recruited her for their first astronaut class to accept women. She was one of the six women selected from over 1,500 female applicants. While training in the astronaut program, Resnik developed software for NASA missions. Also, she focused on her physical fitness, hoping this would increase her chances to be selected for the first U.S. female space mission. In 1984, Resnik became the second American woman in space on the maiden voyage of Discovery. Her duties included operating the shuttle's robotic arm or Remote Manipulation System. Because she helped create the device, she was considered an expert. Judith also deployed and conducted experiments on a solar array wing as a potential way of generating additional electrical power during future space missions. She logged 145 hours in orbit.

During her first mission, Judith held a written sign saying, "Hi Dad," to the cameras. She demonstrated great poise in a live televised broadcast with President Reagan. She told him, "The Earth looks great." When Reagan asked her if the flight was all she hoped it would be, she replied, "It certainly is and I couldn't have picked a better crew to fly with." Later, crew member, Henry Hartsfield, described Resnik as the "astronaut's astronaut." He said, "I was also happy to be crewed with Judy... She was smart, hardworking, and dependable, all the things you would want in a fellow crewmember."

On January 28, 1986, Judith Resnik embarked on her second space flight. Seconds after lift-off, the Space Shuttle Challenger exploded killing the entire crew. Resnik's many contributions to space exploration are remember with several buildings and schools named in her honor. Annually, the Institute of Electrical and Electronics Engineers present the IEEE Judith A. Resnick Award to the individual or team making outstanding contributions to space exploration. Each year, the Society of Women Engineers awards the Resnik Challenger Medal to a woman who has changed the space industry with innovative technology.

Richey, Helen: Legendary American Aviator for British ATA and WASP

Helen Richey has a fascinating aviation journey. She was born in 1909 in McKeesport, Pennsylvania. She was considered a "Tom Boy," in those days. She wore pants, kept her hair short, played with mechanical "boy" toys, and joined the boys in sports. Helen performed well in school, leaned toward math and science. After high school, she attended Pittsburgh's Carnegie Tech. Within a few months, she dropped out to enroll in flight school. Helen was now where she felt she belonged.

In April, 1930, she soloed at Bettis Field with only six hours of instruction. Her father, McKeesport School System Superintendent, placed high value on education. But, Helen's passion for flying was obvious. He financed her first open-cockpit biplane. In a few short months with only thirty hours in her log books, Helen put on a crowd-pleasing aerial performance at the opening ceremony for the new airport near Johnsonburg, Pennsylvania. Helen quickly flew a Curtiss Fledgling biplane to 3,000 feet up in the air. The daring, young woman cut the engine, put the airplane into a death spin, and pulled up at the very last moment. The crowd and media went wild. Helen discovered how electrifying that adrenaline rush felt.

At age 20, she earned her pilot license. She teamed up with record-setting pilot, Frances Marsalis, to gain national attention in an endurance flight over Miami. The Curtiss Thrush monoplane was named "Outdoor

Girl," after their cosmetics company sponsor. The duo took off on December 20, intending to stay aloft with aerial refueling and supplies until the New Year. They experienced harsh weather conditions, and several refueling and resupply mishaps which tore or punctured the airplane fabric. Plucky Helen climbed out each time sewing or patching the fabric, while hanging on to the strut. Fatigue became a factor. On December 30, 1933, after 237 hours and 43 minutes, they eclipsed the previous endurance record set the year before by Marsalis and Louise Thaden. The national press covered their epic flight.

Helen Richey, trailblazing American aviator. (San Diego Air & Space Museum archive)

In 1934, Helen won the first Women's National Air Meet in Dayton, Ohio. Twenty experienced women aviators competed in 20- and 50-mile races. The media coverage elevated Helen's aviation profile even higher. Then, Central Airlines of Greensburg, Pennsylvania, hired Helen, making her the first woman commercial airline pilot. Meanwhile, James D. Condon, the airline president, assured the U.S. Department of Commerce and his male pilots that he hired a woman only for publicity purposes. He did not plan to keep her on his airline flight deck for long. Helen sat in the co-pilot seat on her first flight in the Central Airlines Ford Trimotor flight from Washington, D.C. to Detroit, with scheduled stops in Pittsburgh and Cleveland. The Central Airlines president got the publicity he craved.

The blow back from the male pilots was immediate and intense. The Federal Bureau of Air Commerce mandated that the airline ground Helen during "bad" weather. The male pilots made the few flights Helen was "allowed" to fly very, very difficult. They even threatened to strike, unless Helen was fired. They refused her membership in their union, the Air Line Pilots Association (ALPA). The Bureau of Air Commerce urged the airline to limit Helen to only flying three times a month, at most. Her log book shows just eleven flights in the ten months of her Central Airlines employment. In November, 1935, Helen Richey resigned from Central Airlines.

The more you trust your intuition, the more empowered you become, the stronger you become, and the happier you become.

~ Gisele Bundchen, Super model and helicopter pilot

Next, Helen focused on record-setting and air shows. In 1936, Helen set an international altitude record, reaching 18,448 feet. She joined Amelia Earhart in the prestigious transcontinental Bendix Trophy Air Race. Earhart/Richey finished fifth, besting some of the male teams. In 1940, Helen became the first American woman to earn her flight instructor rating. She instructed air cadets at the Pittsburgh-Butler Airport, in advance of America entering World War II. Richey felt compelled to help Britain fight Germany.

Jackie Cochran encouraged Helen to apply to the British Air Transport Auxiliary. Helen had nearly 2,000 hours of flight time, a commercial pilot license, an instructor rating, and flight instructor experience with the U.S. Army Air Corps. It was a no-brainer that Helen was accepted. Helen left immediately for England. After a short orientation, Helen began transporting aircraft throughout England for the Royal Air Force. Initially ATA women pilots ferried trainers from British factories to air bases. When those restrictions were lifted, Richey was one of the first women to climb into a Hawker Hurricane, a single-seat fighter. In no time, Helen was flying the faster and more powerful fighter, the Supermarine Spitfire. Helen wrote home about the exhilaration she felt flying the Spitfire.

In 1942, famed war correspondent, Ernie Pyle, wrote about Helen Richey in two of his stories. Pyle wrote, "Helen is 33 now and as engaging as ever. She wears a dark blue uniform with slacks for flying and skirt for street wear. She looks very snazzy in her outfit. Their job is a dangerous one. The fatality rate in ferry service is higher proportionally than in the RAF." Then, in April 1943, Helen returned to the United States to join Jackie Cochran at Avenger Field in Texas. Helen became a WASP. She ferried aircraft across the United States. Within a few months, Helen was piloting twin engine Mitchell B-25 bombers to bases throughout the United States. Her stellar aviation skills had been finely honed in the war years.

On December 20, 1944, the military disbanded the WASP. As with many WASP and Rosie the Riveters, women could not find employment. Males returning from the war now filled many of the jobs women worked during the war years. Helen had difficulty adjusting to the new reality of civilian life. She did apply for flight instructor and aviation consultant positions but was not hired. Sadly, on January 7, 1947, Helen Richey was found dead in her New York City apartment. Her death was ruled a suicide. In her thirty-eight years, Helen Richey blazed a wide sky trail. Women in Aviation International included Helen Richey in their list of the 100 Most Influential Women in Aviation and Aerospace.

Riddle, Mary: First Enrolled Native American Licensed Female Pilot

Mary was born in Oregon in 1902. Her Clatsop Tribe members called her "Kus-de-cha" or Kingfisher. Her grandmother named her that because Mary's cries as a baby sounded like a Kingfisher's call. Her Native American tribe was part of the Quinault Indian Nation. When Mary was eleven, she saw an airplane in the Oregon sky. She was mesmerized by an object that reminded her of an eagle. In those early days of aviation, seeing an airplane was a rare event. Mary wanted to fly like an eagle.

When she was seventeen, Mary attended an air show. During the show, a woman pilot was killed. Mary heard people say, "Women should not fly." Mary took that as a challenge. She vowed to fly someday. So, Mary saved her money for two years to attend the Rankin Flying School in Portland. Tex Rankin was a famous barnstormer and aerobatic pilot. Rankin was very welcoming when Mary asked for flight training. Rankin knew there would be a big appetite for a flying circus performed by an all-female stunt team. He suggested to Mary she could do that. Wisely, Mary declined his offer and concentrated on learning how to fly. In May, 1930, she soloed and never looked back.

Just a few months later, Mary performed in the Portland Rose Festival with Dorothy Hester and Edith Foltz, both successful barnstormers in the northwest. Mary was game for the theatrics of the air show. Mary entered the arena riding a beautiful horse. She dressed

Mary Riddle of Seattle, only Indian woman flier, has an important message: "Come on, let's help fill the sky with thunder birds." (See page 3)

A MAGAZINE ABOUT WOMEN AND FLYING

Mary Riddle, the first Enrolled Native American woman to earn her pilot's license, is featured on the cover of the June, 1934, Ninety-Nines magazine. (Image courtesy of The Ninety-Nines, Inc.)

in full Native American clothes with a headband holding a large single eagle feather. Then, Mary dismounted her steed to enter her "air" horse to perform for the enthusiastic crowd. Mary was now flying like an eagle. Mary continued barnstorming, earning even more aviation credentials. In 1933, Mary earned a limited commercial pilot's license. By June, 1934, Mary was featured on the cover of the 99's magazine, sitting on her airplane in Native American dress encouraging more women to "fill the sky with Thunderbirds."

Next, Mary Riddle went to Tulsa, Oklahoma, to learn parachuting at the Spartan School. At the time, the school was all-male. Determined Mary convinced them that she would be an excellent student. True to her word, Mary graduated with honors. By 1937, Mary was again barnstorming across the United States as a stunt parachutist. But one jump almost ended her life when the parachute failed to open property and tangled with her legs. The next year, she suffered a back injury. It was time for Mary to pack away her parachute.

Then, Mary became Chief Stewardess for the Voice of Washington Tri-motor airliner. But when World War II grounded most civilian flying, Mary became an aircraft manufacturing inspector for the U.S. Army Air Corps Civil Service. She is quoted as saying, "I just had to be near airplanes- even if I could not fly them. I was a sort of guinea pig, really, on account of being the only woman, but I got along fine." After the War, Mary continued to fly privately. But, with a lot fewer theatrics.

Ride, Sally Kristen: America's First Woman in Space

Born in Los Angles in 1951, Sally was always interested in science. She was also a gifted athlete. At age 14, she was a nationally ranked junior tennis player. Sally earned a scholarship to attend the private Westlake School for Girls. After graduating, she crossed the country to attend Swarthmore College in Pennsylvania. After three semesters, she returned home to the University of California in Los Angeles, concentrating on physics courses. She entered Stanford University as a junior. She graduated with a Bachelor of Science in English and Physics. She continued at Stanford for her master's (1975) and doctorate in physics (1978). Sally researched astrophysics and free electron lasers.

In 1978, NASA announced in college newspapers across the country for qualified women to apply for the Group 8 astronaut class. Over 1,500 women applied. Sally Ride was one of them. On January 16, 1978, thirty-five astronaut candidates were announced. In Astronaut Group 8, two different kinds of astronauts were selected: pilots and mission specialists. This was also the first NASA class to select women as astronaut candidates. Sally Ride joined five other stellar women, Anna Fisher, Shannon Lucid, Judith Resnik, Rhea Seddon, and Kathy Sullivan.

> *The two most important days in your life*
> *are the day you are born*
> *and the day you find out why.*

In interviews the media often focused on gender, instead of asking about mission responsibilities. When asked, Sally often responded that she saw herself as an astronaut with responsibilities to contribute to the success of each mission. According to the Smithsonian National Air and Space Museum, "As a mission specialist astronaut, not a pilot, Ride was expected to spend fifteen hours a month aloft in the backseat of a T-38, practicing navigation and communication procedures while conditioning herself for high performance flight. Ride, who had previously flown only on commercial airliners, so enjoyed flying in the T-38 that she took lessons and earned her pilot license."

On June 18, 1983, thirty-two year old Ride became the first American woman in space on STS-7 Space Shuttle Challenger. Many spectators at the launch site and nationwide watching on their home televisions sported "Ride, Sally Ride," t-shirts. The slogan came from lyrics from Wilson Pickett's popular song, "Mustang Sally."

Sally focused on the mission to deploy two communications satellites, and to conduct experiments within the shuttle cargo bay. Part of Ride's responsibility was to operate the robotics arm to deploy and retrieve the valuable Shuttle Pallet Satellite-SPAS-1. The SPAS was a reusable free-flying vehicle which could be deployed, and retrieved by the U.S. Space Shuttle's Remote Manipulator System arm.

In 1984, Ride again made history. On Challenger STS-41-G, Sally became the first American woman to travel into space a second time. That mission lasted nine days. Ride spent 343 hours in space. On this important space mission, Ride again operated the robotic arm to remove ice from the shuttles exterior and readjust a critical radar antenna. Sally Ride did train extensively for eight months for a third mission, STS-61-M, which was immediately cancelled with the Challenger disaster. Ride was named to the Rogers Commission to investigate the causes. Also, she led the subcommittee on operations. Following the Challenger investigation, Ride was assigned to NASA headquarters to author a road map for strategic planning. The report titled, NASA Leadership and America's Future in Space, resulted in the founding of NASA Office of Exploration.

Sally Ride, shown floating in the Challenger flight deck in space, later described the STS-7 launch as "exhilarating, terrifying and overwhelming all at the same time." (NASA photograph)

In 1987, Ride left NASA to return to Stanford. She co-founded the Sally Ride Science education company with her partner, Tam O'Shaughnessy. They coauthored award-winning children's science books. Because of her astronaut status, Sally Ride became a role model for many young women who loved exploration and science. She said in the Harvard Business Review, "Young girls need to see role models in whatever careers they may choose, just so they can picture themselves doing those jobs someday. You can't be what you can't see."

In 2012, Sally Ride lost a battle with pancreatic cancer. However, her space legacy lives on with several elementary schools named for her. She received many awards and honors during and after her lifetime: National Astronaut Hall of Fame, National Women's Hall of Fame, National Aviation Hall of Fame, and WAI Pioneer Hall of Fame. In 2018, the U.S. Postal Service issued a Sally Ride forever postage stamp. Ride, Sally Ride!

Savitskaya, Svetlana Yevgenyevna: Russian Cosmonaut and First Woman to Spacewalk

Born in 1948 in Moscow, Svetlana's father was a highly-decorated WWII fighter pilot. Later, he became Deputy Commander-in-Chief of Soviet Air Defense. Svetlana's mother was a Moscow Communist Party leader. Svetlana was a good student. She graduated from the Bauman Higher Technical School. Always adventurous, Svetlana began parachuting at age sixteen. She never mentioned her extracurricular activity until her father discovered a parachute knife in her school bag. He was pleased that she was interested and encouraged her. By her seventeenth birthday, she had 450 parachute jumps. The next year, she jumped 46,758 feet setting a stratospheric parachute world record. Over her career, Svetlana had three world-record stratospheric parachute jumps, and 15 world-record parachute jumps from jet planes.

Did I mention she was adventurous? By 1966. Svetlana was enrolled in the Moscow Aviation Institute (MAI) for flight training. Beginning in 1969, she was an important member of the Soviet national aerobatic team. At the 1970 World Aerobatic Championships, flying a Yak-18,

Svetlana won the world championship with her female teammates. At that time, a United Kingdom journalist nicknamed her, "Miss Sensation." Svetlana excelled. The world noticed.

Svetlana Savitskaya, world-record setting aviator and Soviet Cosmonaut. (New Mexico Museum of Space History)

By 1971, Svetlana was a flight instructor. In 1972, upon her Fedotov Test Pilot School (FTPS) graduation, she continued setting FAI World Aviation records. In May, 1978, Svetlana became a test pilot for the aircraft manufacturer, Yakovlev. By 1981, Svetlana set fourteen FAI world aviation records for altitude and speed in MiG-21, MiG-25, Yak-50, and Yak-40K. She flew twenty different aircraft with 1,500 hours of flight time.

Next, she joined the Soviet Space Program. During her cosmonaut training, Svetlana continued her meteoric rise through test after test. Svetlana prepared for her first space flight. As a research cosmonaut, she became Russia's second woman in space. America had not yet launched a woman into space. In 1984, still not done making space history, Svetlana became the first woman in the world to launch into space twice. But wait, there is more. During this important mission, Svetlana also because the first woman in the world to perform a spacewalk or EVA-Extravehicular Activity. This 36-year-old, record-setting woman spent over three hours EVA repairing the spacecraft.

Svetlana's two space missions were 19 days and 17+ hours. Originally, the Soviets hoped Svetlana and an all-female cosmonaut crew would launch. However, because of many technical problems and the aging spacecraft that mission was cancelled. Svetlana served in the cosmonaut program until her retirement in 1993. Svetlana received Hero of the Soviet Union recognition twice during her outstanding air and space career. After her retirement as a cosmonaut, Svetlana followed in her mother's footsteps serving in elected and appointed positions in the Soviet government.

Schweizer, Virginia Mayer (Bennis) "Ginny:" American First Lady of Soaring

Born in 1922, Ginny Mayer grew up on New York farmland. In those early years of aviation, the area was home to many famous aviation names and aircraft companies. During her teen years, the Long Island AirHoppers Gliding and Soaring Club flew on weekends off a vacant field near her home. Curious, Ginny found the atmosphere fun, friendly, and exciting. Soon, Ginny was hooking up towlines and steadying the glider wings before take-off. Of course, she was invited to start her flight lessons with her new weekend air friends. In those days, single-seat gliders were the norm. Student's early flights were straight ahead with the instructor sitting on the tow vehicle facing the student. Hand signals were used to tell the student what to do next.

Easing the student into increasing altitudes, speed, and even turns took time. But, students built confidence. By 1941, the soaring club moved to a more formal location at Helms Farm, later called Wurtsboro airport. By now, Ginny was soaring on her own. Then, on Sunday, December 7th word came about the Japanese attack at Pearl Harbor. Any private flying was now over for Ginny and her soaring club members for the duration of the war. Ginny worked for Grumman and Republic Aircraft during the war. She continued to keep soaring members connected with a newsletter. As soon as World War II was over, Ginny went to the Schweizer Glider Factory in Elmira, New York.

Schweizer Glider factory began in the early 1930s. There Ginny earned her commercial glider license. She became the first woman in the United States to do so. She could now instruct in the sport she loved. Which she did. In New York soaring was seasonal. Ginny partnered with Steve Bennis, an instructor and tow plane pilot. They used war surplus gliders for a soaring operation in Florida in winter. Their new soaring business became one of the first in the nation. The business qualified for GI Bill approved soaring flight training. Ginny instructed. She checked out tow plane pilots, too.

With her growing experience, Ginny competed in soaring competitions. She set many altitude and distance records. In 1947, Ginny became the National Women's Champion. That year, Ginny became the first American woman to earn the Silver "C" soaring award (#86). This prestigious award shows that the glider pilot achieved an altitude gain of at least 3,281 feet, flew a five-hour or longer flight, and soared cross-county for a minimum distance of 50 km or over 30 miles. The three elements can be achieved simultaneously or in separate flights.

Ginny Schweizer was passionate about the sport of soaring. (National Soaring Museum)

Unfortunately, in 1948, a glider student froze at the controls. Ginny could not overpower him. Both were badly injured in the crash. Ginny had difficulty walking for the rest of her life. However, her passion for soaring operations continued. She returned to New York to care for her widowed father. Close enough to Elmira to soar often. Her long-time friendship with soaring legend, Paul A. Schweizer, grew into romance. In 1967, Soaring Royalty wed. The "First Lady of Soaring" united with the "Soul of American Soaring." They became an inseparable team, traveling the world promoting the air sport they both loved.

In 1971, Ginny joined Paul as a Laureate in the National Soaring Hall of Fame. In 1996, she received the National Aeronautical Association Katharine Wright Memorial Trophy. The U.S. Women's Soaring Pilots Association created the "Virginia M. Schweizer Competition Trophy," awarded to the female glider pilot with the highest score in the annual soaring championship. Ginny's dedication and passion reminds me of a poster at a glider port, "God created all women equal. But, the best soar!"

Scott, Blanche Stuart (Betty Scott): American Aviation Pioneer Early Bird

Born into a successful, Rochester, New York, family in the 1880s, Scott was adventurous and loved exploring outdoors. Her mother considered her a "tomboy." As Blanche was growing up, America started its love affair with transportation. Cars were expensive and roads rudimentary. But, that would soon change. Scott became an early enthusiast of the automobile. With no age restrictions on driving, Blanche drove the family car as a teenager. She loved to speed. Several Rochester citizens and city council members unsuccessfully tried to ban her from driving. Eventually, her mother sent her to "finishing school."

Blanche Stuart Scott at the controls of a Curtiss Model D, circa 1910. (Library of Congress)

That did not change Scott's adventurous spirit. In fact, in 1910, Scott drove a Willys-Overland Company automobile westward from New York City all the way to San Francisco, California. Scott was the first woman to drive west across the United States. Blanche took a woman reporter, Gertrude Buffington Phillips, as her passenger. On May 16th, they left New York in the automobile named, "Lady

Overland," headed for California. They reached San Francisco on July 23. The New York Times and many other newspapers trumpeted the story far and wide.

Back in New York, pilot, Jerome Fanciulli, on the famed Glenn Curtiss Flying Exhibition Team, contacted Blanche with an exciting proposition. She could be the first woman to learn to fly under the direction of Glenn Curtiss, America's pioneering aviator and aeroplane inventor. Scott immediately understood that this would keep her in the media spotlight. Glenn Curtiss was a "reluctant" instructor for "this woman." Jerome had not thoroughly "staffed" his brilliant idea with Curtiss first. Nevertheless, Blanche arrived in Hammondsport, New York, to begin flying lessons. Luckily, Scott was a determined woman, who was used to men thinking she could not succeed. She actually enjoyed proving them wrong.

Blanche began flying in a one-seat, Curtiss Pusher. Curtiss stood on the ground shouting instructions to her in the pilot seat. What she did not know was that Curtiss had fitted a limiter on the throttle to insure the airplane would not gain too much speed and become airborne while she practiced taxing on her own. On the historic day of September 6, either the limiter moved, or a gust of wind lifted her plane as she taxied, or maybe both, she went airborne. She flew to an altitude of forty feet before she gently landed. Although, short and possibly unintended, the Early Birds of Aviation credit Blanche as the first American woman to solo an airplane. Although, the Aeronautical Society of American credits Bessica Raiche on September 16 as the first American woman to make an intentional solo.

Quoted in several sources, Scott said about her flight, "I got down all right. After that, I wasn't going to stay on the ground any more, and I never did." She was the first and only woman Glenn Curtiss ever taught how to fly. On October 23, 1910, Scott made her first professional appearance as a female air star on the Curtiss Exhibition Team in Fort Wayne, Indiana. Her flying name was "Tomboy of the Air." Her stunts were breathtaking. She flew upside down. She flew "death dives" from 4,000 feet and suddenly pulled up only 200 feet from the ground. She was a crowd favorite. During her exhibition career, she reportedly earned up to $5,000 a week, appearing in meets with such aviation luminaries as Lincoln Beachey and Harriet Quimby. In 2021 dollars, Scott earned about $150,000 a week. In 1910, the average American worker earned $200 to $400 for an entire year.

In the spring of 1911, Scott joined the Thomas Baldwin Exhibition Group, flying a Baldwin Red Devil. This plane was more sophisticated and powerful than the Curtiss Pusher. On July 30, 1911, Scott set a new world distance record on a ten-mile flight. A month later, she broke her own record with a 25-mile flight. Because she did not earn a pilot's license, Scott was not allowed to compete or fly in exhibition events sanctioned by the Aero Club of New York. Scott moved to California

Next, she played the lead role in the first movie about flying called The Aviator's Bride. In 1912, she joined Glenn L. Martin, a pioneer aircraft designer and pilot. Scott became his first female test pilot flying Martin designs. Scott also joined Martin's flying circus. Again, she was only allowed to participate in events not sanctioned by the Aero Club of New York due to her lack of license. Although she witnessed several fatal aircraft crashes, including that of Harriet Quimby, Scott continued to fly. On Memorial Day of 1913, Blanche crashed after her Red Devil's throttle wire broke. After a year of recovery, she resume flying. But, in 1916, Scott retired from flying.

She joined the California entertainment industry with the same determination of her earlier pursuits. Blanche worked as a screenwriter for nine years for studios as RKO, Universal, Warner Brothers, and others. She wrote, produced, and played "Roberta" in a very successful, long-running radio show. In September of 1948, Scott was invited for a ride in a jet airplane as a passenger. The pilot was aviator, Chuck Yeager, a United States Air Force Officer. They flew in TF-8oC, which was a prototype of the T-33. Knowing Scott's history as a stunt pilot, Yeager treated her to some snap rolls and a 14,000 foot dive in the subsonic American jet! In the early 1950s with aviation back in her mind, Scott became a special consultant for the Air Force Museum at the Wright-Patterson Base. During her years there, she collected $1.25

million worth of aviation artifacts. In 1970, she flew West from her home in Rochester, New York. Blanche Scott's trailblazing in the air is honored with inclusion in the WAI Pioneer Hall of Fame and the National Women's Hall of Fame.

When I thought I couldn't go on, I forced myself to keep going. My success is based on persistence, not luck.

~ Estee Lauder

Seddon, Margaret Rhea: NASA Astronaut

Born in 1947 in Murfreesboro, Tennessee, Rhea attended St. Rose of Lima Catholic School. In 1965, she graduated from Central High School. In 1970, Rhea earned a bachelor's in physiology from the University of California, Berkeley. By 1973, she completed a doctorate from the College of Medicine at the University of Tennessee. Next, Seddon completed a surgical internship and three years of residency in general surgery in Memphis. She served as an Emergency Department physician at hospitals in Mississippi, Tennessee, and in the Houston area as her time allowed. Her clinical research focused on the nutritional impact of radiation therapy in cancer patients.

In 1978, when NASA opened the astronaut training program to women candidates, Dr. Seddon was one of over 1,500 female applicants. She was one of the six women selected. In August, 1979, Rhea was now an astronaut. Her duties focused on Orbiter software. Of course, she worked on the Shuttle medical kit and checklists. She served on launch and landing rescue helicopter physician support crew for STS-6. Dr. Seddon served on the NASA Aerospace Medical Advisory Committee.

She became a Capsule Communicator (CAPCOM) in the important Mission Control Center.

Rhea Seddon flew on three Space Shuttle flights as a mission specialist. Her flights hours in space on STS-51D-Discovery (1985), STS-40-Columbia (1991), and as the payload commander on STS-58-Columbia (1993) totaled 722 hours with 480 Earth orbits. On terra firma, Dr. Seddon served in several NASA management and communications positions. In 1996, NASA detailed her to Vanderbilt University Medical School in Nashville, Tennessee, in preparation for the cardiovascular experiments on the 1998 Space Shuttle Columbia Neurolab flight.

Astronaut Dr. Rhea Seddon working in space on Discovery STS-51 mission in 1985. (NASA photograph)

In 1997, after almost 20 years on the NASA space team, Dr. Rhea Seddon retired. Married to former astronaut, Robert "Hoot" Gibson (1981), mother of four children, she wrote, Go for Orbit, a memoir of her journey into outer space. Today, Rhea Seddon shares her many life experiences as a surgeon, private pilot, astronaut, wife, mother, manager, author, and now successful public speaker. In 2015, Seddon was inducted into the United States Astronaut Hall of Fame.

Sharman, Helen Patricia: First British Person in Space
Born in 1963 in England, Helen enjoyed science, especially chemistry. In 1984, she graduated from the University of Sheffield with a chemistry degree. By 1987, Helen earned her doctorate in chemistry. She worked in British industries in research and development technology in London. She landed as a chemist for Mars, Incorporated, enhancing the tastes and properties of chocolate.

Helen heard a radio announcement about Project Juno, which was a cooperative British-Soviet Union program to put the first British space explorer into orbit with Soviet cosmonauts. Qualified candidates were encouraged to apply. Nearly, 13,000 did so. Selection criteria included scientific, educational, and aerospace backgrounds, and the ability to learn a foreign language because the 18-month training program took place in Russia's Star City. On November 25, 1989, on live ITV-Independent Television network in London, Helen was introduced to the world. Immediately, the British tabloids began calling Helen, "The Girl from Mars," because of her scientific employment at the British chocolate company.

The Project Juno mission was to be privately-funded from British companies, working with the Soviet Space Program, to train a British Cosmonaut. Not enough private funds materialized. The Anglo-Soviet Juno mission was almost cancelled. Understanding the important impact on international relations, the Soviet Government agreed to proceed. However, several expensive space experiments were eliminated. Helen used her time to learn Russian. Then, she spent 18 months in Star City in intense training for space. Her milestones were constantly reported back home by the UK Press.

On May 18, 1991, Soyuz TM-12 launched into space with British Cosmonaut, Helen Sharman, and Soviets Cosmonauts, Anatoly Artsebarsky and Sergei Krikalev, on a mission to the Mir Space Station. Sharman's tasks included medical and agricultural tests, and photographing the British Isles. She obtained a ham radio operator license for a radio broadcast with British children from space. Helen became the first British person in space. She became the first Western European woman in space. Sharman became the first privately-funded woman in space. Helen also became the first woman to visit and work in the Mir Space Station.

British Cosmonaut, Helen Sharman, is a woman of many firsts. (The National Space Centre)

Upon her return from outer space, Helen shared her science experience with the public. She became one of Britain's Ambassadors of Science. In 1993, she wrote her autobiography, Seize the Moment. In 1997, she authored the children's science book, The Space Place. She presented science programs on radio and television as part of the BBC Schools broadcasts. By 2011, Helen was a Group Leader at the British National Physical Laboratory. Later, she became an Operations Manager at the Imperial College of London Department of Chemistry.

Her pioneering science efforts have earned her numerous recognitions to include Order of the British Empire (OBE), Honorary Fellow of the Royal Society of Chemistry, and many more. Multiple British schools are named in her honor. In 2011, the President of the Russian Federation awarded Helen their medal, "For Merit in Space Exploration." As a pioneering woman of STEM, Helen Sharman said, "People are fascinated by space flight. It makes them interested in science, gets them asking questions and motivates them."

Smith, Elinor Regina Patricia Ward (Sullivan): America's "Flying Flapper of Freeport"

Born in 1911 into a vaudeville family living in Freeport, New York, Elinor led an exciting life filled with firsts and extremes encouraged by her family of performers. Her father changed their name from Ward to Smith. Tom was popular and appeared in many stage productions. In 1914, the family packed up for Europe to accompany Tom in the touring production of The Wizard of Oz. Tom played the iconic role of the scarecrow. That adventure was cut short when Archduke Ferdinand was assassinated and triggered World War I. The family escaped on the last ship to sail from France before War was declared.

Elinor took her first airplane ride at only age six in a Farman pusher biplane. She was hooked. In 1917, she spent that entire summer begging rides from famous French pilot, Louis Gaubert. He was performing in New York and "adopted" the family of Francophiles. Gaubert allowed little Elinor to "fly." Upon landing, he informed her father, "She has the touch." Her father began hiring pilots to fly him to his performances with Elinor invited to fly along. At age ten, she began informal flying lessons. Her mother insisted she learn French, piano, and tap dancing, too! Elinor soloed at 15. At age 16, she became America's youngest pilot ever to receive a license, female or male. Her licensed was signed by Orville Wright.

On the very same day she earned her FAI pilot license, she broke the world's altitude record. Flying her father's Waco biplane to 11,874 feet. At age 17, she became the first and only pilot to successfully fly under all four New York City East River bridges--the Williamsburg, Manhattan, and Queensboro bridges – dodging several ships along the way. She flew sideways beneath the Brooklyn Bridge. She put a finishing flourish on her epic flight by circling the Statue of Liberty…twice!

Of course the media-savvy family alerted the press. The flight was caught on news reels and was front-page news. The press dubbed her, "The Flying Flapper of Freeport." Several government agencies tried to ground Elinor for the stunt. But, the Mayor of New York intervened. All of which only continued to fuel the publicity. In fact, Elinor was offered a job by Waco to demonstrate and deliver planes to their clients in the Northeast. She was paid a wage equal to male Waco company pilots. Customers enjoyed having their new purchase flown in by this celebrity female pilot. Some even called the local press to cover the event.

Then, Elinor was approached by the Brunner Winkle Aircraft Corporation to set an endurance record with their newest Bird biplane. Elinor knew Viola Gentry set the record for women at eight hours. Then, Bobbi Trout broke that solo endurance record at 12 hours. In January, 1929, Smith bested both, managing 13 hours and 16+ minutes in the air. Then, Louise Thaden quickly surpassed Elinor's record. On April 24, 1929, Elinor then took to the sky again. She set the women's solo endurance record of 26 hours, 23 minutes, and 16 seconds!!

In 1930, Elinor was voted the best woman pilot in the United States. In 1931, Elinor set another altitude record of 32,576 feet. She continued a record-setting aviation career as the first woman test pilot for both Fairchild and Bellanca aircraft companies. Elinor, the entertainer, became an aviation correspondent for NBC radio. Later, Smith became the aviation editor of the popular general interest weekly news magazine, Liberty. Elinor became the first woman to appear on a Wheaties cereal box.

Record-setting pilot, Elinor Smith, in 1942. (Library of Congress archival photograph)

In 1933, Elinor took time away from aviation to raise a family. She married Patrick Sullivan, a New York State Assemblyman. Together they raised four children. In 1956, she took to the sky again. Enjoying the freedom of the air. At nearly 90 years young, she became the oldest pilot to master a shuttle landing on the NASA Space Shuttle flight simulator. Next, she flew an experimental C33 Raytheon AGATE. Proving "she still had the touch." In 2001, for her contributions to aviation, Elinor Smith joined the many trailblazers honored in the Women in Aviation International Pioneer Hall of Fame. She flew West a few months short of age 99. A rather appropriate number for one of America's pioneer women pilots.

Stinson, Katherine (Otero): America's "Flying Schoolgirl"
Born in Alabama in 1891, Katherine Stinson's life turned upside down when her father abandoned his wife and four children. Gathering their meager belongings, Katherine and her family moved to Mississippi. Katherine learned to drive the family clunker at age 14. Everyone learned self-reliance. Katherine was a good student. She was introduced to the sky at age 16 when she won a raffle for a balloon ride. She loved it. She began learning about the big money being made by female stunt pilots. Katherine dreamed of being a concert pianist. Stunt flying could be a way to finance her music studies. She even sold her beloved piano to pay for flight instruction.

Her flight instructor was Max Lillie, a Swedish immigrant. Max was an Early Bird of Aviation. He earned the first "Expert Aviator Certificate" issued by the Aero Club of America. Katherine was an excellent student. She soloed in few hours. In July, 1912, Katherine became a licensed pilot, the fourth woman in the United States to do so. She immediately began her career as a stunt pilot. At air exhibitions, Katherine was billed as the "Flying Schoolgirl." She became a crowd favorite. She was youthful, friendly, and flew her modified Wright B in stunt after stunt. She set records for aerobatic maneuvers, distance, and endurance. In 1913, with Katherine's barnstorming money, she teamed with her mother to form the Stinson Aviation Company to rent and sell airplanes. They were the first American women to own an aviation business.

Katherine Stinson, an Early Bird of Aviation member, began flying in 1912. (Library of Congress)

Then, in 1915, the growing Stinson aviation business moved to Texas to open the Stinson School of Flying. In their new San Antonio location, Marjorie Stinson, Katherine's younger sister, joined the women as Chief Flight Instructor. Because Canada had no formal flight training schools, Stinson's contracted with the Canadian government to train Canadian pilots. Katherine continued to perform in air meets to underwrite some of the Stinson Aviation Company expenses.

Katherine became famous for her "dippy twist" loop, a variation of the loop-the-loop aerobatic maneuver. Katherine hit the top of the vertical bank, did a wingover before continuing the loop. At a Los Angeles night performance, she used magnesium flares "writing" C A L in the dark night sky. In 1913, while performing at a four-day fair in Helena, Montana, Katherine picked up mail from the fairgrounds and delivered it to the center of town each day. Katherine became an ambassador of aviation. She was the first female to fly in Canada. She was the first American woman to fly over London, England. In 1917, she became the first woman to fly in China, and Japan. During her six-month tour in the Orient, fan clubs idolizing the daring American "Air Queen" started.

During World War I, because she was a woman, the U.S. Army Air Corps rejected her aviation services. Katherine tirelessly crossed America raising funds for the Red Cross. For example, In June, 1917, she flew from Albany, New York, to Washington, D.C. to raise money for the Red Cross. In December of 1917, Katherine became the first person to fly nonstop, solo from San Diego to San Francisco. This was a national distance and duration record of 610 miles. She later broke this record with her 783-mile flight from Chicago to New York.

As with many in America in 1918, Katherine developed influenza during the flu pandemic. This so weakened her immune system that she next contracted Tuberculosis. Both so damaged her health that at only age 25, this legend of aviation was grounded. Fortunately, she lived. She became an award-winning architect. In 1928, she married Judge Michael Otero, Jr., a pilot of World War I. In 1969, Katherine Stinson received the National Aeronautic Association Elder Statesman of

Aviation Award. She died in 1977. In 2002, she was inducted posthumously into the International Air & Space Hall of Fame.

Stinson, Marjorie Claire: America's "Flying Schoolmarm"

Born in 1895 into the Stinson Family, mother, Emma and four children was abandoned by their father in Alabama. They relocated to Mississippi. The five formed a close and lasting bond. Older sister, Katherine, became a celebrated air star. In 1913, Emma partnered with her daughter, Katherine, to found the Stinson Aviation Company. Younger Marjorie watched how her brother, Eddie, the aircraft mechanic, worked on the airplanes. Soon, Marjorie began flight training.

In 1914, Marjorie earned her pilot license at the Wright Flying School in Dayton, Ohio. Then, Marjorie debuted as a stunt pilot in Brownwood, Texas. Marjorie performed throughout the year gaining practical knowledge and experience. In 1915, when the Stinson Flying School opened in San Antonio, Marjorie joined her mother and older sister as Chief Flight Instructor. Brother, Eddie, was their aircraft mechanic and airplane designer. Later, his successful Stinson Detroiter became a popular cabin airplane.

The Stinson family had an agreement with Canada to train pilots. In November, 1915, their first class graduated. Many headed to the Royal Air Force in England to fight in World War I. Before Marjorie was 22 years old, she trained over 100 male Canadian pilots. She was called the "Flying Schoolmarm" because of her Chief Flight Instructor status. Marjorie Stinson was the only woman granted a pilot's license by the Army and Navy committee of aeronautics during World War I. In early 1917, when America entered World War I, civilian flying was grounded. The Stinson's had to close their successful flight school.

As she could, Marjorie continued to barnstorm across the nation at fairs and air meets until 1928. By 1930, she folded up her wings to work in the Aeronautical Division of the U.S. Navy. She was still in aviation but with an eye for designs of the future. In 1928, Marjorie became a founding member of the Early Birds of Aviation. Pilots who soloed before December 17, 1916 were eligible for membership. Membership was limited to those who piloted a glider, gas balloon, or airplane. The date of December 17 honored the first flight of Wilbur and Orville Wright in 1903. Because of the large number of aviators trained in 1917 for World War I, 1916 was the cut off year limiting membership to pioneering aviators.

Marjorie Stinson learned to fly in 1914 at the Wright Flying School in Dayton, Ohio. (Library of Congress)

Membership grew to 598 pioneering aviators, although many early aviators as Harriet Quimby would have been eligible. Quimby died before this group was created. Twelve pioneering women aviators are listed as Early Bird members, including Marjorie and her sister, Katherine. The others are: Alys McKey Bryant, Jeanette Doty Caldwell, Helen Hodge Harris, Jean Marie Landrey, Ruth Bancroft Law, Bernetta Miller, Matilde Josephine Moisant, Lucille Belmont Rutshaw, Blanche Stuart Scott, and Dorothy Rice Sims.

In 1968, Marjorie received the National Aeronautic Association Elder Statesman of Aviation Award. She died April, 1975. Her ashes were scattered over Stinson Field in Texas from a 1931 Curtiss Pusher. In 2003, Women in Aviation International added Marjorie to their list of the 100 Most Influential Women in the Aviation and Aerospace Industry.

Sullivan, Kathryn D. "Kathy:" First American Woman to Walk in Space.

Born in 1951, in New Jersey, Kathy grew up in California. She enjoyed exploring and science. After her Taft High School graduation, Sullivan earned a Bachelor of Science in Earth Science from the University of California at Santa Cruz. In 1978, Dr. Sullivan graduated from Dalhousie University in Halifax, Nova Scotia. That year, qualified women were encouraged to apply for NASA Astronaut Group 8. She was selected as one of the six female astronaut candidates. At age 26, Kathy was also the youngest.

Quoted in the Association for Women in Science Magazine, summer, 2005, "I was always interested in exploring. Maps and landscapes appeal to me and I have always had a desire to explore. When I was growing up, we as a nation were involved in two grand adventures: the space program and underwater exploration. I was fascinated by both." In October, 1984, her exploration of outer space began when she joined Sally Ride on STS-41G on Challenger space shuttle. It was the first American mission to have two female astronauts onboard. But, Dr. Sullivan would make more history on this flight.

As the third American woman is space, she became the first NASA female mission specialist to spacewalk. Any time an astronaut gets out of a vehicle while in space, it is called a spacewalk. A spacewalk is also called an EVA. EVA stands for extravehicular activity. Working with astronaut David Leestma, they successfully tested a new satellite refueling technique. Their EVA lasted over three hours. For this important first, Dr. Sullivan was later inducted into the International Space Hall of Fame.

Kathryn Sullivan prepares for a potential spacewalk. In October, 1984, she became the first American woman to walk in space. (NASA photograph)

In 1990, Kathy returned to space on STS-31 on the Discovery crew. She assisted in the deployment of the Hubble Space Telescope. According to NASA, "The Hubble Space Telescope is a large telescope in space. Hubble is as long as a large school bus. It weighs as much as two adult elephants. Hubble travels around Earth at about 5 miles per second. That is as fast as driving a car from the East Coast of the United States to the West Coast in 10 minutes. Hubble faces toward space. It takes pictures of planets, stars and galaxies. Hubble has seen stars being born. Hubble has seen stars die. It has seen galaxies that are trillions of miles away. Hubble also has seen comet pieces crash into the gases above Jupiter. Scientists have learned a lot about space from Hubble pictures."

In May, 1992, Sullivan returned to space on a third mission. On STS-45, she was the payload commander in charge of the Atmospheric Laboratory for Applications and Science or ATLAS-1. The first Spacelab dedicated to NASA's Mission to Planet Earth. During the 9-day mission, the crew conducted experiments that produced detailed measurements of atmospheric chemical and physical properties, which contributed significantly to scientific understanding of Earth's climate and atmosphere.

As a veteran astronaut, Dr. Sullivan spent over 532 hours in orbit. After her NASA service, Sullivan joined the National Oceanic and Atmospheric Administration as Chief Scientist. She oversaw the agency's $5 million research and technology program. In 2006, Dr. Sullivan was named the first director of the Battelle Center for Mathematics and Science Education Policy at the John Glenn School of Public Affairs at Ohio State University. In 2019, her book, Handprints on Hubble: An Astronaut's Story of Invention, was published.

In 2020, she continued to make history. She became the first woman to travel to the deepest part of the ocean floor. As part of the Challenger Deep expedition, Sullivan descended 35,810 feet to the lowest part of the Marianas Trench in the South Pacific Ocean. She is the first woman in the world to fly in outer space, walk in space, and reach the deepest part of the ocean floor.

Sullivan is in the Astronaut Hall of Fame. Dr. Sullivan joined other Sky Stars in the Women in Aviation International Pioneer Hall of Fame. The list of her awards and honors reflects her many accomplishments in the sky when she flies her Super Decathlon, in outer space, and in our ocean depths.

Women are seeking freedom. Freedom in the skies! They are soaring above temperamental tendencies of their sex which have kept them earth-bound. Flying is a symbol of freedom from limitation.

~ Margery Brown, Charter member of The International Ninety Nines in 1929.

5

T-Tango to Z-Zulu

You must believe in yourself and allow your dreams to soar.

~ Shaesta Waiz, an American pilot, the first female certified civilian pilot born in Afghanistan, and the youngest woman to fly solo around the world in a single-engine airplane

Tereshkova, Valentina Vladimirovna: First Woman in Space
Born in 1937 in the Soviet Union, early in her childhood Valentina's father was killed in World War II. Valentina and her two brothers were raised by their widowed mother in Yaroslav, northeast of Moscow. In 1953, Valentina, a bright and hard-working student, graduated from Soviet Girls High School #32. However, the family's finances required that Valentina work in the local textile mill. She began correspondence classes at night in textile engineering. Several of her friends coaxed Valentina to join them at the Yaroslav Air Sports Club for parachuting. In May, 1959, Valentina made her first jump. By age 26, Valentina had completed 126 jumps.

The next year, Valentina completed her textile engineering degree. Because the Soviets were aggressively launching "manned" spaceflights, Valentina boldly wrote to the Supreme Soviet suggesting women should train as cosmonauts. It is often said, "Luck is what happens when preparation meets opportunity!" Because parachuting was one of the skills cosmonauts needed, Valentina had that. She interviewed when the USSR officials were in Yaroslav. As usual, Valentina performed well. Next, she had physical and mental testing. On March 2, 1962, the Soviet Government proudly introduced Valentina, and three other female Cosmonaut candidates. She became a junior officer in the Soviet Air Force. Immediately, Valentina moved to Star City for the extensive Cosmonaut training. Valentina loved the rigor and excelled.

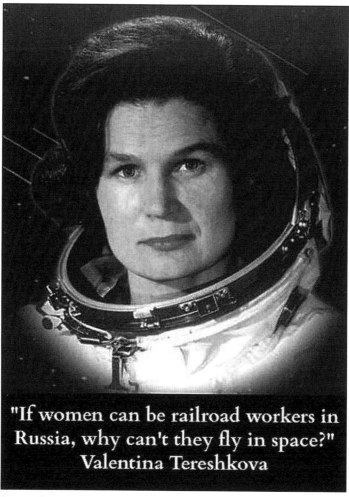

"If women can be railroad workers in Russia, why can't they fly in space?"
Valentina Tereshkova

Soviet Cosmonaut, Valentina Tereshkova, is the first woman in space. (Wikimedia source)

Valentina became a Soviet Cosmonaut. On June 16, 1963, Valentina Tereshkova launched into space alone in the Vostok-6 spacecraft. This was an historic victory for the Soviet Union in the "space race," a Cold War competition between the United States and the Soviet Union to develop aerospace capabilities, including artificial satellites, unmanned space probes, and human spaceflights. Unknown to the world outside the Soviet Space program, the Vostok-6 was programmed for ascent, but not descent. Soviet ground control engineers had to very quickly design a new program. Valentina orbited the Earth 48 times in two days, 22 hours, and 50 minutes, while the reprogramming was completed. It worked. Valentina safely parachuted out of the spacecraft to Earth. For years, Valentina and the Soviet government kept secret the dangerous situation Valentina faced. Valentina asked that the engineer who nearly cost her life not be punished. The Soviet Government asked Valentina never to reveal the truth. She never spoke of it until documents were unclassified.

With this space flight, Valentina because the first woman in the world to fly solo into space. She became the youngest woman, too. She was given a parade in Red Square. She became a decorated national hero. The Soviets used her international celebrity to worldwide advantage. Tereshkova represented the Soviet Union at numerous international conferences. She received the Gold Space Medal from the *Fédération Aéronautique Internationale*-FAI. She became a member of the World Peace Council. At home, she was elected to the Yaroslav Supreme Soviet. She became president of the Soviet Women's Committee.

In May, 1969, Valentina graduated from the Zhukovsky Air Force Engineering Academy as an aerospace engineer. In 1985, she became a member of the International Space Hall of Fame. She said, "One cannot deny the great role women have played in the world community. My flight was yet another impetus to continue female contribution." To this day, Valentina Tereshkova remains the only woman on earth to have flown a successful, solo space mission.

Thaden, Iris Louise McPhetridge: First Woman to Win the Bendix Trophy

Born in November, 1905, in Bentonville, Arkansas, Louise was intelligent and daring. Flying fascinated her from childhood. At age 7, she survived jumping off a barn while holding a large umbrella to see if she could fly. By age 15, she entered the University of Arkansas for journalism and physical education. After two years of classes, Louise looked for adventure. It was the Roaring '20s with economic prosperity and dramatic social changes. Louise moved to Wichita, Kansas, for a building materials job. In Wichita, Louise noticed the busy airfield. She loved looking at the airplanes. She spent many days there dreaming of flying. She put her dream of flight on hold because of finances. But, fate brought an answer very quickly.

Luckily, in the fall of 1926, Walter Beech, the aviation entrepreneur, hired Louise as an assistant for his West Coast Travel Air distributor in San Francisco. Louise would be surrounded by airplanes. Louise worked as a top-notch secretary during the day. At night, she took flying lessons, as part of her employment benefits. In just a few month, Louise earned her pilot's license. She continued to fly airplanes from the Travel Air fleet. Soon, Louise logged enough flight hours to qualify for her transport license.

On December 7, 1928, Louise set a new altitude record of 20,200 feet, besting Lady Sophie Heath's record of 16,438 feet. Three months later, she set a new endurance record of over 22 hours. Between December 1928 and April 1929, Louise set three aviation records—in altitude, endurance, and speed (156 mph). She is the first American woman to hold these records simultaneously.

In 1929, Louise met Herbert Thaden, an ex-army pilot and aeronautical engineer, at the local airport. They married in Reno, Nevada. With support from her husband and Walter Beech, Louise entered the first Women's Air Derby. This was the first official all-women air race in the United States. She proudly piloted a Travel Air designed for her by Walter Beech. On August 18, 1929, female flyers left Santa Monica, California. The Derby ended 2,800 miles away at the

Cleveland Municipal airport. On August 26, 1929, an estimated 18,000 people gathered in Cleveland, Ohio, to greet the women pilots at the end of the race. Louise Thaden finished the race first. She won the heavy class with the fastest time of 20 hours, 19 minutes and 4 seconds.

Louise Thaden set numerous aviation records. She is the first American woman to hold altitude, speed, and endurance records simultaneously. (San Diego Air and Space Museum archive)

In November, 1929, Louise and many of the other pilots of the Women's Air Derby formed the Ninety-Nines organization. Thaden served as Vice-President (1931-36), and as Treasurer (1930-34). In July, 1930, the Thadens welcomed their first child. A week later, Louise was airborne again. In 1932, Thaden was invited by Curtiss Exhibition flight team member, Frances Marsalis, to take part in a publicity stunt. On August 14, the daring duo took to the air. Eight days later, they did it. They beat the earlier non-stop, endurance flight record by 73 more hours, flying 196 hours. They celebrated this aviation milestone at a White House dinner with Herbert Hoover.

In 1933, Louise welcomed her second child. By 1935, Thaden joined her good friend, Phoebe Omlie, in the Bureau of Air Commerce in air marking America's airports. Thaden was assigned the western part of the United States because of her knowledge of that area. Louise was back in the air. In July, 1936, in a borrowed plane, she set yet another speed record. Then, she was invited to race in the 1936 Bendix Transcontinental Air Race. This one of the most prestigious air races in Thaden's entire career. She teamed with co-pilot, Blanche Noyes. They both were thrilled with the opportunity to compete with the men but didn't think they would actually win. Both gals wanted to "put on a good show."

Flying a Beech Staggerwing C17R, when they landed their plane at the finish, they were surrounded by a huge, cheering crowd. They WON! Later, Thaden's husband confessed he had not expected such a great performance from such a worn airplane engine. Louise and Blanche were awarded the $4,500 first place money, along with the coveted Bendix Air Trophy. That would be the equivalent of around $85,000 today. But, wait there is more. They also won the $2,500 prize for the first female team to cross the finish line. Today, that would be close to $50,000. Louise won the 1936 Harmon Trophy for Outstanding Aviator.

Louise maintained a life-long friendship with Walter and Olive Beech. For many years, Thaden was a demonstration pilot for the famed Beech Aircraft Company. During World War II, Louise volunteered to train pilots for the Civil Air Patrol (CAP). She flew CAP search and rescue missions. She volunteered with Ruth Nichols for Relief Wings. Louise worked with her husband at their Thaden Engineering Company. They tested and manufactured flight equipment for the U.S. Navy. Upon his death in 1969, Louise continued the company until she flew West in 1979. In her book, *High, Wide and Frightened*, she wrote, "Flight is the essence of the spirit. It nurtures the soul. It is awesome. Often ethereal. Glorious. Emotionally wondrous and all-pervading. Intangible."

In 1951, her hometown honored her by naming the Bentonville Municipal Airport, Louise Thaden Field. In 1999, Louise was named to the National Aviation Hall of Fame. In 2000, she joined the luminaries of the WAI Pioneer Hall of Fame.

Thornton, Kathryn C. "Kathy:" NASA Astronaut-Four Space Flights & Three Spacewalks

Born in 1952 in Montgomery, Alabama, Kathy was always interested is how things worked. At Auburn University, she studied science and physics. In 1994, after graduation, Kathy continued her study in physics. In 1977, she earned a Master of Science from the University of Virginia. By 1979, she earned a doctorate in physics there. As a stellar scholar, Thornton was awarded a one-year NATO Postdoctoral Fellowship to continue her research at the Max Planck Institute for Nuclear Physics in Heidelberg, West Germany. Upon her return to the United States, Thornton was a physicist at the U.S. Army Foreign Science and Technology Center in Virginia. In May, 1984, she began NASA astronaut training. In July, 1985, Kathy joined the astronaut corps.

In 1989, Thornton's first flight as a Mission Specialist was on Discovery space shuttle STS-33. Thornton became the first American woman to fly on a military space mission for the Department of Defense. In May, 1992, on her second flight, Thornton served on STS-49, which was the maiden flight of the new Endeavor space shuttle. Kathy made her first spacewalk. She performed important extravehicular tasks, including retrieving, repairing, and redeploying the International Telecommunications Satellite (INTELSAT).

Nuclear physicist, Kathryn Thornton, is a veteran of four NASA space missions. (NASA photograph)

In 1993, Thornton's second and third spacewalks were on her third flight on STS-61 as a Mission Specialist aboard Endeavor. This important space flight included capturing and restoring the Hubble Space Telescope to full capacity. Despite problems with her spacesuit, Thornton, and crew member, Tom Akers, replaced Hubble's two solar arrays, which provides power to the telescope. On Thornton's next spacewalk, the Hubble High Speed Photometer was replaced.

In 1995, on her fourth space flight, Kathy was promoted to payload commander on STS-73 on Columbia space shuttle. This important mission focused on numerous scientific experiments. On her four NASA space missions, Kathryn Thornton logged more than 975 hours in space, including 21 hours of extravehicular activity. While in space, she deployed satellites, conducted research, helped repair the important Hubble Space Telescope, and tested systems for the construction of the International Space Station.

When not in outer space, Thornton performed NASA technical assignments, including flight software verification, Vehicle Integration Test Team (VITT) member, and CAPCOM spacecraft communicator. In 1996, Astronaut Kathryn Thornton left NASA to serve on the aerospace engineering faculty of her alma mater, the University of Virginia. In 1996, Thornton received NASA's Distinguished Service Medal. In 2010, she was inducted into the Astronaut Hall of Fame.

Trout, Evelyn "Bobbi:" Record Setting American Aviator
Born in 1906, in Illinois, Trout had an early interest in aeroplanes. By age 12, her eyes were skyward at the sound of any plane. Evelyn loved fixing things. She enjoyed sports. At age 14, her family moved to California. Mr. Trout was less than reliable. Evelyn's mother, Lola opened a gas station called "The Radio Station." Customers would drive up to hear music or radio comedy blasting out of speakers, while Evelyn would fill their car with gas and wash their windshield. One day, Evelyn came home with her hair in a "bob." Silent screen actress and ballroom dancer, Irene Castle, popularized the short, boyish hairstyle favored by the flappers in the 1920s. Now, Evelyn was called Bobbi.

Bobbi told her gas station customer, W.E. Thomas, how she dreamed of flying. He owned a Curtiss JN-4 Jenny. He invited Bobbi to fly with him. On December 27, 1922, flying from the Rogers Airport, west of Los Angles, Bobbi Trout's life changed forever. She was determined to fly. Bobbi worked hard and saved money for flight lessons. In January, 1928, with $2,500, Bobbi began training at the Burdett Fuller Flying School. This was a big commitment for Bobbi.

Unfortunately, on one of her early flight lessons the young flight instructor told Bobbi to three-quarter turn at low altitude. The biplane began to spiral. The resulting crash completely wrecked the plane. Undeterred, Bobbi completed her solo flight in April, obviously in another plane. Lola Trout bought her daughter an International K-6 biplane. By September, 1928, Bobbi earned her pilot license from the United States Department of Commerce.

Bobbi Trout began flying at age 16. Her pilot license was signed by aviation pioneer, Orville Wright. (Wikicommons)

In January, 1929, Trout shattered Viola Gentry's women's flight endurance record by more than four hours. Bobbi flew 12 hours and 11 minutes. But, just a few weeks later, Elinor Smith broke Bobbi's record. On February 10, 1929, Bobbi took to the sky again in her prototype R.O. Bone Company Golden Eagle. Trout set a new *Fédération Aéronautique Internationale* (FAI) Women's Solo World Record for Endurance of 17 hours, five minutes. Also, Bobbi set the record for the first all-night flight by a woman, landing February 11, 1929 at Mines Field, now Los

Angeles airport. Just five weeks later, March 17, 1929, Louise Thaden would break Bobbi's record.

Later in 1929, flying a 90-horse power Golden Eagle Chief, Bobbi Trout set a new altitude record of 15,200 feet. After some modifications, a 100-horse power engine was installed for Bobbi to compete in the 1929 Women's Air Derby aka Powder Puff Derby. Mechanical problems hampered her flight. Later that year, she became a founding member of the Ninety-Nines. By 1931, Bobbi was flight instructing for the Los Angeles-based, Cycloplane Company. She was hired as an aviation editor. She solicited sponsors for a planned flight from Los Angeles to Honolulu. However, she never attract enough funding. On January 11-12, 1935, Amelia Earhart became the first woman to make the record-setting solo flight from Honolulu to Oakland, California.

In 1938, Trout started the Aero Reclaiming Company. She was a good businesswoman. She discovered a knack for inventing improvements for airplanes. She remained active in aviation. She provided museums and historians with early aviation artifacts. In 1976, Trout was named Pioneer Woman of the Year by the iconic OX5 Aviation Pioneers. In 1984, she joined the OX5 Aviation Pioneers Hall of Fame. In 1993, Trout was named to the WAI Pioneer Hall of Fame. In 1996, Bobbi became the first woman to receive the Howard Hughes Memorial Award from the Aero Club of Southern California. On her ninetieth birthday, the Los Angeles Police Department flew Trout over the city in honor of her contributions to aviation history.

Quoted in a July, 2001, *Airports Journal* article, Bobbi Trout explained her devotion to aviation, "What do I love about it? What does anybody love about it? You can go places and fly like a bird." In 2003, Bobbi Trout flew West.

Vollick, Eileen: Canada's First Licensed Female Pilot
Born in 1908 in Hamilton, Ontario, Eileen grew up with mechanical equipment and cold winters on Lake Ontario. Growing up near the airport, she watched out her bedroom window as it was constructed. As a young teen, she watched as planes flew at the Jack V. Elliot Air

Service. She wondered, "Can girls fly?" Her first job was as a textile analyst near the new Hamilton Airport. Still curious, Eileen visited the J.V. Elliott Flying School where she did not receive the warmest of greetings to the new world of aviation. In fact, after Eileen requested flying lessons, Mr. Elliot sent her request all the way to Canada's Department of National Defense for written approval. In June, 1929, when the Government sent him the approval, his next strategy was to assign his toughest flight instructor, Earl Jellison, to dissuade the young woman.

Apparently, what neither of them knew was that Eileen, as a fearless teenager, gained some fame earlier that summer as Canada's first "girl" parachutist. Eileen jumped from an airplane into the water from 2,800 feet. Perhaps the males at the Elliot Flight School missed the extensive newspaper coverage. Flight Instructor Jellison was sure he was "man-enough" to get the job done. So, he told Eileen to get in. He proceeded to do spins, rolls, any aerobatic maneuver he knew to get her airsick and scared. Upon landing, Eileen thanked him for the great flight. She scheduled her next lesson…and wanted to be sure Mr. Jellison was available!

Eileen's mother altered one of her father's mechanic suits, cutting it down to a small size. This protected Eileen during flying. Often, Eileen would layer clothes underneath it for warmth. Vollick loved flying. Eventually, the flight instructors and male students began to admire the young woman. Her determination was obvious, even to a casual observer. She would faithfully appear at the flight school every morning at 6:30 a.m. She had to be at the Hamilton Cotton Company for work at 8:30 a.m. She never missed a flight lesson. Eileen never missed a day of work at the textile mill. In March, 1928, 19-year-old Eileen Vollick made Canadian aviation history when she took off in a ski-plane on frozen Burlington Bay near Hamilton. The Curtiss JN-4 aka "Jenny" was equipped with skis in place of wheels.

Weighing only 89 pounds and only 5'1," Eileen used her bed pillows on the pilot's seat to lift her high enough to see. For her flight test from the Canadian Government Civil Aviation examiner, Eileen skillfully put the biplane through take-offs and landings on the frozen bay. The air was cold on her face but the feeling of exhilaration with each successful take-off and landing warmed her to her core. The test was thorough. All applicants made four landings from 1,500 feet and had to land within 150 feet of a designated point on the ground. An additional landing with the motor off was required. Other requirements of the test included executing five figure-eight turns between two designated points, and completing a cross-country trip.

In 1928, Eileen Vollick became Canada's first licensed female pilot. (Royal Aviation Museum of Western Canada)

On March 13, 1928, Eileen Vollick made more Canadian aviation history when she passed the flight test. She became the 77th Canadian to earn a pilot license. Eileen was the first Canadian woman to do so. Of the thirty five male flight students from the Elliot Flying School testing that day, ten passed.

Throughout the years, Eileen Vollick continued to fly and encourage women in aviation careers. She died in 1968. Posthumously, her important legacy is recognized. In 1975, The Ninety-Nines awarded her their Amelia Earhart medallion. In 2008, on the 100th anniversary of her birth, Vollick earned the distinction of being the first woman in Canada to have an aviation facility named in her honor. The two-story Wiarton Keppel International Airport passenger terminal is named after Eileen. Also, in 2008, Vollick was celebrated as Canada's first licensed female pilot with a Canadian postage stamp designed by the Canadian Ninety-Nines. Eileen Vollick definitively answered her own question, "Yes, girls can fly!"

Wagstaff, Patricia Combs "Patty:" First Female U.S. National Aerobatic Champion

Born in 1951 into an aviation family, Patty lived and traveled worldwide because of her Air Force pilot father. Later, as a Japan Airlines pilot, he introduced his precocious daughter to the flight deck. As early as age ten, Patty sat at the DC-6 controls with her Dad. By nature and nurture, Patty was destined to be a sky star. After high school in California, Patty searched for her purpose. Secretarial school in Tokyo, barmaid, emergency medical technician, even a short-lived marriage to an Australian abalone fisherman were clearly not the answers. Soon, Patty found herself in Alaska. Aviation is very important in Alaska so Patty began flight lessons. That was the answer all along.

In her 1997 *Fire and Air: A Life on the Edge* book, Patty explains the passion she feels. "This is where I belong and where I feel alive, even joyous. Each time I fly aerobatics, I feel more at home in my machine and in the air. I believe in the elements: air, earth, water, and fire. I believe that people are basically elemental, drawn instinctively and specifically to one or two of them, like the animals that we are. Air and fire are seductive to me. I feel them. Air and fire—my equation for the airplane." Obviously, with this passion, Patty flew her way to ratings and fame. She quickly earned single, multi-engine, seaplane, commercial, and instrument ratings. Then, she qualified for Certified Flight and Instrument Instructor ratings. Later, she earned a commercial rotorcraft rating.

Patty Wagstaff believes flying represents Adventure, Freedom, and Challenge. (Courtesy photo from https://pattywagstaff.com)

Her flight instructor, Bob Wagstaff, soon became Patty's second husband. In 1982, Patty began her aerobatics training. To say the rest is aviation history would be shortchanging her meteoric rise. The list of titles and awards is dazzling. In 1991, Patty won the U.S. National Aerobatic Championship, three years in a row, making aviation history. She is also a six-time member of the U.S. Aerobatic Team-Gold, Silver, and Bronze Medal Winner in International Aerobatic Competitions. Wagstaff is a four-time winner of the Betty Skelton First Lady of Aerobatics Trophy. Patty is a fan favorite on the Air Show circuit with her high-powered aerobatic performances. Always eager for new opportunities and adventures, Patty performs stunt flying in Hollywood movies and television programs.

Did I mention her high-energy level? She writes articles and books about aviation and aerobatics. She owns and teaches in her very successful Aerobatic flight school in St. Augustine, Florida. Patty Wagstaff Aviation Safety trains pilots from all over the world. An important commitment to Earth, one of her four elements, is her dedication to animal protection and conservation. In 2001, Patty began annual trips to Africa providing flight instruction to the brave pilots of the Kenya Wildlife Service (KWS). Patty teaches bush-piloting skills and aerobatic evasive flight. Because wildlife poachers on the preserves are now more aggressive and armed, the KWS pilots often must take evasive measures and make quick maneuvers.

In 1997, Wagstaff received her first Hall of Fame induction into both the Women in Aviation International Pioneer Hall of Fame, and the Arizona Aviation Hall of Fame. Over the years, the accolades have accumulated: National Aviation Hall of Fame, International Council of Air Shows Foundation Hall of Fame, and their Sword of Excellence Award, International Air and Space Hall of Fame, Living Legends of Aviation, Smithsonian National Air and Space Museum Trophy for Current Achievement in Aviation, National Aeronautic Association (NAA) Paul Tissandier Diploma, NAA Katherine and Marjorie Stinson Award, and NAA Katharine Wright Award. Also, the Philip J. Klass Award for Lifetime Achievement, Wings Club of New York

Outstanding Aviator Award, and the Bill Barber Award for Sportsmanship for superb air show performance. Aviation organizations poll readers about their favorite woman airshow performer. Patty Wagstaff usually tops their list.

In recent years, Patty has added more fire to her aviation life as a wildfire pilot. She uses her immense aerobatic skill and discipline in flying a twin-turboprop OV-10A Bronco as an observation and forward air control aircraft to fight forest fires. Patty is part of a team of aerial firefighters. No cheering crowds below her on these missions. Just fire and smoke from the burning forests. Patty Wagstaff's commitment to protecting the four elements- air, earth, water, and fire is authentic.

The race goes not always to the swift ...

but to those who keep on flying.

Walton, Nancy-Bird: Pioneering Australian Aviator

Born in 1915 in New South Wales, Australia, Nancy Bird always dreamed of flying from a very early age. However, as a teenager during the Depression, Nancy left school at age 13 to help her family financially. Over the years, Nancy always had her eyes on the sky. Not far away, famed aviator, Sir Charles "Smithy" Kingsford, who in 1928 was the first to fly from the United States to Australia, opened a flying school in Sydney. In 1933, Nancy followed her dream to his flight school. Smithy sensed her commitment to flying. He welcomed her as one of his first flight students. At age 18, Nancy became Australia's youngest woman to earn her pilot's license. She did not stop. She next earned a commercial pilot's license. With a small inheritance and borrowed money, Nancy bought her first airplane, a de Havilland Gipsy Moth.

Nancy-Bird Walton in a Gipsy Moth at Kingsford Smith Flying School in 1933. (State Library of New South Wales)

Gutsy Nancy became a barnstormer. She flew at fairs across Australia. The de Havilland was often the first airplane many had ever seen. Then, to have a young girl flying it was magical to see this brave, young Australian woman. Nancy's aviation destiny was set in 1935. Reverend Stanley Drummond wanted her to join him providing medical services in the outback of New South Wales. They named the new humanitarian and rescue organization, Royal Far West Children's Health Scheme. Nancy's own Gipsy Moth became an air ambulance. Over time, this important medical air service expanded to neighboring Queensland and other remote areas. Soon, Nancy earned the name "The Angel of the Outback."

Next, Nancy won the 1936 Ladies' Trophy at the Adelaide to Brisbane air race. Nancy took at short break from flying to work in Europe for the Dutch airline company, KLM, in their headquarters. Soon after World War II broke out, Nancy returned to her beloved Australia. She began training women in aviation, similar to the United States WASP program. The purpose was to free male pilots flying in the Royal Australian Air Force. Not long after, Nancy met and married, Englishman, Charles Walton. Because he called her "Nancy-Bird," that name stuck.

After World War II, Nancy-Bird continued her contributions to Australian aviation, especially women aviators. In 1950, Nancy and other women pilots formed the Australian Women Pilots Association (AWPA). She served as President for five years. In later years, she served as their Patron. In 1966, for her significant contributions to Australian aviation, charities, and medical air services, Nancy-Bird Walton was invested with the Order of the British Empire (OBE). The next year, The National Trust of Australia declared her an "Australian Living Treasure."

Given all of the rugged terrain and remote, dangerous flying conditions in early aviation, miraculously Nancy-Bird Walton never had an aviation accident. She saved many lives of rural Australians in need of emergency medical services. In 1990, Nancy-Bird Walton was appointed an Officer of the Order of Australia (AO). In 2001, she was inducted into the Victorian Honour Roll of Women. Qantas named its first Airbus A380 for Nancy-Bird Walton. Shortly before her 2009 death, Nancy-Bird participated in the feature-length documentary film, *Flying Sheilas*, about Australia's early women flyers. In March 2019, the Western Sydney Airport was named Western Sydney International Nancy-Bird Walton Airport. All because a young Australian girl dreamed of flying and never stopped looking to the sky.

Warner, Emily Hanrahan Howell: America's First Female Airline Captain

Born in 1939 into a large Irish family in Denver, Emily and her twin, Eileen, were always adventurous. Back in the early 1950s, Emily thought of being an airline stewardess (flight attendant today). In 1958, Emily took her first airplane flight from Denver to Gunnison. She found the Frontier Airlines flight thrilling. On the return Denver flight, the DC-3 only had one passenger, Emily. She boldly asked the crew to allow her in the flight deck. This was long before airline security closed and locked the doors to the airplane cockpit. The male pilots were happy to show Emily the view.

Emily said in a 2001 interview, "It was love at first sight. When I looked through that airplane windshield at the blue sky and gazed at the control panel, I knew from that moment what I wanted to do. My whole world changed." Emily began saving for flight lessons. She did not buy ice cream or records as her teenage friends did. Emily knew she needed every penny to pursue her dream of flying.

Flight lessons were $12.75 an hour. That would be around $100 an hour today. Emily only earned $50 a week, working as a department store clerk. She paid her parents $20 a week for room and board. Emily was determined to be a pilot. Secretly, Emily started flying lessons at Clinton Aviation at the busy Stapleton Airport. The owner was impressed with young Emily. He offered her a new job as the flight school receptionist. Emily told her parents. They told Emily, if that is what she wanted, do it. But, be careful!

Emily would manage the flying school front office during the week. She took flying lessons on her days off and weekends. She was a natural at the controls because she loved flying. In less than a year, Emily earned her private pilot license. She said, "After I earned my private, Clinton Aviation would allow me to fly one of the school planes in good weather to Greeley or Colorado Springs to pick up airplane parts. They could not pay me, but I was getting free flying experience." As her flight hours grew, Clinton Aviation sent Emily to Wichita, Kansas, to fly back brand new Cessna 150 airplanes.

In 1976, Emily Warner became America's first female airline Captain.
(Hamilton Collection)

Emily would set the compass for 279 degrees when she left Wichita. She would dead reckon to Denver. In most of the flights, the Cessna did not have a radio installed yet. As she neared Denver, she landed at another airport. She telephoned the Denver Air Traffic Control Tower that she was coming in to land. When she got to Stapleton, the tower would turn on a green light so Emily knew she was cleared to land! She said, "I did anything because flying was such a joy to me." Emily soon became a flight instructor. Students flocked to her because she was so passionate about flying. One of her students was Julius Warner, a former World War II V-12 Navy College Training Program student. Later, they married.

During those years, Emily logged over 7,000 flight hours. She continued to upgrade her aviation ratings. As an Instrument Flight Instructor, many of her male students were hired by the airlines. At that time, the airline executives closed the door to women based on their gender, not their flight experience. Emily began to apply to Frontier, United, and Continental for an interview. Emily periodically updated her airline applications with her additional flight time and ratings. No airline called her.

Then, in 1973, Frontier released its list for the new airline pilot class. Emily Warner was not on the list. Emily literally marched into Frontier Headquarters She asked for a private interview with Frontier chief pilot, Ed O'Neill. In the kindest possible way, Emily explained that she was more than qualified. She asked the airline to explain their hiring less qualified males. Never underestimate a determined woman. Ed O'Neill thought he would put Emily in a flight simulator and throw every trick he could to demonstrate to her she was not as qualified as she thought she was. After dozens of instrument approaches over several hours, Emily flew flawlessly. Mr. O'Neill, by now exhausted, said, "Emily, you are hired. Now, what will you wear?" That was on January 29, 1973, fifteen years after Emily decided she was going to be an airline pilot.

On February 6, 1973, Emily wore a pants suit as her new Frontier uniform. The Frontier Airlines flight from Denver to Las Vegas received extensive media coverage. In 1974, she became the first female member of the Air Line Pilots Association-ALPA, something denied to Helen Richey in the 1930s. This opened airline flight decks to women. In 1976, Emily Howell Warner became America's first female airline Captain. Her uniform is enshrined in the Smithsonian Air & Space Museum. Emily believed her role was to mentor and encourage women in aviation and the airlines. She is a founding member of the International Society of Women Airline Pilots (ISA+21).

After Frontier, Emily flew for Continental Airlines, and United Parcel Service (UPS). In 1990, she joined the Federal Aviation Administration (FAA) as a Flight Examiner. Emily was the FAA Aircrew Program Manager for United Airlines Boeing 737 fleet. During her career she flew over 21,000 hours and conducted over 3,000 check rides. She earned the FAA Wright Brother's Award. Highly respected, Emily was honored with induction into the National Aviation Hall of Fame. National Women's Hall of Fame, Women in Aviation International Pioneer Hall of Fame, Living Legends of Aviation, International Ninety-Nines Award of Achievement for Contributions to Aviation, Irish-American Hall of Fame, Colorado Aviation Hall of Fame, and Colorado Women's Hall of Fame. In July, 2015, her home airport in Granby, Colorado, was named Emily Warner Field.

Weber. Mary Ellen: NASA Astronaut and Record Setting Skydiver
Born in 1962 in Ohio, Mary Ellen grew up enjoying sports and science. After high school, she earned a Bachelor of Science degree in chemical engineering, with honors, from Purdue University. During her undergraduate student years, she interned at Ohio Edison, Delco Electronics, and 3M. In 1983, she also discovered skydiving. The precision and focus skydiving requires is similar to the rigor of scientific pursuits. During her doctoral studies at the University of California at Berkeley, she explored the physics of gas-phase chemical reactions involving silicon. After her 1988 graduation, Dr. Weber joined Texas Instruments (TI) to research new processes for making computer chips. TI assigned her to a consortium of semiconductor companies, SEMATECH, and subsequently to Applied Materials. She created a revolutionary reactor for manufacturing computer chips. She received one patent, and published eight papers in scientific journals.

Not satisfied with scientific accomplishments, in 1991, Weber earned a silver medal at the U.S. National Skydiving Championship 20-Way Freefall Formation event. In 1992, Weber joined the NASA Astronaut class. In 1995, her first space mission was on Space Shuttle Discovery. On STS-70, Dr. Weber deployed satellites and performed biotechnology experiments. The STS-70 mission completed 142 orbits of the Earth, after traveling 3.7 million miles in 214 hours and 20 minutes.

Dr. Mary Ellen Weber floating in outer space in a yoga position on STS-70 in 1995. (NASA photograph)

Upon her return from space, Weber continued to compete is precision skydiving competition. In 1996, she participated in the world's largest freefall formation, a 297-way. On the ground for NASA, Weber assisted in launching shuttles at the Kennedy Space Center. She worked on payload and robotic developments. In 2000, on her next NASA space mission, STS-101, Dr. Weber flew on Atlantis. Weber's two primary responsibilities were flying the 60-foot robotic arm to maneuver a spacewalk crewmember along the Station surface, and directing the transfer of over three thousand pounds of equipment to the International Space Station. The STS-101 mission was accomplished in 155 orbits of the Earth, after traveling 4.1 million miles in over 236 hours.

Maybe YOU belong in the sky among the stars!

In her space flights, Dr. Weber flew 450 hours and performed critical tasks for successful missions. She said her goals as an astronaut were, "Being an effective crew member, and making the mission successful, that is what I am striving for." In 2001, she left NASA. She joined the staff of the University of Texas Southeastern Medical Center in Dallas as their Vice-President of Government Affairs and Policy. Over the years, Weber has been a frequent keynote speaker and television news guest.

Dr. Mary Ellen Weber is an instrument-rated aviator with over 800 hours of flight time, including 600 in jet aircraft. She has over 6,000 parachute jumps. She holds a world skydiving record, and 19 U.S. National Skydiving Championship Medals. She is a dynamic conference speaker sharing her passion and experience in space and in the sky. Quoted in 2011, Weber said, "It was sky diving that triggered my fascination for aviation and I wanted to merge my passion for science and aviation." She urges young women to pursue technical fields, to keep on open mind about new things, and have a difficult goal which inspires aspiring astronauts to work hard.

Weeks, Samantha: Air Force Thunderbird Pilot

Born into an Air Force family, Samantha knew at age 6 she wanted to be a U.S. Air Force fighter pilot. Flying home to the United States from serving overseas, the family was inside the cavernous cargo area of a KC-135. During the flight, Samantha was invited to watch out the Boom Operator window as the Stratotanker refueled a combat fighter F-111. Samantha was mesmerized. She told her father, she wanted to do that. He thought she wanted to be the crewmember controlling the refueling boom and pumping jet fuel into the F-111 Aardvark. Samantha replied she wanted to be the F-111 fighter pilot. Her dad smiled, patted her on the back and said, "Girls don't do that!"

In 1993, Samantha entered the U.S. Air Force Academy. That same year, Congress passed legislation allowing military female aviators to fly combat aircraft. Basically, Congress said, "Now, girls CAN do that." Samantha was even more focused on her goal as an Air Force Cadet. Samantha graduated in 1997, earning a Bachelor of Science in Biology. Next was Air Force Specialized Undergraduate Pilot Training. Samantha flew the F-15C, Eagle fighter jet. Later, she flew in support of Operations Northern and Southern Watch in Iraq. In 2001, Weeks flew in Operation Nobel Eagle-ONE, a joint U.S. and Canadian military operation related to homeland security. From 2004 to 2006, Weeks was an Instructor Pilot. Apparently, "girls do that now!"

Over time, Samantha built up 2,200 flying hours with 105 of those in combat/combat support. Then, in late 2006, the ultimate dream aviator job of U.S. Air Force Thunderbird aerial demonstration team member became hers. Weeks became the second woman to join the Thunderbirds. After transition training to the F-16 Fighting Falcon, Weeks flew the #6 Opposing Solo and #5 Lead Solo. She was the first woman to fly the Solo Role. The Thunderbirds perform precision aerial maneuvers, demonstrating the capabilities of the U.S. Air Force high performance aircraft. The Thunderbird Demonstration pilots fly a mix of formation flying and solo routines. The four-aircraft diamond formation demonstrates the training and precision required of Air Force fighter pilots. The solo aircraft highlight the capabilities of the F-16 Fighting Falcon.

U.S. Air Force Captain, Samantha Weeks, entering her F-15C Eagle, a highly-maneuverable combat jet. Weeks became the second woman selected to fly with the United States Air Force Thunderbirds Air Demonstration Team. (USAF photo by SSgt. Rhiannon)

Thunderbird pilots fly about 30 maneuvers in each performance. The season lasts from March to November. The squadron performs about 75 precision flight demonstrations each year. Over the years, the Thunderbirds have flown in more than 4,000 aerial demonstration in all 50 United States and 58 foreign countries. Demonstration pilots fly a two-year assignment with the squadron. Winter months are used to train, and practice, practice, practice. Samantha Weeks served as an Instructor Pilot for new team members, too.

Over her 23-year Air Force career, Colonel Samantha Weeks was assigned as an Air Force Fellow to the Office of the Deputy Secretary of Defense, Washington D.C., and was chosen for a Lorenz Fellowship where she was awarded her Doctorate in Military Strategy, focusing on leadership development. Samantha earned a Masters in Human Relations from the University of Oklahoma. She graduated from the Air War College. She successfully commanded several Air Force Squadrons and Wings.

Today, Samantha Weeks is a popular speaker with Athena's Voice-Wisdom of Women Warriors. She is quoted in a *Sooner Magazine* article giving this sage advice, "Many people will hold back from trying something for fear of failure. They won't fail, but they won't succeed and reach their full potential." Samantha says her motto is: Be Bold! Use your voice, and never look back!

Welch, Ann Edmonds Walker: British Pioneer Glider Pilot & ATA Women's Section World War II Pilot
Born in London in 1917, Ann loved aeroplanes. When her family moved to Kent, Ann kept a diary of every aeroplane she saw flying over her house. At age 13, she took her first flight in a Fairey biplane. In her autobiography, *Happy to Fly*, Ann wrote "I knew that all I ever wanted was to fly, to just float around the cool sky, looking at the land and sea below, toy-like and beautiful." Ann acquired a motorbike so she could visit the local aerodromes often. She was encouraged to take flying lessons. In 1934, one month after her 17th birthday, Ann qualified for her Royal Aero Club pilot's license. Just three years later, Ann began

her gliding career at the London Gliding Club. The Anglo-German Fellowship held a gliding camp. Of course, the Nazi regime sent over two of their top glider pilots. One was Hanna Reitsch, Germany's most famous woman flyer.

Ann was hooked on soaring. Ann became a gliding instructor. In 1938, with the help of the Douglas family, who owned Redhill Aerodrome, Ann opened the Surrey Gliding Club. It was immensely popular. The Douglas family, particularly Graham, a pilot, loaned the club money to purchase gliders and a winch. At age 21, Ann was the club's chief, and only, gliding instructor. Eventually, Ann and Graham married.

When World War II began, Graham flew for the Royal Air Force (RAF). Of course, all civilian flying ended. Ann stored the gliders hoping the Surrey Gliding Club would open again soon. In 1940, Ann joined the Air Transport Auxiliary (ATA) Women's Section. She wrote in her book, "The war was just beginning to get serious. I had to be involved; it had to be in flying. Nothing else could even be contemplated." The ATA was a select group of experience pilots. Their mission was to deliver new aircraft from the factories to RAF airfields.

For Ann, in February, 1942, a routine flight became dangerous. Her mission was to fly a Spitfire only 50-miles to the RAF Colerne airfield, north of Bath. Ann was grounded for three days waiting for England's notorious rainy weather to lift. Most pilots say, "It's better to be on the ground wishing you were the air, than in the air wishing you were on the ground." But, this was war time. Delivering the Spitfire to the RAF was priority because it was needed to defend the besieged island of Malta. Very long story cut short. Ann flew the Spitfire at only 300 feet above the ground, and sometimes even lower scud running. She even flew with flaps down to fly more slowly to pick her way through the fog banks and icy clouds. No other Spitfires made it to the RAF in Colerne that day but Ann's. During her time in the ATA, Ann flew many different types of aircraft, including Tiger Moth trainers, Blenheim fighter-bombers, Spitfire and Hurricane fighters, as well as Wellington bombers. Ann recalled often she had only half an hour to familiarize herself with the controls of a new plane. By the end of the war, her log book listed 150 aircraft types. In 1944, her work as an ATA pilot came to an end with the birth of her first daughter.

Ann Welch in 1934 after her first solo flight. (KenleyRevival.org)

In 1948, Ann and Graham divorced. Ann restarted her beloved Surrey Gliding Club. The gliders stored during the war were rotted or destroyed. The few salvageable parts had been used during the war. Ann was joined at Surrey by former RAF pilot, Lorne Welch. In 1953, they married. The dynamic duo became a major force in International Soaring. Together, they penned books about techniques and history for the gliding and soaring sport community. With technical backup from Lorne, Ann led British international championship gliding teams for many years, winning in Spain in 1952, and in France in 1956. In 1961, during the world contest at Lezno, in Poland, Ann set a British women's record for distance.

Ann Welch was an organizer and doer. Ann worked hard to re-establish the British Gliding Association. She managed the British Team at the World Gliding Championships between 1948 and 1968. In 1974, she formed the British Hang-Gliding Association, and served as their president. Ann was also president of the British Microlight Association. She was also a Fellow of the Royal Aeronautical Society. In 1997, she was elected as an Honorary Fellow of the Royal Institute of Navigation. Ann received the Fédération Aéronautique Internationale (FAI) Gold Air Medal for her contributions to the development of four air sports - gliding, hang gliding, paragliding, and microlight flying.

Ann was awarded Member of the Order of the British Empire-MBE for her outstanding achievements and service to the British Commonwealth. Later, she was awarded the Order of the British Empire-OBE for her many aviation accomplishments. Ann Welch soared to greatness over her 85 years. She blazed trails for women in flight instruction, military aviation, sailplanes, hang gliders, and ultralights.

Wells, Helen Fay Gillis "Fay:" Historic American Aviator
Born in 1908 in Minneapolis, Helen was called Fay by family and friends. Because her father's skills were in great demand, the family lived in many towns in the United States and Canada. Fay was outgoing and made friends quickly over the years. In 1925, she graduated from

high school in New Jersey. She began study at Michigan State University. In August, 1929, Fay took her first flying lesson. She knew her future was in the sky. On September 1, Fay soloed. The very next day, Fay was invited to co-pilot an experimental airplane. Apparently, it was not yet ready for flight because midair the flight vibrations loosened the engine. The plane plummeted toward earth. Fay joined the Caterpillar Club when she pulled her parachute ripcord and landed safely.

> *Do not allow anyone to turn your sky into a limiting ceiling.*

Founded in 1922, the Caterpillar Club membership "eligibility" requirements are: "A person must have jumped from a disabled aircraft with a parachute to save their life." The motto, "Life depends on a silken thread" is because at one time parachutes were made of silk. Fay immediately flew the next day. By October, 1929, Fay earned her pilot's license at the Curtiss Flying School on Long Island. Curtiss-Wright Corporation hired Fay to demonstrate and sell Curtiss-Wright aircraft. In November, 1929, Fay became a founding members of the Ninety-Nines. Fay represented Curtiss-Wright across the nation. Her flight hours increased. In 1930, she received her commercial pilot's license.

During 1930-34, because her father was working in the Soviet Union, Fay joined the family. With her aviation and journalism contacts, Fay arranged to write articles for the *New York Herald Tribune*. *The New York Times* and the Associated Press made her their special reporter. Fay was building her aviation and journalism credentials. In 1933, she used her connections in Russia to arrange logistics for famed aviator, Wiley Post, on his solo round-the-world flight. In 1935, Wiley invited Fay to co-pilot with him in another round-the-world flight. Fay declined because she eloped to marry Linton Wells, a distinguished Foreign Correspondent.

The Wells immediately became a dynamic go-to foreign correspondent team for the International Press. In 1935, they covered the Italo-Ethiopian War for the *New York Herald*. Fay and Linton pioneered foreign reporting radio broadcasting. In 1939, Fay began the Overseas Press Club. Upon their return from foreign reporting, they both continued newspaper and radio reporting. In 1964, Fay was hired by Storer Broadcasting Company to cover the White House. At that time, Storer was the largest privately-owned radio and television broadcaster in the United States. Fay became the first woman to be an accredited White House correspondent. Fay covered Presidents Johnson, Nixon, Ford, and Carter in the White House. In 1972, she was one of only three women reporters selected to cover the historic Nixon trip to China. Fay retired in 1977.

During her many years in journalism-broadcasting, aviation was always in her heart. In 1962, using her extensive government and media contacts, the U.S. Postal Service issued the Amelia Earhart Airmail postage stamp. Fay and Linton were key supporters of the creation of the International Forest of Friendship in Atchison, Kansas. In 1976, Fay began actively planning events there. The arboretum and memorial forest is dedicated to celebrating aviation and space explorers. For many years, Fay co-chaired the International Forest of Friendship.

Over her lifetime, Fay Gillis Wells received many awards in the fields of aviation and broadcasting: 1972 Woman of the Year by OX5 Aviation Pioneers, 1984 Women's Aerospace Achievement Award, 1992 WAI Pioneer Hall of Fame, 1998 Esther Van Wagoner Tufty Award for broadcasting and personal achievement, 2001 National Aeronautic Association Katharine Wright Award for outstanding contributions to aviation, 2002 Amelia Earhart Pioneering Achievement Award, and the American Women in Radio and Television Lifetime Achievement Award. In 2002, Lillian Brinnon and Howard Fried penned an entire book about this remarkable trailblazer, *Fay Gillis Wells: In the Air & On the Air*.

Fay Gilles Wells was a founding member of the Ninety-Nines. She is a member of the Caterpillar Club, too. (International Women Air & Space Museum)

Whitson, Peggy Annette: Record Setting NASA Astronaut

Born in 1960, on an Iowa farm, Peggy always loved science. In 1969, Peggy, along with an estimated 530 million television viewers worldwide watched the Apollo 11 Moon landing with awe and fascination. Peggy made the decision she would become an astronaut. In 1978, after she graduated from high school, she began studying biology and chemistry at Iowa Wesleyan College. After her 1981 graduation with a Bachelor of Science, she was accepted for advanced studies at Rice University. By 1986, Dr. Whitson had earned her degrees in biochemistry. Rice offered her a Robert A. Welch Post-doctoral Fellowship. That year, she married Dr. Clarence F. Sams, a biochemist and aviator.

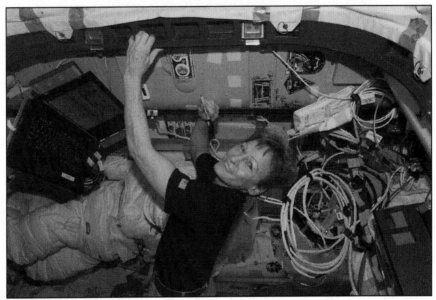

Record-setting Astronaut, Dr. Peggy Whitson, works in space on the International Space Station. (NASA photograph)

From 1989 to 1993, Peggy Whitson was a research biochemist in the NASA Biomedical Operations and Research Branch. Whitson was a key member of the US-USSR Joint Working Group in Space Medicine and Biology. She was named the project scientist of the Shuttle-Mir Program. Her roles and responsibilities increased. From 1993 through 1996, Whitson held the additional responsibilities of Deputy Division Chief of the Medical Sciences Division. Then, in 1995, Peggy was elevated to co-chair of the U.S.-Russian Mission Science Working Group.

In April, 1996, Dr. Whitson was selected as a NASA astronaut candidate. She began the two-year training program .In 1998, as an astronaut, she was assigned technical duties in the NASA Astronaut Office Operations Planning Branch. Additionally, Peggy was the lead for the Crew Test Support Team in Russia. In 2002, Whitson flew her first space mission, with an extended stay aboard the International Space Station. She was a member of Expedition 5. When she returned to terra firma, in June, 2003, Whitson served as the commander of the NEEMO-5 (NASA Environment Mission Operations) mission aboard the Aquarius underwater laboratory. The team lived and worked underwater for fourteen days. Dr. Whitson had flown to outer space and a few months later she was on the Atlantic Ocean floor about three miles off Key Largo, Florida.

In 2007, when Peggy Whitson returned to outer space, she made space history becoming the first female commander of the ISS with Expedition 16. When she returned in 2017, Dr. Whitson became the first female NASA female astronaut to command the International Space Station twice. She broke the record for the longest single-space flight by a woman of 289 days in orbit. Peggy flew back to Earth aboard Soyuz-MS-04. Peggy Whitson holds the record for the oldest woman spacewalker. She set the record for total spacewalks by a woman. Her cumulative EVA time is 60 hours, 21 minutes. At age 57 on her final space flight, she also became the oldest female astronaut ever in space at that time. On September 3, 2017, upon her return to Earth, Peggy Whitson accrued a total of 665+ days in space over her record-setting NASA career. She was NASA's most experienced astronaut at that time. She spent more time in space than any other American, and any other woman worldwide.

On June 14, 2018, Dr. Whitson retired from NASA. She became a consultant for Axiom Space, a privately funded space infrastructure developer. Recently that American space company announced, Dr. Whitson was selected to command Axion Mission 2 which will launch to the International Space Station in the fall, 2022. Dr. Whitson continues to make space history. Peggy is already honored in the International Air and Space Hall of Fame. *Time* named her one of the 100 Most Influential People of 2018. Dr. Peggy Whitson said, "I am not sure what the future holds for me personally, but I envision myself continuing to work on spaceflight programs." She continues to contribute her experience, talent, and enthusiasm for space exploration.

Wideroe, Turi: Norway's First Female Airline Pilot

Born in 1937 into a Norwegian aviation family, Turi became a frequent passenger on her father's Wideroe Airline, which began in 1934. Today, Wideroe is the largest regional airline operating in the Nordic countries. Wideroe Airline fleet of Bombardier Dash 8 and Embraer E190-E2 aircraft serves over 40 domestic and international destinations. Initially, Turi focused on art and design. She was educated as a book designer. She graduated from the Norwegian National Academy of Arts & Crafts. Her book designs won awards and acclaim. Turi worked in the publishing industry with several top companies in Norway. In 1960, she became the assistant editor for the National Association of Norwegian Architects magazine.

But, soon, Turi heard the siren call of the sky. In 1962, she began flight lessons. She grew up in aviation so when she had questions, she had a large network of support, knowledge, and mentoring available to her. After her flight training, she began flying for an ore research mining company in northern Norway in rugged terrain and harsh weather conditions. In 1965, Turi earned her commercial and ATP license. Turi began piloting Twin Otters on scheduled, and even mercy flights north of the Arctic Circle for Wideroe.

In 1968, Scandinavian Airlines System-SAS hired Turi. In 1969, after graduating from the SAS Flight Academy, Turi was certified as a co-pilot on Convair 440 Metropolitan, which is a large twin turboprop, usually configured for 52 passengers. Turi Wideroe became Norway's first female airline pilot. Turi also became the first woman pilot in the entire major scheduled airline industry. In 1970, Turi was awarded the Harmon Aviatrix Trophy, recognizing her historic role in commercial aviation.

Later, Turi flew Scandinavian Airlines System first jet aircraft, the Caravelle. The Caravelle is a French regional jet airliner. Turi was now a SAS airline Captain. Before Turi left Scandinavian Airlines System flight deck, she ended her airline career flying the DC-9, which is a twin-engine jet manufactured for frequent, short flights. Turi's SAS uniform is displayed at the Smithsonian Air and Space Museum. Always eager to have other women in the airline flight deck, on the historic day of February 6, 1973, when America's Emily Warner piloted the Frontier Airlines jet from Denver to Las Vegas, Turi sent Emily a bouquet of flowers and her congratulations.

In 1969, Turi Wideroe, flying for Scandinavian Airlines System, became the first female pilot for a major airline. (WikiCommons)

In 2005 in Paris, Turi received the FAI Paul Tissandier Diploma. The *Paul Tissandier Diploma* is a perpetual international award established in 1952 by the *Fédération Aéronautique Internationale* in memory of Tissandier, who was FAI Treasurer and its Secretary General from 1913 to 1945. The diplomas are awarded to those persons who have served the cause of aviation by their work, devotion, or other endeavors.

Using her original training in book design and publishing, Turi wrote the 40th Anniversary history of Wideroe Airline. After ending her flight career, Turi worked for the Norwegian Broadcasting Corporation and other media companies. She focused on cultural institutions.

Williams, Sunita Lyn "Suni": U.S. Navy Test Pilot and NASA Astronaut

Born in 1965 in Ohio, Suni's father, Deepak Pandya, was a neuroanatomist. Her mother was Slovene American. The family placed high value on education. Suni was an excellent student. She was appointed to the U.S. Naval Academy. In 1987, Ensign Williams graduated with a Bachelor of Science. After several short rotations in the fleet, and in diving operations, Suni was selected for U.S. Naval Flight School. As a stellar student, Suni began Sea Knight H-46 Rotary Wing Training. The Sea Knight is a medium-lift tandem-rotor transport helicopter. In July, 1989, Suni earned her U.S. Navy Golden Wings. Williams joined U.S. Naval Squadrons in support of several military operations. Her overseas deployments were in the Mediterranean, Red Sea, and Persian Gulf for Operations Desert Shield.

In January, 1993, Suni was selected for U.S. Naval Test Pilot School. She graduated at the end of the year. She was the Project Officer for H-46. She was the Squadron Safety Officer. She flew test flights on multiple rotary wing assets. In 1995, Suni earned a Master's degree in engineering at Florida Institute of Technology. In December, 1995, she went back to the Naval Test Pilot School as an instructor in the Rotary Wing Department and as the school's Safety Officer. There she instructed in the UH-60 Sikorsky Black Hawk, OH-6 Hughes Cayuse, and the OH-58 Bell Kiowa. After that assignment, Williams was deployed on the USS Saipan, a Tarawa-class amphibious assault ship. She was the Aircraft Handler and Assistant Air Boss when her selection for NASA Astronaut training was announced. In 1998, Suni had logged more than 3,000 flight hours in more than 30 aircraft types.

Sunita "Suni" Williams is a NASA record-setting Astronaut and U.S. Navy Test Pilot. (NASA photograph)

In June, 1998, Suni began her NASA astronaut training. Scientific and technical briefings, intensive instruction in space shuttle and International Space Station systems, physiological training, even ground school for T-38 flight training are packed into the program. Candidates have additional water and wilderness survival training. Williams was assigned additional duty to work in Moscow with the Russian Space Agency on the Russian contribution to the space station and the first Expedition 1 Crew. After Expedition 1, Williams was assigned within the Robotics branch on ISS Robotic Arm.

She was a NEEMO 2 crew member, where she lived on the floor of the Atlantic Ocean in the Aquarius habitat for nine days. Suni's first space flight was in December, 2006. She launched with the crew of STS-116 docking with the ISS on December 11. As a member of the Expedition 14 crew, Suni was a Flight Engineer. While onboard, Williams established a world record for women with four spacewalks totaling 29 hours and 17 minutes. In June 2007, Suni returned to Earth with the STS-117 crew, landing at Edwards Air Force Base.

After her first flight, she served as NASA Deputy Chief of the Astronaut Office. She continued to train for her next space launch. In July, 2012, Williams launched from the Baikonur Cosmodrome in Kazakstan, along with Russian Soyuz commander Yuri Malenchenko, and Japanese Aerospace Exploration Agency Flight Engineer, Akihito Hoshide. On July 17, 2012, they were welcomed at the ISS. Williams conducted research for four months. She conducted three spacewalks. In November, 2012, after 127 days in space, Suni returned to Earth, landing in Kazakhstan. The slogan says, "Join the Navy. See the world." That was sure true of Suni's experience.

Williams continues to work with NASA. She has earned multiple awards and recognition for both her military and her space accomplishments. In 1970, she was awarded the Harmon Aviatrix Trophy. The Ninety-Nines awarded her their Amelia Earhart Medal. In 2005, the FAI awarded the Paul Tissandier Diploma to Suni Willians. She explained her path from air to space, "Understanding how things work and being an engineer led me to become a helicopter pilot, and eventually to NASA. The path doesn't necessarily have to be straight, but don't limit yourself to what you know. Go out and try new things."

Wilson, Stephanie Diana: NASA Astronaut and Second Black American Woman in Space

Born in 1966, her parents worked in the sciences. Stephanie's father, Eugene, used his electronics experience in the U.S. Navy to earn a degree from Northeastern University. He had a long and successful career at Raytheon, Sprague Electric, and Lockheed Martin. Stephanie's mother, Barbara, was a production assistant at Lockheed Martin. In a pre-launch NASA interview in 2010, Stephanie said, "When I was about thirteen, I was given a school assignment in a Career Awareness class to interview someone that worked in the career field in which I was interested. I interviewed a local area astronomy professor. I thought that astronomy was a fantastic career, being able to teach, being able to see events in the heavens, and to do the observations. Later, I became more interested in engineering and decided that I would study engineering in college and perhaps that aerospace engineering would be a good combination of my interests in astronomy and my interest in engineering."

In 1988, after high school, Stephanie attended Harvard University, earning a Bachelor of Science degree in engineering science. In 1992, Stephanie graduated from the University of Texas, earning her master's in aerospace engineering. She was hired by the Jet Propulsions Laboratory in Pasadena, California. She focused on the Galileo spacecraft systems there. In 1996, she was selected by NASA as an Astronaut Candidate. By August, Stephanie was at the Johnson Space Center to begin the two-years of training and evaluation.

Stephanie qualified for space flight assignment as a Mission Specialist. Initially, Stephanie was assigned technical duties in the Astronaut Office Space Station Operations Branch. She worked on Space Station payload simulations and procedure check lists. She served in the Astronaut Office CAPCOM Branch working directly with Mission Control as the prime communicator with orbiting crews. Next,

Stephanie moved to the Shuttle Operations Branch involving the Space Station Main Engines, External Tank, and Solid Rocket Boosters. All critical functions for the crew members.

Stephanie Wilson made NASA space history. (NASA photograph)

Finally, On July 4, 2006, on STS-121 Space Shuttle Discovery, Stephanie Wilson and crew launched to the International Space Station. Stephanie returned on Discovery on July 17, 2006. Stephanie Wilson became the second Black American woman in space. Her next mission launched October 23, 2007 for the ISS with the Harmony connecting module for the International Space Station. Astronaut Wilson flew a third time. In April 2012, on STS-131 Space Shuttle Discovery again reaching the International Space Stations. This marked an historic space milestone for women when for the first time in history four women served together: Stephanie Wilson, Tracey Caldwell Dyson, Dorothy Metcalf-Lindenburger, and Japanese JAXA Astronaut Naoka Yamazaki.

Upon her return to Earth, Wilson again made more space history for women when Stephanie served as the ground controller and CAPCOM in Houston for the first all-women spacewalk. On October 18, 2019, Wilson coordinated the EVA by Christina Koch and Jessica Meir. Stephanie Wilson is one of the NASA astronauts being considered for the 2024 Artemis program. She might be the first woman to walk on the moon and the first Black American on the Moon. Currently her 42 days in space are the most of any female Black American female in NASA.

Yamazaki, Naoka: JAXA Astronaut 2nd Japanese Woman in Space
Born in 1970, Naoka grew up in Hokkaido, Japan's northernmost island. She discovered a passion for the stars and sky at an early age. She would study the stars in the night sky. At age 15, she watched the televised Challenger Space Shuttle Disaster. Naoka decided to dedicate her life to the exploration of space. "I remember thinking that this wasn't science fiction. The people who perished in the disaster were real. That's when I first thought that I wanted to become a part of future space programs." Naoka knew in her heart that many space workers and scientists worked tirelessly to support the Challenger crew from the ground. She wanted to be part of a space team, working to reach the stars.

In 1989, Naoka graduated from high school to enter the University of Tokyo. Her laser focus was on science and the sky. In 1993, Yamazaki earned a Bachelor of Science in Aerospace Engineering. She continued her studies there. In 1996, Naoka earned a Masters in that subject. That year, a dream opportunity at the National Space Development Agency of Japan opened for Naoka. She joined a development team for the Japanese Experimental Module (JEM). JEM is nicknamed Kibō, which means "Hope" in Japanese. JEM is a Japanese science module for the International Space Station developed by JAXA. It is the largest single ISS module, and is attached to the ISS Harmony module.

Next, in 1998, Nakota became part of the International Space Station Centrifuge Team with focus on life science experimentation. In 1999, Naoka was selected as an astronaut candidate for Japan .Next, Naoka began rigorous training with the International Space Station (ISS) Astronaut Basic Training program. Astronaut candidates in regions from around the world train for space missions before, during, and after their space flights. They undergo medical tests, physical training, extra-vehicular activity (EVA) training, crew management and communications, and ISS systems orientation. This in-depth training is conducted at both NASA Johnson Space Center in Houston, and in the Soviet Union in Star City.

Virtual and physical training facilities have been integrated to familiarize astronauts with the conditions they will encounter during all phases of flight and prepare astronauts for a microgravity environment. Naoka also participated in ISS Advance Training, specifically on the operation of the Japanese Experimental Module. In 2004, Yamazaki completed the Soyus Flight Engineering training at the Yuri Gagarin Cosmonauts Training Center in Russia's Star City.

Undergoing nearly two years of extreme training – including a survival camp in minus-20 degrees Celsius in Russia, where Naoka and other astronaut candidates had to cut trees to start a fire. Another was in the United States. In this test Naoka had to escape out of a simulated crashed helicopter sinking in water. The harshness of these training sessions, however, is what made her stronger, she recalls. "Thanks to those lessons in failure, we could get ready for almost all emergencies in space."

Japanese Aerospace Exploration Agency, JAXA, astronaut, Naoko Yamazaki flew on the STS-131 NASA Discovery space shuttle to the International Space Station. (NASA photograph)

She was selected as a NASA Mission Specialist in 2006. In November 2008, JAXA announced that Yamazaki would become the second Japanese woman to fly in space on STS-131 on Space Shuttle Discovery to the International Space Station. On April 5, 2010, STS-

131 launched. Because Discovery was retired in 2011, Naoka is the last Japanese astronaut to ever fly on that space shuttle. She made more space history with this flight. When STS-131 docked with the ISS, this mission marked the first time that four women were together is space. Naoka teamed with NASA Astronauts Tracy Caldwell Dyson, Dorothy Metcalf-Lindenburger, and Stephanie Wilson. STS-131 set a record as the longest Discovery space shuttle mission as well, lasting more than 15 days. On April 20, 2010, Naoka returned to Earth on Discovery.

In August, 2011, Yamazaki retired from JAXA. She continued her studies and space research at the University of Tokyo. Naoka promotes STEM education in Japan. In July, 2018, Yamazaki co-founded the Space Port Japan Association to open Japan to spaceport development in partnership with private companies and government. Close to her heart is her leadership as an adviser to the Japan Young Astronaut Club, and to the Women in Aerospace Program of the Japan Rocket Society.

Yang, Liu: People's Republic of China's First Female Taikonaut in Space

Born in 1978, into a worker's family in Zhengzhou in Henan Province, Liu was taught to work hard. Zhengzhou is the capital and largest city in the province. Today, over 12 million live there because it is an important hub for the Chinese national transportation network of railways. It has an international airport, and several large universities. Liu was an excellent student. In 1997, Yang joined the PLA Air Force. She graduated from the PLA Air Force Aviation University. She qualified as a transport pilot. Liu is a precise and excellent aviator. She became the deputy head of a flight unit. She earned the rank of Major in the PLAAF. Liu, flew over 1,680 hours before she entered the Taikonaut Training Program.

Taikonaut is derived from the Chinese word, *Taikong* meaning outer space. A Taikonaut is a Chinese Astronaut. After two rigorous years of space training, Liu excelled in the testing before she was selected as a candidate for the Taikonaut Corps. At the end of the space training, Liu was chosen. Liu said, "From day one, I have been told I am no different from the male astronauts. As a pilot, I flew in the sky. Now that I am an astronaut, I will fly in space."

Liu Yang, People's Republic of China, first woman Taikonaut is space. (Wikicommons)

In 2003, the first Chinese male Taikonaut launched into space. Over the years, the Chinese government built a space station named Tiangong-1. The Shenzhou-9 mission would be the first crewed mission to dock with the space station. On March 12, 2012, China announced the initial crew selection roster for the mission, which for the first time included two female Taikonauts, Liu Yang and Wang Yaping.

On June 15, the Shenzhou-9 Taikonaut crew members were introduced to the world community. Liu Yang was selected. Shenzhou 9, the 9th space flight in China's program, was the fourth crewed spaceflight. On June 16, 2012, Liu became the first Chinese woman in space. The June 16, 2012, Shenzhou-9 launch was an historic day for the People's Republic of China. But, also, the date was chosen because it was the 49th anniversary of the first female Russian space cosmonaut, Valentina Tereshkova, launch in Vostok 6.

During this important Shenzhou-9 crewed space mission, Taikonaut Liu performed experiments in space medicine. On June 18, the Shenzhou-9 docked with the Tiangong-1 space station. This was the first crewed spacecraft to do so. This marked the first woman Taikonaut to launch into space. On June 29, Shenzhou-9 returned to Earth by parachute in the Inner Mongolia Autonomous Region.

Colonel Liu Yang explored space for 300 hours in her first flight. On her return, she said, "I believe in preserving. If you persevere, success lies ahead of you."

Trust yourself.

Know that you're capable and be bold in

going after what you want.

~ Stephanie Chung

Yeager, Jeana: First Women to Receive the Collier Trophy

Born in 1952 in Texas, horses and sports were her interests. She enjoyed adventure and challenge. One of her first jobs, as an aeronautical draftsman, was with Project Private Enterprise. Their goal was to use private enterprise to fund manned space flight. While there Jeana learned a great deal about aerodynamic design and rockets. In 1978, at the age of 26, she earned her private pilot's license. In 1980, she met Dick Rutan, a retired U.S. Air Force fighter pilot of 300 Vietnam War missions, and a respected test pilot. Together, both were record-setters in a number of experimental aircraft for speed and distance. Dick's brother, Burt, was a noted aerospace engineer and visionary designer of fuel efficient aircraft.

Jeana Yeager inside Voyager. In 1986, she earned her Trailblazer title by circumnavigating the globe, non-stop without refueling. (Smithsonian Air and Space Museum archive)

They set an impossible goal to circumnavigate the world, non-stop, without refueling. They were told many times, "they were dreaming the impossible dream." Very long story cut short, as Amelia Earhart once said, "Never interrupt someone doing something you said couldn't be done." It took almost six years of meticulous planning, testing, and more testing to perfect the Rutan Voyager.

The Voyager was the first aircraft constructed primarily of lightweight graphite honeycomb composite materials. The Voyager was 20% lighter with composite material instead of aluminum. The composite was seven times tougher. The wing span was 110-feet. The cost was over two million which was raised with sponsorships, donations, and even t-shirt sales. Weight is always a factor in aviation, Jeana even cut her hair very short because every ounce of unnecessary weight mattered. Jeana was 100 pounds, five-feet four inches tall.

The cockpit was about 42 inches by 84 inches or about the size of a phone booth. The odyssey began on December 14, 1986. A support team on the ground constantly monitored systems, just a NASA mission control does when a space shuttle is launched. They were in constant communication with pilots, Yeager and Rutan. The record-setting flight took nine days, three minutes, and forty-four seconds. Between December 14 through December 23, 1986, Voyager's flight was the first-ever, non-stop, unrefueled flight around the world. The intrepid duo set six new world records. The flight circumnavigated the world, flying 26,366 statute miles. The average altitude flown was about 11,000 feet. The Voyager took off from and landed at Edwards Air Force Base in California. The absolute world distance records set during that flight remained unchallenged today. The Voyager now hangs at the Smithsonian Air and Space Museum.

Four days after their Voyager landing, President Ronald Reagan presented Jeana Yeager and Dick Rutan, the Voyager crew, and Burt Rutan, Voyager designer, with the Presidential Citizenship Medal, awarded only 16 times previously in history. Jeana Yeager became the first woman in history to be awarded the Collier Trophy. The Collier Trophy is awarded annually "for the greatest achievement in aeronautics or astronautics in America, with respect to improving the performance, efficiency, and safety of air or space vehicles, the value of which has been thoroughly demonstrated by actual use during the preceding year."

In recognition of the 1986 Voyager flight, Yeager received both the Harmon Aviatrix Trophy, and the National Air and Space Museum Trophy. Both pilots were recognized by many aviation organizations and publications for their daring voyage. In 1992, Jeana Yeager joined the Women in Aviation International Pioneer Hall of Fame.

Zvereva, Lydia: Russia's First Female Pilot

Born in Saint Petersburg into a prominent military family, Zvereva studied at the Czar Nichol I Institute for Girls. In an effort to modernize, Czar Nicholas II invited pioneering French and German aviators to demonstrate their aeroplanes in a series of exhibitions in Russia. French pilot, Raymonde de Laroche, the first woman in the world to be a licensed pilot, performed. Raymonde wowed the crowd. In a gathering after her air performance, Raymonde encourage other women to fly, including Lydia.

Lydia had always been fascinated by the sky and flying. She was a voracious reader of books and articles about mechanical things. She learned about the early French balloonists. She sought out mechanical and complex toys. She even built some models of ships and wagons. She was determined to fly just like the Baroness de Laroche. It did not bother her than the early aeroplanes were quite dangerous and flimsy. If Ramonde could do it, so could she.

Lydia enrolled at the Gamayun private flying school just outside Saint Petersburg. The newspapers got wind of this story. But, when they wrote the story about a Russian woman taking flying lessons, they referred to her only as "Miss Z." Just in case Lydia quit or crashed, the Russian newspapers wanted to respect her privacy. In fact, Lydia did have several serious accidents during her quest. But, thankfully, she had minor scratches or bruises, no broken bones or worse.

The early aeroplanes were flimsy. A strong gust of wind could tear the fabric on the wings. Often, the crashes were because of the equipment and not the skill of the pilot. In August, 1911, 21-year-old Lydia Zvereva earned pilot license No. 31. She became the first woman licensed to fly in the whole Russian Empire. Lydia continued to build her skill in the air. She loved high altitudes which attracted great attention.

In 1912, Lydia and her pilot husband, and former flight instructor, Vladimir Slyusarenko, made a good living flying exhibitions. It was called "barnstorming" in America. At one performance in windy conditions in Riga, the wind pushed Lydia's Farman toward the grandstands. She tried to gain altitude but the wind was gusting even stronger. The wind flipped the plane, but Lydia was able to fly the upside down plane to the ground. The newspapers reported that Lydia "was barely alive because the wreckage pinned her until the crowd rushed to lift the aeroplane off her lifeless body." Well, this was a bit of hyperbole. Lydia almost broke her leg. She may have punctured a lung. But, with rest the doctors felt she would "probably not get galloping consumption."

Lydia Zvereva's 1911 diploma. Russia's first woman pilot. (Wikicommons)

In a few months, Lydia did recover and was back in the air. In fact, Riga invited her back to perform. The large Baltic town was the center of Russian aviation at that time. Many aircraft engines were built there. In 1913, the enterprising aviation couple opened their flying school in Riga. They priced the cost of flying lessons as the lowest in the Russian Empire to encourage students to learn how to fly. They even started an aeroplane repair workshop. Next, was a construction workshop with Lydia as the aircraft designer.

Lydia loved teaching and designing. This was a dream come true for her. In 1914, in an exhibition performance, Lydia even flew an aerobatic maneuver, a loop, to the amazed crowd. When World War I started, the couple's aircraft workshop was moved. A real factory employing 300 people built military aircraft. Periodically, Lydia would test fly the aeroplanes. Because of the war, public performances largely ended. Sadly, on May 16, 1916, Lydia Zvereva, who had cheated death numerous times in the air, died from typhoid fever. The 26-year-old aviator was mourned with a Squadron of pilots in Farmans flying over the cemetery giving this Russian trailblazer an aerial salute.

Never let fear stand in the way of an opportunity.

~ Jessica Cox, World's first licensed armless pilot.

6

Trailblazing Groups

We remain committed to creating an industry that is as diverse as our communities.
~ Allison McKay, Women in Aviation International CEO

ATA Air Transport Auxiliary Women's Section of World War II
Originally, the ATA excluded many female pilots who applied because of gender. Prominent British aviatrix, Pauline Gower, protested this insanity. By 1940, she was "given permission" to form the Women's Section of the ATA. Eight women were selected: Winifred Crossley, Margaret Cunnison, Margaret Fairweather, Mona Friedlander, Joan Hughes, Gabrielle Patterson, Rosemary Rees, and Marion Wilberforce. They were based at the Hatfield Air Base in England.

This select World War II corps of female pilots flew newly-manufactured aircraft from factories to Royal Air Force (RAF) military airfields. All the women were experienced pilots before their selection into this elite civilian flying corps. Their purpose was to free-up RAF male pilots for air battle. Some ATA women even flew air ambulances. Most ferried aircraft to RAF airfields across the United Kingdom. Their motto was *Aetheeris avidi,* Latin for "Eager for the Air."

Initially, they were only allowed to ferry smaller aircraft as the Tiger Moth. They were paid 20% less than male ferry pilots. The stellar female pilots came through the winter without losing one plane and without one accident. In May, 1940, as their high performance was obvious, Gower was "given permission" again to expand the ATA women flyers. Famed British aviator, Amy Johnson, and two women pilots for the Polish Air Force, Jadwiga Pilsudska and Anna Leska, who had escaped the German invasion of their country, joined.

The British ATA-Air Transport Auxiliary Women's Section made significant contributions to the Allied success in World War II. (Wikicommons)

In 1942, Jacqueline Cochran recruited 25 American women to join her in the ATA, even though America was not yet officially in World War II. Women of the ATA were billeted in combat areas under constant threat from German bombers. Finally, in June, 1943, the British Parliament decreed that women ferry pilots receive equal pay for equal work with their male counterparts. A revolutionary concept for the time.

Although most ATA members were from the United Kingdom, others in the Women's section came from America, Argentina, Australia, Canada, Chile, New Zealand, Poland, South Africa, and The Netherlands. During the war, the ATA flew 415,000 hours and delivered more than 309,000 aircraft of 147 types, including Spitfires, Hawker Hurricanes, Mosquitoes, Mustangs, Lancaster bombers, Halifaxes, Fairey Swordfish and Barracudas, and Flying Fortresses.

The ATA Women's section grew to over 165 aviators. Tragically, toward the end of World War II, ATA women pilots were asked to ferry planes into more dangerous areas as the Allies advanced on Germany.

Fifteen died in aviation loses. ATA Women's Section was disbanded in November, 1945, two months after the end of World War II. The famous British slogan used during the toughest times in World War II of "Stay Calm and Carry On!" was certainly true of these trailblazing ATA women. These brave aviators were recognized by Women in Aviation International in their Pioneer Hall of Fame.

Betsy Ross Air Corps 1931-33

Founded in 1931, by pioneering aviator, Opal Kunz, the new organization was named in honor of the Revolutionary War patriot, Betsy Ross, who supposedly sewed the American flag in Philadelphia. Opal's vision for the Betsy Ross Air Corps was for a paramilitary air cadre to provide humanitarian emergency service across America. Kunz earned her pilot license in 1929. She was a founding member of the Ninety-Nines. In 1930, she became the first woman to race in an open competition with men at the Philadelphia American Legion Benefit Air Meet. She won that air race. Opal hoped to offer flight instruction for women in the Betsy Ross Air Corps. Opal served as the commander of the Betsy Ross Air Corps for the two years of its existence. Kunz partially funded the organization. At its zenith, about 100 members were part of the Betsy Ross Air Corps. In 1933, the Betsy Ross Air Corps was disbanded because it was never recognized nor supported by the U.S. Army Air Corps. Nevertheless, Opal Kunz continued to be active in American aviation and in flight instruction.

Two stonecutters were asked what they were doing. The first said, "I'm cutting these stones into blocks."

The second replied, "I'm on a team that's building a cathedral."

Early American aviator, Opal Kunz, was a charter member of the Ninety-Nines. She founded the Betsy Ross Air Corps. Later, in the 1940s, she was co-founder of the Women Flyers of America, Inc. (Wikicommons photograph)

ISA+21 International Society of Women Airline Pilots

Founded in 1978, with twenty-one pioneering women airline pilots, their global mission was to be a unifying voice for female airline pilots, to support and advocate for women on the flight decks of the airline industry, and to inspire women to join them in this exciting career.

Today, membership has grown to over 35 countries with women pilots flying for ninety airlines worldwide. To form this important organization, Beverley Bass and Stephanie Wallach wrote letters to the chief pilot of every U.S. airline. They asked that their letter of invitation to attend the first convention be given to every female pilot on their airline staff. The inaugural convention was held in Las Vegas. Continental Airlines sponsored this organizational meeting which formed the International Society of Women Airline Pilots.

ISA+21 Founding members: Beverley Bass, Denise Blankenship, Jane Bonny, Julie E. Clark, Sandy Donnelly, Gail Gorski, Sharon Griggs, Jean Haley Harper, Karen Kahn, Angela Masson, Holly Ann Mullins, Norah O'Neill, Lennie Muttick-Sorenson, Lynn Rhoades, Terry London Rinehart, Mary Bush Shipko, Claudia Simpson-Jones, Maggie Stryker-Badaracco, Valerie Jene Walker, Stephanie Wallach, and Emily Howell Warner,

iWOAW Institute for Women of Aviation Worldwide

Founded in Canada by Mireille Goyer, an airline-rated pilot and aviation educator, the iWOAW mission is to foster gender balance in the air and space industry worldwide. In late 2009, Goyer wanted to celebrate the 100th anniversary of the world's first female licensed aviator, Raymonde de Laroche. The centennial was on March 8, 2010. Mireille found nothing was scheduled. Determined to celebrate this historic event and other important milestones for female aviation pioneers, Mireille used her extensive promotional skills to launch a worldwide campaign for other pilots to join her to Fly It Forward® by introducing a woman or a girl to flying in a small aircraft. Using her own money, Goyer offered world titles and awards for the pilots and airports who introduced the most women and girls to flight. As a result, more than 1,600 women and girls discovered the joys of flying in thirty-six countries on four continents.

Lines of women and girls waiting for a chance to experience aviation, hands-on, plus hundreds of photos of their smiles told the positive story. As a result, an industry previously content to dismiss women as "not interested" was forced to examine its outreach and inclusion of women. Then, Goyer launched the annual Women of Aviation Worldwide Week initiative. This annual full week in March focuses global awareness and outreach to "help change the face of aviation." Their slogan is "Let's Add Some Pink in Aviation!" Moyer is widely recognized as an industry leader for gender equity. She received numerous awards. The outreach for iWOAW grew with industry newsletters, collaboration with corporate partners, and promotional opportunity for females in this important global industry.

Mireille Goyer (top) with the women and girls to whom she gave a Fly It Forward® flight at the Hawthorne Airport, CA, USA, in March, 2010. (Courtesy of the Institute for Women of Aviation Worldwide-iWOAW)

Mercury 13

In 1958, NASA accepted applications for its astronaut program. However, in addition to a college degree, future astronauts needed to be not only rated aviators, but military jet test pilots. At the time, women were excluded from flying as military jet test pilots. Consequently,

America's Mercury 7 Astronauts were all male with "the right stuff." The world-famous aviator, Jacqueline Cochran, funded a private testing program at the Lovelace Clinic. This secret testing program was by invitation only for experienced women in aviation. The women participated in testing similar to that of the male astronauts. Stellar women committed themselves to this important research. They were:

Myrtle Cagle - a pilot with 4,300 hours of flight time and a licensed aircraft mechanic, age 36;

Jerrie Cobb - ATP rating, age 28. She was ferrying military fighters worldwide to foreign Air Forces. Cobb had flown 64 types of propeller aircraft;

Jan Dietrich - age 35, had 8,000 flying hours as a pilot for a large company. Her twin sister, **Marion**, was an aviation journalist and pilot with 1,500 hours;

Wally Funk - the youngest, at age 23. She was a flight instructor with 3,000 hours;

Sarah Gorelick (Ratley) - 28 years old, an engineer and pilot with 1,800 hours;

Jane "Janey" Briggs Hart - oldest of the Mercury 13 at age 40. She earned her pilot's license during World War II;

Jean Hixson-age 38, a school teacher, U.S. Air Force Reserve Captain with 4,500 flight hours;

Rhea Hurrle (Woltman) - age 31, worked as an executive pilot with 1,500 hours;

Irene Leverton - also an executive pilot, had accrued 9,000 hours by age 35;

Jerri Sloan (Truhill) - age 31, owned an aviation company. She had 1,200 hours;

Bernice "Bea" Steadman - age 36, owned and operated an aviation service company. She had 8,000 hours;

Gene Nora Stumbough (Jessen) - only 25 years old with 1,450 hours as a professional pilot for an aircraft company.

In 1995, seven of the Mercury 13 First Lady Astronaut Trainees (FLATs) stood outside Launch Pad 39B near the Space Shuttle Discovery. (L-R) Gene Nora Jessen, Wally Funk, Jerrie Cobb, Jerri Sloan Truhill, Sarah Gorelick Ratley, Myrtle Cagle, and Bernice Steadman. (NASA photograph)

Their fight for female NASA astronauts was lost on Capitol Hill. Congress voted to support NASA's decision to not use women in their astronaut program. In 1978, NASA allowed women to apply for their Group 8 NASA astronaut class. But, just as we now honor and remember our World War II WASP, the Mercury 13 women blazed a trail for today's women in space. They are in the WAI Pioneer Hall of Fame. Recently, Netflix produced an original documentary titled, *Mercury 13,* about these stellar trailblazers.

NASA First Female Astronaut Class

In 1978, because industries were pressured by government regulators and new Equal Opportunity legislation, NASA finally selected women for their astronaut training program. Astronaut Group 8 was organized as pilots and mission specialists. Group 8 was composed of 29 males and six women. All six women completed the astronaut training. All of them participated in space missions. In 1983, Sally Ride became the first American woman in space.

In 1978, NASA selected six women for their first female astronaut candidates. (L-R) Shannon W. Lucid, Margaret Rhea Seddon, Kathryn D. Sullivan, Judith A. Resnik, Anna Lee Fisher, and Sally K. Ride. In August, 1979, all six joined the NASA Astronaut Corps. (NASA photograph)

Judith Resnik flew in 1984 as the second. Resnik logged 145 hours in orbit, traveling to space on the first flight of the shuttle orbiter Discovery. Tragically, in 1986, Resnik was killed in the Challenger disaster. Kathryn Sullivan and Sally Ride were the first two female astronauts to fly on a mission together. Kathy Sullivan became the first American woman to perform a spacewalk. Shannon Lucid was our first American woman to serve on a mission on the Russian Mir Space Station. In April, 1985, Dr. Rhea Seddon became the first female surgeon in space. Anna Lee Fisher, a physician and chemist, flew on STS-51-A Discovery as a Mission Specialist. In 1996, Fisher became Chief of NASA Space Station Branch. Before her retirement, Anna served as International Space Station Capsule Communicator (CAPCOM) in Mission Control Center. These Spacefarers blazed the trail to outer space for the many women who followed.

Night Witches of World War II Russian 588th Night Bomber Regiment

These amazing women flew old, noisy airplanes with limited support from the Russian military. They wore oversized men's clothes and boots. They flew missions mostly at night to bomb the German positions. In order to complete their missions, these intrepid Russian women sometimes shut down their engines... They would glide down, drop their bombs, restart their engines, fly back to refuel, and then fly another mission.

The 588th was given old canvas and plywood Polikarpov-Po-2 biplanes which had been crop dusters and early basic flight training machines. Typically, the pilot sat up front and the navigator, who also was the bombardier, sat in the rear. These stealth flyers struck fear in the enemy men when they would hear the whooshing sound of the Russian female pilots often too late to shoot them out of the sky. German soldiers thought of the women as flying on broomsticks. They named the daring Russian women pilots, "Nachthexen" or "Night Witches."

Night Witch, Nadezhda "Nadya" Popova, at only age 19, flew 852 missions. Due to the weight of the bombs they carried, they did not even have parachutes onboard. The 588th flew over 23,000 sorties, dropped over 3,000 tons of bombs and 26,000 incendiary shells. They were the first women military combat pilots of World War II. Soviet Aviation Pioneer, Marina Raskova, also recruited Russian women for aviation training in the 586th Fighter Aviation Regiment and the 587th Bomber Aviation Regiment. But, the 588th was the most highly decorated female unit in the Soviet Air Force, with many pilots having flown over 800 missions by the end of the war. Twenty-three Night Witches were awarded the Hero of the Soviet Union medal. Thirty-two of the 588th Night Bomber Regiment died during the war.

Order of Fifinella

In November of 1944, the Women Airforce Service Pilots-WASP established the Order of Fifinella at Maxwell Air Field, one month before the WASP program was deactivated. The purpose of the organization was to disseminate information about re-employment opportunities, to maintain communication among the WASP, to form a unified organization to influence legislation, and to encourage potential employers in aviation. By December 20, 1944, the organization had 300 members. By 1945, membership was over 700. Officers were appointed with an advisory council with representatives from all the WASP classes. The organization grew in membership, produced bi-annual newsletters, coordinated reunions across the country, and maintained a roster for all its members. In 2008, the last reunion was held in Irving, Texas. By the next year, the organization was officially dissolved.

Fifinella was a good, female gremlin adopted by the WASP as their official mascot. Fifi was painted on flight jackets, airplanes, and a symbol of WASP protection. Created by Walt Disney for an animated film, the Disney Company granted the WASP permission to use Fifinella. (Wikicommons)

Rosie the Riveters of World War II

Rosie the Riveter became a cultural symbol, representing the 6,000,000 American women who worked in factories and shipyards during World War II. Many of whom produced munitions and war supplies. Many others worked in the airplane factories and some became aircraft mechanics. After the Japanese attack on America on December 7, 1941, an increasing number of American men volunteered or were drafted for the war effort. Women were needed to fill those jobs. In recent years, the Rosie the Riveter image has become a symbol for women in the workforce and of female independence.

Iconic image to inspire American women of World War II. (Library of Congress)

The Ninety-Nines, Inc.: International Organization of Women Pilots

On November 2, 1929, twenty-six female aviators launched The Ninety-Nines, International Organization of Women Pilots. Amelia Earhart was their first President. (Library of Congress)

On November 2, 1929, at Curtiss Field in Long Island, Amelia Earhart invited the other 116 licensed women pilots to join a new international organization to provide networking, mentoring, and flight scholarships for women. Although twenty-six women attended that initial meeting, a total of ninety-nine women expressed interest in joining the organization. Hence the name, Ninety-Nines, was adopted. Amelia served as the first President. This legendary organization for women pilots in now worldwide. Even today, the Amelia Earhart Memorial Scholarship and Award program follows the original mission of support of the new generation of women pilots through education, mutual support, and sharing the passion for flight. In addition to a worldwide network of Chapters, the organization supports the Museum of Women Pilots, Amelia Earhart Birthplace Museum, mentoring programs, and promotes aviation careers.

Charter Members of the Ninety-Nines

Mary C. Alexander	Melba M. Gorby	Blanche W. Noyes
Mary Bacon	Geraldine Grey	Gladys O'Donnell
Barbara W. Bancroft	Candis I. Hall	Margaret F. O'Mara
Bernice C. Blake	Sacha Peggy Hall	Phoebe Fairgrave Omlie
Ruth T. Bridewell	Ruth E. Halliburton	Neva Paris
Margery H. Brown	Frances Marsalis Harrell	Peggie J. Paxson
Myrtle Brown	Lady Mary Heath	Achsa Barnwell Peacock
Vera Brown	Jean David Hoyt	Elizabeth F. Place
Thelma Burleigh	Katherine F. Johnson	Lillian Porter
Myrtle R. Caldwell	Angela L. Joseph	Thea Rasche
Ruth Elder Camp	Mildred E. A. Kauffman	Mathilda J. Ray
Mildred Helene Chase	Betsy Kelly	Meta Rothholz
Irene J. Chassey	Madeline B. Kelly	Gertrude Catherine Ruland
Bonnie M. Chittenden	Cecil "Teddy" Kenyon	Joan Fay Shankle
Marion Clarke	Cecelia Kenny	Hazel Mark Spanagle
Margaret Perry Cooper	Florence E. Klingensmith	Ruth W. Stewart
Helen V. Cox	Opal Logan Kunz	Marjorie G. Stinson
Jean Davidson	Eleanore B. Lay	Mildred Stinaff
Jane Dodge	Eva May Lange	Dorothy L. Stacker
Marjorie Doig	Jean LaRene	Louise M. Thaden
Amelia Earhart	Dorothea Leh	Margaret Thomas
Thelma Elliott	Marjorie May Lesser	Nancy Hopkins Tier
Frances Ferguson	Ethel Lovelace	Evelyn "Bobbi" Trout
Sarah Fenno	Lola L. Lutz	Esther M. Vance
Adeline F. Fiset	Edwyna McConnell	Mary E. Von Mach
Phyllis Fleet	Retha McCulloh	Wilma L. Walsh
Edith Foltz	Helen Manning	Vera Dawn Walker
Ila Fox	Olivia "Keet" Matthews	E. Ruth Webb
Viola Gentry	Jessie Keith-Miller	Nora Alma White
Betty Huyler Gillies	Agnes A. Mills	Nellie Z. Willhite
Fay Gillis	Sylvia Anthony Nelson	Margaret Willis
Phyllis M. Goddard	Ruth Nichols	Josephine Chatten Wood
Mary Goodrich	Mary N. Nicholson	Alberta B. Worley

U.S. Air Force UPT Class 77-08- First Women Aviators of the Undergraduate Pilot Training Program

On September 2, 1977, ten female U.S. Air Force officers earned their Silver Wings as graduates of the Undergraduate Pilot Training Program (UPT) at Williams Air Force Base in Arizona. Graduates include: Captain Connie Engel, Captain Kathy La Sauce, Captain Mary Donahue, Captain Susan Rogers, Captain Christine Schott (Schott is the first woman in the U.S. Air Force to qualify and serve as an aircraft commander), 1st Lt. Sandra Scott, 1st Lt. Victoria Crawford, 2nd Lt. Mary Livingston, 2nd Lt. Carol Scherer, and 2nd Lt. Kathleen Rambo. These U.S. Air Force aviators completed their training with 36 male colleagues, becoming the first female military aviators in the United States Air Force.

In 2016, the entire UPT Class 77-08 of ten U.S. Air Force female pilots was inducted in the Women in Aviation Pioneer Hall of Fame. (U.S. Air Force photograph)

U.S. Army First Women Rotary Wing Aviators

On June 4, 1974, U.S. Army officer, Sally D. Murphy, became the first female U.S. Army helicopter pilot to graduate from Rotary Wing Flight School at Fort Rucker, Alabama. During the early 1970s, four Army lieutenants and five warrant officers proved women had a place in military aviation and blazed the sky trail for future generations of Army women aviators. In addition to Murphy, Linda Horan DuMoulin, Susan Dunwoody Schoeck, Beverly Birkholtz, and Warrant Officers Jennie Vallance, Diane Dowd, Susan Boring, LaVern Farnsworth, and Mary Reid earned U.S. Army Aviator Wings.

Each has a unique story of persistence to earn their wings. Army pilots assist with both offensive and defensive operations. They perform air assaults in addition to transporting both cargo and personnel. Recently, Women in Aviation International inducted the U.S. Army First Women Rotary Wing Aviators into their Pioneer Hall of Fame. These pioneering, military helicopter aviators had what author, Shannon Huffman Polson, the Army's first female attack helicopter pilot, calls "The Grit Factor." These pathbreakers opened the sky for today's U.S. Army women aviators.

U.S. Coast Guard First Black American Female Pilots aka "Fab Five"

On March 4, 1977, U.S. Coast Guard Lt. Janna Lambine became the first woman to earn Gold Wings in fixed wing aviation. Janna was the only female in a class of 400. She transferred to U.S. Coast Guard Helicopter training. Soon, she was rated to fly the U.S. Coast Guard Sikorsky-61 helicopter in search and rescue.

It was not until June 24, 2005, that Jeanine Menze became the first Black American female to earn U.S. Coast Guard Aviation designation in the HC-130 Hercules. Soon, four other African American women joined the U.S. Coast Guard Aviation ranks. La'Shanda Holmes became the first Black female helicopter pilot, flying a MH-65 Dolphin. Next, Chanel Lee, Angel Hughes, and Ronaqua Russell joined U.S. Coast Guard aviation. Soon, these five Black female pilots were called "Fab Five."

Each aviator has her own unique path and story. All five are frequent speakers sharing the exciting opportunities for women who fly. In 2019, Lt. Ronaqua Russell, became the first African American woman aviator in the U.S. Coast Guard to earn an Air Medal. Flying during Hurricanes, Harvey, Maria, and Irma, in an Ocean Sentry-HC-144, Russell provided life-saving equipment and personnel in the storm-damaged areas. Today, the Fab Five continue to serve. Lt. Cdr. Menze currently flies the C-130. Lt. Cdr. Holmes flies the H-65. Lt. Cdr. Lee is also a helicopter pilot flying the H-60. Lt. Cdr. Hughes serves as an aircraft commander and instructor pilot on the C-144. In 2015, Angel Hughes founded Sisters of the Skies, Inc. (SOS), a 501 (c)-3 national aviation organization, composed of "women of color cultivating and promoting minority women in the aviation industry through scholarship, mentorship, and most of all emotional support." This organization works to support and inspire more Black females to enter the aviation workforce. The U.S. Coast Guard Fab Five obviously lives the motto, *Semper Paratus*-Always Ready!

U.S. Marine Corps First Class of Women Aviators

In 1993, as soon as the U.S. Marine Corps opened aviation slots for female Marines to apply, Sarah Deal boldly applied. In college, Sarah had earned her single and multi-engine ratings. She performed very well on the Kent State Precision Flight Team. In 1992, after graduating with a Bachelor of Science in Aerospace Flight Technology, Deal entered the U.S. Marine Corps as a Second Lieutenant. The U.S. Marine Corps sent her to Air Traffic Control School. When selected by the U.S. Marine Corps for Naval Aviation training, Sarah began flight training in a Beechcraft T-34C Turbo Mentor at Pensacola Naval Air Station. Quickly, Sarah moved from this single-engine trainer to the TH-57 Sea Ranger helicopter for more advanced training in rotary wing. On April 21, 1995, Sarah earned her aviators wings. Sarah Deal became the U.S. Marine Corps first woman aviator qualified for the rotary wing. Sarah qualified to pilot the Sikorsky Super Stallion, the Marine Corps primary heavy-lift helicopter.

Nine trailblazing women joined Sarah "Dimes" Deal as U.S. Marine Aviators: Traci "Powder" Hoffman, Susan "Xena" Jenkins, Melinda "Tink" Rizer Gould, Alison "Rocky" Thompson, Donna "Gidget" Hesterman, Karen Fuller "Stump" Brannen, Jeanne "Xena"

Woodfin, Keri "NAG" Berman, and Christine "Mulan" Westrich. In 2021, these ten U.S. Marine Aviators were inducted into the WAI Pioneer Hall of Fame.

U.S. Navy First Class of Women Aviators

In 1974, the U.S. Navy was the first of the military services to open aviator training slots for women. The first class of Women Naval Aviators to earn their Naval Aviation Wings of Gold are: Barbara Ann Allen, Joellen Drag, Rosemary Merims (Mariner), Judith Neuffer, Jane Skiles, and Ana Marie Scott. These six became the first women to be designated full-fledged U.S. Navy pilots. Their determination and success made it possible for subsequent female naval aviators. In 2017, Women in Aviation International honored the U.S. Navy First Class of Women Aviators with inclusion into their Pioneer Hall of Fame.

WAFS Women's Auxiliary Ferrying Squadron

On September, 10, 1942, with the support of the U.S. Air Transport Command, experienced aviator, Nancy Harkness Love, was appointed Commander of the new Women's Auxiliary Ferry Squadron (WAFS). The purpose of the WAFS was delivery of planes from the factory to military bases. The female pilots were Civilian Civil Service Employees. The women had to pay for their WAFS uniform. They paid their own transportation costs to the WAFS Delaware Headquarters at New Castle Army Air Base.

> *When everything seems to be coming against you, just remember airplanes take off against the wind, not with it.*

The WAFS were recruited from among commercially licensed American women pilots with at least 500 hours flying time and a 200-

hp rating. WAFS pilots selected actually averaged about 1,100 hours of flying experience. Many were flight instructors. The first woman to qualify and join as a WAFS pilot was Betty Gillies. During the WAFS existence, no more than 25 to 28 women flew. However, many of the WAFS were historic. A few were: Nancy E. Batson, Bernice Batton, Delphine Bohn, Cornelia Fort, Barbara Erickson, Teresa James, Gertrude Meserve, and Evelyn Sharp.

Although their original mission was to ferry U.S. Army Air Corps trainers and light aircraft from the factories, soon they were delivering fighters, bombers, and transports. Betty Gillies and Nancy Love became the first women to pilot and ferry the Boeing B-17 Flying Fortress, four-engine heavy bomber. The WAFS members made significant contribution toward winning World War II.

In August, 1943, a new organization was created, the Women Airforce Service Pilots (WASP). The WAFS were merged with the Women's Flying Training Detachment (WFTD), which was under the leadership of Jacqueline Cochran. Many of the original WAFS members joined the WASP-Women Airforce Service Pilots.

WAFS commander and pilot, Nancy Harkness Love, with B-17 Flying Fortress bomber named "Queen Bee." (National Archives)

WASP Women Airforce Service Pilots

Because of World War II, in August, 1943, the Women Airforce Service Pilots-WASP were formed with the merger of the Women's Auxiliary Ferrying Squadron (WAFS) and the Women's Flying Training Detachment (WFTD. Although flying under military command, the women pilots of the WASP were classified as civilians. They were paid through the civil service. The WASP had to pay their own transportation to Avenger Field in Texas. They were charged room and board which was deducted from their monthly pay.

Women Airforce Service Pilots, Frances Green, Margaret "Peg" Kirchner, Ann Waldner, and Blanche Osborn, leave their B-17 Flying Fortress aircraft, "Pistol Packin' Mama," during their ferry training at Lockbourne Army Airfield, Ohio, 1944. (U.S. Air Force archival photograph)

When Jacqueline Cochran called for patriotic women to apply for the WASP, over 25,000 American women answered. Only 1,879 women were selected for the 27-week training at Avenger Airfield.

During the 16-months of the WASP existence, 18 classes graduated 1,074 WASP. These pilots became the first women in American history to fly military aircraft. WASP flew every type of U.S. Army Air Force airplane--from trainers, target tow planes, fighters, and bombers, and even tested experimental equipment. They flew over 60 million miles in ferrying 12,000 new and repaired aircraft from the factories and repair stations to military bases.

The WASP flew military aircraft and military personnel from 120 Army Air Bases across America. The only woman to receive the Air Medal throughout all of World War II was WASP Barbara Erickson London. She flew a five-day, 8,000 mile air mission. Barbara first delivered a DC-3 from her Long Beach, California base to Fort Wayne, Indiana. There, she picked up P-47 Thunderbolt for delivery to California. Next, Barbara flew a P-51 Mustang to Fort Wayne, Indiana again. She picked up yet another P-47 to fly to Long Beach again. On the last leg of this whirlwind mission, she flew a P-61 Black Widow to Sacramento.

During WASP training or on air missions, thirty-eight died. Because WASP were considered civilians, the military did not pay to have their remains shipped home to their families for burial. Often, the other WASP donated money, if the family could not afford the cost. Those 38 families were not even allowed to display the traditional Gold Star in their window, indicating a family member lost their life while serving our Nation in the armed forces. In 1977, it took Congressional action for WASP to retroactively have veteran status and benefits. It was not until 1984, almost 40 years after the end of World War II, that WASP were awarded their World War II Victory Medal. For those serving more than a year, they were awarded the American Theater Medal. In 2010, WASP were awarded the Congressional Gold Medal, the highest civilian expression of National appreciation, for their World War II contributions. Today, the stories of our World War II WASP continue to inspire.

Whirly Girls International Women Helicopter Pilots

Founded on April 28, 1955, the Whirly Girls, International Women Helicopter Pilots, began with only thirteen members: Hanna Reitsch from Germany (1938 first woman in the world to fly a helicopter); Ann Carter (America's first woman helicopter pilot); Pat Swenson; Nancy Livingston Stratford (1947 helicopter rating); Marilyn "Lyn" Grover Heard Alexander; Dr. Valerie Andre (highly decorated French pilot and physician); Ethel Sheffler; Jacqueline Auriol (French Record-setting aviator), Marilyn Himes Riviere (U.S. first woman helicopter instructor); Edna Gardner Whyte; Clara Livingston; Mary Rosholt; and Jean Howard-Phelan (Founder and Whirly Girls President, 1959-73).

Dora Jean Dougherty Strother, Whirly Girl #27, was a World War II WASP and B-29 Superfortress demonstration pilot. In 1961, as a Bell Helicopter test pilot, she broke a helicopter altitude record (at 19,406 feet) in a Bell 47G-3. She is congratulated by Bell chief test pilot, R.C. Buyers, (at left) and company president, E.J. Ducayet, (at right). She earned the first doctorate in aviation science from New York University and received many awards during her career for achievements in flight and engineering. In 1979-81, Dr. Dora Jean Dougherty Strother was Whirly Girls President. (Smithsonian Institution archive)

A unique feature of the Whirly-Girls organization is that each member is assigned a number upon joining that is hers forever. The Whirly Girls logo was inspired by a U.S. Army helicopter recruiting show in the early 1950s. Four helicopters performed a square dance, choreographed to the song, "Turkey in the Straw." Two of the helicopters were painted with big cartoon character, "Betty Boop," eyes with blonde mops for hair to represent female helicopters. The now iconic logo is sported today by almost 2,000 Whirly Girls members worldwide.

In 1968, a scholarship program in memory of Doris Mullen (WG #84) began. Over the years, Whirly Girls has expanded flight training scholarships. In the early years, a major initiative of the International Women Helicopter Pilots was medical and hospital heliport development and expanded use of helicopters in medical and emergency services. In 1998, Women in Aviation International honored Whirly Girls in their Pioneer Hall of Fame.

Your attitude definitely determines your altitude.

Women Flyers of America

In April, 1941, Women Flyers of America, Inc. (WFA) was founded. Women Flyers of America membership was open to any woman with any interest in aviation. The original founders were Opal Kunz, an early aviator and charter member of the Ninety-Nines, and Chelle Janis, first woman manager of the New York Aviation Training Academy. In August, 1940, Vita Roth, a WFA member and 1920s women's parachute jumping record holder, took over leadership. Vita found members were younger, between 20 to 35 years of age, were working, were adventurous, and were concerned about national defense. WFA focused on training opportunities and lower cost flight instruction. Soon, WFA became a national organization with chapters all over America. By December 1941 American women wanted to contribute to the war effort. Local training in flight schools, air traffic control, parachute-rigging, and an All-Women's Aircraft and Engine Mechanics training program at Teterboro airport propelled the growth of WFA chapters. Women Flyers of America ceased operations in 1954 in the post-war years.

Women in Aviation International-WAI

Women in Aviation International is a worldwide nonprofit organization to provide networking, education, mentoring, scholarships, and career opportunities in aviation and aerospace. WAI began with Dr. Peggy Baty Chabrian, the Dean of Academic Support at Embry-Riddle Aeronautical University in Prescott, Arizona. In 1990, the first annual conference was held. The headliners were Moya Lear, Jeana Yeager, Dr. Shannon Lucid, and Bobbi Trout. With this momentum, an informal organization was created.

By 1994, WAI was formally incorporated. By 1996, Dr. Chabrian was named CEO and the first full-time President by the WAI Board of Directors. By 1998, WAI had 3,000 members. Chapters are now International, providing mentoring to women and students. Over the years, the mission has expanded from the annual conference which draws thousands to network, learn, and meet with industry leaders. In 1992, the WAI Pioneer Hall of Fame began highlighting the many notable women in the aviation and aerospace industry. By 2015, the annual Girls in Aviation Day, held on the last Saturday in September, reaches thousands of girls from eight to 17.

Over the years, WAI has expanded its professional development and scholarship opportunities which has become a major benefit of membership. In just over thirty years, WAI has become a powerhouse of innovation and industry leadership.

Women Military Aviators-WMA

Formed in 1978, WMA promotes and preserves the historic role of women aviators, navigators, and aircrew in the service of their country during war and peace. Membership is worldwide. Networking, mentoring and support of women in military aviation are key missions of WMA.

In addition to electronic publications, WMA members gather annually at the Women in Aviation International conference, at local luncheons, informal networking meetings, and at WMA Biennial Convention. A scholarship program for women pursuing an aviation degree or pilot license is offered.

Aviation is still considered a man's world by many. The time to reach young ladies is during their first years of school. Research has shown that although children may change their minds several times about their eventual careers, the possibilities of them selecting a non-traditional role must be nurtured at an early age.

~ Dr. Peggy Baty Chabrian, founder of Women in Aviation International

AFTERWORD

By Cindy Lovell, Ph.D.

In 1999, Danny and Amy Perna established Epic Flight Academy in New Smyrna Beach, Florida. Danny is a third-generation aviator who holds an A&P certificate and CFII. When the Pernas first opened as Epic Aviation, they were the complete staff. The fleet consisted of a used Cessna 152. Danny kept the plane serviced and instructed students. Amy kept the books and ran the office. The young couple had no idea at that time how Epic would grow.

Today, Epic Flight Academy employs 115 people and trains pilots from more than 80 countries. Epic graduates are employed at 300+ airlines. Recently, we expanded to include a Part 147 aircraft mechanic school. In 2021, we launched Epic Airways, offering charters and scheduled flights.

Epic Flight Academy has been a champion of women in aviation since the beginning. Four female high school students have won Epic flight training scholarships, and several of Epic's female mechanic students also earned scholarships. We invite all aspiring aviators to apply for our generous scholarships, including full aircraft mechanic scholarships offered through Women in Aviation International, Latino Pilots Association, Organization of Black Aerospace Professionals, and the National Gay Pilots Association.

A few years ago, Epic began painting the tails of its training aircraft pink for breast cancer awareness. Pilots in the New Smyrna Beach area commented how distinctive these were and easier to spot. This evolved into the practice of painting all of Epic's tails bright red in the interest of safety. Epic is also known as the site of a special aviation landmark:

a decommissioned DC-7 that was once part of the American Airlines fleet. We invite you to stop by and see this vintage aircraft.

When we learned of Penny Rafferty Hamilton's latest project, *101 Trailblazing Women of Air and Space*, we were eager to support her work. Penny has been inspiring females in the profession of aviation for many years, as has Captain Judy Rice, who penned the foreword for this important book. We salute both of these inspiring ladies for their dedication to the field of aviation.

Here at Epic Flight Academy, we continue our practice of training and hiring female pilots and mechanics. You've met some inspiring ladies in this book. We now invite you to join them in the most exciting profession of all: aviation.

Cindy Lovell, Ph.D., Director of Education Epic Flight Academy, New Smyrna Beach, Florida

https://epicflightacademy.com/

Epic Flight Academy promotes aviation history with the outdoor display of the iconic Douglas Aircraft Company DC-7 low-wing, four-radial engine airliner. (Photographer Cindy Lovell)

EXPLORE MORE

Books about/by Trailblazers

These stories bring our collective experiences to life in the minds of readers--our history, our challenges, and our successes. ~ Liz Booker, retired U.S. Coast Guard helicopter pilot and creator of The Aviatrix Book Review.

Ackmann, Martha, foreword by Lynn Sherr. *The Mercury 13: The True Story of thirteen women and the dream of space flight.* New York: Random House Trade Paperbacks reprint edition, 2004.

Albion, Michele Wehrwein, editor. *The Quotable Amelia Earhart.* Albuquerque, NM: University of New Mexico Press, 2015.

Anderson, Nina. *Flying Above the Glass Ceiling: Inspirational Stories of Success from the First Women Pilots to Fly Airline and Corporate Aircraft.* Garden City NY: Square One Publishers, 2009.

Ansari, Anousheh with Homer Hickman. *My Dream of Stars: From Daughter of Iran to Space Pioneer.* New York: St. Martin's Press, 2010.

Aragon, Cecilia. *Flying Free: My Victory over Fear to Become the First Latina Pilot on the US Aerobatic Team.* Ashland OR: Blackstone Publishing, 2020.

Arlen, Alice. *The Huntress: The Adventurers, Escapades, and Triumphs of Alicia Patterson: Aviatrix, Sportswoman, Journalist, Publisher.* New York: Pantheon, 2016.

Armstrong, Erika. *A Chick in the Cockpit: My Life Up in the Air.* Coraopolis, PA: Behler Publications, 2005.

Atkins, Jeannine. *Wings and Rockets: The Story of Women in Air and Space*. New York: Farrar, Straus, and Giroux, 2003.

Bartels, Diane Ruth Armour. *Sharpie: The Life Story of Evelyn Sharp-Nebraska's Aviatrix*. Lincoln NE: Great Americans Publishing, 2005.

Bondar, Roberta. *Touching the Earth*. Toronto, Canada: Key Porter Books, 1994.

Borden, Louise and Mary Kay Kroeger. *Fly High! The Story of Bessie Coleman*. New York: Aladdin, 2004.

Bosca, Caro Bayley. *Women Airforce Service Pilots, Class of 43-W-7: Letters 1943-44*. Denton TX: Texas Woman's University Special Collections, 1995.

Bower, Jennifer Bean, foreword by Cris Takacs. *North Carolina Aviatrix Viola Gentry: The Flying Cashier*. Charleston, SC: The History Press, 2015.

Bragg, Janet Harmon as told to Marjorie M. Kriz. *Soaring Above Setbacks: The Autobiography of Janet Harmon Bragg*. Washington, DC: Smithsonian Institute Press, 1997.

Bridges, Donna, Jane Neal-Smith and Albert Mills, editors. *Absent Aviators: Gender Issues in Aviation*. London: Ashgate Publishing, 2014, paperback edition 2020.

Briggs, Carole S. *Women in Space: Reaching the last frontier*. Minneapolis, MN: Lerner Publications, 1988.

Burgess, Colin, foreword by Grace George Corrigan. *Teacher in Space: Christa McAuliff and the Challenger Legacy*. Lincoln, NE: University of Nebraska Press, 2020.

Butler, Susan. *East to the Dawn: The Life of Amelia Earhart*. New York: Da Capo Press, 1999.

Cadogan, Mary. *Women with Wings: Female Flyers in Fact and Fiction*. Chicago: Chicago Academy Publishers, 1993.

Carl, Ann Baumgartner. *A WASP Among Eagles*. Washington DC: Smithsonian Institution Press, 1999.

Cavallaro, Umberto. *Women Spacefarers: Sixty Different Paths to Space*. New York: Springer Praxis Books, 2017.

Clark, Julie with Ann Lewis Cooper. *Nothing Stood in Her Way: Captain Julie Clark*. West Alexandria, OH: Women in Aviation Intl., 2004.

Cobb, Jerrie. *Jerrie Cobb, Solo Pilot*. Sun City Center, FL: Jerrie Cobb Foundation, Inc., 1997.

Cobb, Jerrie and Jane Rieker. *Woman Into Space: The Jerrie Cobb Story*. Whitefish, MT: Literary Licensing LLC, 2012.

Collins, Col. Eileen M. with Jonathan H. Ward. *Through the Glass Ceiling to the Stars: The Story of the First American Woman to Command a Space Mission*. New York: Arcade Publishing, 2021.

Cooper, Ann Lewis. *Weaving the Winds, Emily Howell Warner*. Bloomington, IN: 1st Books Library, 2003.

Cooper, Ann Lewis and art by Sharon Rajnus. *Stars of the Sky, Legends All: Illustrated Histories of Women Aviation Pioneers*. St. Paul, MN: Zenith Press, 2008.

Cox, Jessica. *Disarm Your Limits: The Flight Formula to Lift You to Success and Propel You to the Next Horizon*. Rightfooted Publishing: Tucson AZ, 2005.

Cummins, Julie with illustrations by Marlene R. Laugesen. *Flying Solo: How Ruth Elder Soared into America's Heart*. New York: Roaring Brook Press, 2013.

Cummins, Julie. *Tomboy of the Air: Daredevil Pilot Blanche Stuart Scott*. New York: HarperCollins Publishers LLC, 2001.

Diehn, Andi and Katie Mazeika illustrator. *Space Adventurer: Bonnie Dunbar, Astronaut*. White River Junction VT: Nomad Press, 2019.

Donnelly, Karen J. *American Women Pilots of World War II*. New York: Rosen Publishing Group, 2004.

Douglas, Deborah G. *American Women and Flight since 1940*. Lexington, KY: University Press of Kentucky, 2004.

Draude, Loree and Dave Hirschman. *She's Just Another Naval Pilot: An Aviator's Sea Journal*. Newport RI: U.S. Naval Institute Press, Updated 2020.

Duckworth, Tammy. *Every Day is a Gift: A Memoir*. New York. Twelve, 2021.

Earhart, Amelia. *20 Hours, 40 Minutes: Our Flight in the Friendship*. Washington DC: National Geographic reprint edition, 2003.

Ellis, Mary as told to Melody Foreman. *A Spitfire Girl: One of the World's Greatest Female ATA Ferry Pilots Tells Her Story*. Barnsley UK: Frontline Books, reprint edition 2019.

Erisman, Fred. *From Birdwomen to Skygirls: American girls' aviation stories*. Fort Worth TX: Texas Christian University Press, 2009.

---*In Their Own Words: Forgotten Women Pilots of Early Aviation*. West Lafayette IN: Purdue University Press, 2021.

Fleming, Candace. *Amelia lost: the Life and Disappearance of Amelia Earhart*. New York: Schwartz & Wade Books, 2011.

Freni, Pamela. *Space for Women: A History of Women with the Right Stuff*. Santa Ana, CA: Seven Locks Press, 2002.

Funk, Wally as told to Loretta Hall, foreword by Eileen Collins. *Higher Faster Longer: My Life in Aviation and My Quest for Spaceflight*. Franklin, TN: Traitmaker Books, 2020.

Garratt, CarolAnn. *Upon Silver Wings: Global Adventures in a Small Plane*. Ocala FL: Garratt Publisher, 2004.

---. *Upon Silver Wings II: World Record Adventures*. Ocala FL: Garratt Publisher, 2009.

---.*Upon Silver Wings III: People and Places Around the World*. Ocala FL: Garratt Publisher, 2012.

Garstecki, Julia. *WASPS*. North Mankato MN: Black Rabbit Books, 2017.

Gibson, Karen Bush. *Women Aviators: 26 Stories of Pioneer Flights, Daring Missions, and Record-Setting Journeys*. Chicago: Chicago Review Press, 2013.

---. *Women in Space: 23 Stories of First Flights, Scientific Missions, and Gravity-Breaking Adventures*. Chicago: Chicago Review Press, 2020.

Gosnell, Mariana. *Zero 3 Bravo: Solo Across America in a Small Plane*. New York: Knopf, 1993.

Hale, Julian. *Women in Aviation*. London: Shire Publications, 2019.

Hall, Ed. Y. *Harriet Quimby: America's First Lady of the Air.* Spartanburg, SC: Honoribus Press, 1990.

Hall, Loretta. *Space Pioneers in their own words.* Rio Grande Books, 2014.

Hamilton, Penny Rafferty. *Inspiring Words for Sky and Space Women: Advice from Historic and Contemporary Trailblazers.* Granby, CO: Mountaintop Legacy Press, 2020.

Harris, Grace McAdams. *West to Sunrise.* Ames IA: Iowa State University Press, 1980.

Harrison, Jean-Pierre. *The Edge of Time: The Authoritative Biography of Kalpana Chawla.* Los Gatos, CA: Harrison Publishing, 2011.

Haydu, Bernice "Bee" Falk. *Letters Home 1944-1945: Women Airforce Service Pilots.* Jupiter, FL: TopLine Printing and Graphics, 2003.

Haynsworth, Leslie and David Toomey. *Amelia Earhart's Daughters: The Wild and Glorious Story of American Women Aviators from World War II to the Dawn of the Space Age.* New York: Perennial, 1998.

Hegar, Mary Jennings. *Shoot like a Girl: One woman's dramatic fight in Afghanistan and on the home front.* New York: Berkley, 2018.

Hertog, Susan. *Anne Morrow Lindbergh: Her Life.* New York: Anchor Books, 2000.

Hickson, Mandy. *An Officer Not a Gentleman: The inspirational journey of a pioneering female fighter pilot.* Independently published, 2020.

Hodgman, Ann, and Rudy Djabbaroff. *Sky Stars: the History of Women in Aviation.* New York, NY: Atheneum, 1981.

Hodgson, Marion Stegeman. *Winning My Wings: A Woman Airforce Service Pilot in World War II.* Annapolis, MD: Naval Institute Press, 1996.

Holden, Henry with Captain Lori Griffith. *Ladybirds: The Untold Story of Women Pilots in America.* Freedom, NJ: Black Hawk Publishing Co., 1991.

Holden, Henry with Lori Griffith. *Ladybirds II-The Continuing Story of Women in Aviation.* Freedom, NJ: Black Hawk Publishing Company, 1993.

Holden, Henry M. *Hovering: The History of the Whirly-Girls: International Women Helicopter Pilots.* Freedom NJ: Black Hawk Publishing Company, 1994.

---Women in Aviation: *Leaders and Role Models for the 21st Century.* Freedom, NJ: Black Hawk Publishing Company, 2001.

Howden, Sarah, Illustrator Nick Craisen. *Roberta Bondar: Space Explorer.* Honley, Great Britain: Collins, 2020..

Hyams, Jacky foreword by Richard Poad MBE. *The Female Few: Spitfire Heroines.* Cheltenham, England: The History Press, 2016.

Jackson, Libby. *Galaxy Girls: 50 Amazing Stories of Women in Space.* New York: Harper Design, 2018.

Jaros, Dean. *Heroes without Legacy: American Airwomen, 1912-1944.* Niwot: University Press of Colorado, 1993.

Jemison, Mae. *Find Where the Wind Goes: Moments from My Life.* New York: Scholastic Press, 2001.

Jessen, Gene Nora. *Powder Puff Derby of 1929: The True Story of the First Women's Cross-Country Air Race.* Napierville, IL: Sourcebooks, 2002

-----*The Fabulous Flight of The Three Musketeers: A Rollicking Airplane Adventure With A Few Thrills.* Charleston, SC: BookSurge Publishing, 2009.

Jessen, Gene Nora, foreword by Eileen Collins. *Sky Girls: The True Story of the First Women's Cross-Country Air Race.* Naperville, IL: Sourcebooks, 2018.

Johnson, Caroline with Hof Williams. *Jet Girl: My Life in War, Peace, and the Cockpit of the Navy's Most Lethal Aircraft, the F/A-18 Super Hornet.* New York: St. Martin's Press, 2019.

Kennard, Gaby. *Solo Woman: Gaby Kennard's World Flight.* New York: Bantam Books, 1990.

Kerr, Leslie. *Harriet Quimby: Flying Fair Lady.* Atglen PA: Schiffer Publishing, 2016.

Kessler, Lauren. *The Happy Bottom Riding Club: The Life and Times of Pancho Barnes*. New York: Random House, 2000.

Kevles, Bettyann Holtzmann. *Almost Heaven: The Story of Women in Space*. Cambridge MA: The MIT Press, 2006.

Krasner, Helen. *The Helicopter Pilot's Companion: A Manual for Helicopter Enthusiasts*. Wiltsshire, Great Britain: The Crowood Press, 2014.

Lambert, Paul F. *Never Give Up! The Life of Pearl Carter Scott*. Ada OK: The Chickasaw Press, 2009.

Landdeck, Katherine Sharp. *The Women with Silver Wings: The Inspiring True Story of the Women Airforce Service Pilots of World War II*. New York: Crown, 2020.

Lang, Heather and Raul Colon illustrator. *Fearless Flyer: Ruth Law and Her Flying Machine*. Westminster, MD: Calkins Creek, 2016.

Langley, Wanda. *Flying Higher: The Women Airforce Service Pilots of World War II*. Linnet Books, 2002.

Larson, Kirsten W. and Tracy Subisak illustrator. *Wood, Wire, Wings: Emma Lilian Todd Invents an Airplane*. Toronto: Calkins Creek, 2020.

Lebow, Eileen F. *Before Amelia: Women Pilots in the Early Days of Aviation*. Washington, DC: Brassey's Inc., 2002.

Lohrenz, Carey D. *Fearless Leadership: High-Performance Lessons from the Flight Deck (second edition)*. Excelsior, MN: CareyLohrenz Enterprises, 2018.

London, Martha. *Bessie Coleman: Bold Pilot Who Gave Women Wings*. North Mankato MN: Capstone Press, 2020.

Lovell, Mary S. *Straight On Till Morning: the Biography of Beryl Markham*. New York: St. Martin's Press, 1987.

Maloney, Linda (editor). *Military Fly Moms: Sharing Memories, Building Legacies, Inspiring Hope*. Tannenbaum Publishing Co, 2012.

Markhan, Beryl. *West with the Night*. Boston, MA: Houghton Mifflin Company, 1942.

Mason, Fergus. *Night Witches: A History of the All Female 588th Night Bomber Regiment*. Anaheim, CA: History Caps, 2014.

McCarthy, Meghan. *Daredevil: The Daring Life of Betty Skelton*. Holland OH: Dreamscape Media, 2013.

McSally, Martha. *Dare to Fly: Simple Lessons in Never Giving Up*. New York: William Morrow & Company, 2020.

Meloche, Renee Taft and illustrator, Bryan Pollard. *Betty Greene: Flying High* (Heroes for Young Readers series). Seattle WA: YWAM Publishing, 2004.

Merry, Lois K. *Women Military Pilots of World War II: A History with Biographies of American, British, Russian, and German Aviators*. Jefferson, NC: McFarland & Co., 2011.

Merryman, Molly. *Clipped Wings: The Rise and Fall of the Women Airforce Service Pilots (WASPs) of World War II*. New York: New York University Press, 1998.

Mextel, Kathy. *Australian Women Pilots: Amazing True Stories of Women in the Air*. Sydney, Australia: NewSouth Publishing, 2021.

Miller, William M. *To Live and Die a WASP: 38 Women Pilots Who Died in WWII*, Seattle WA: CreateSpace Independent Publishing Platform, 2016.

Mitchell, Charles R. and Kirk W. House. *Flying High: Pioneer Women in American Aviation*. Charleston, SC: Arcadia Publishing, 2002.

Mock, Jerrie. *Three-Eight-Charlie: 1st Woman to Fly Solo around the World-1964*. Phoenix, AZ: Phoenix Graphix Publishing Services, 2014.

Moggridge, Jackie. *Spitfire Girl: My Life in the Sky*. London: Head of Zeus, 2015.

Morey, Eileen. *The Importance of Amelia Earhart*. San Diego: Lucent Books, 1995.

Muir, Elizabeth Gillan. *Canadian Women in the Sky: 100 Years of Flight*. Toronto Canada: Dundurn Group, 2015.

Mulley, Clare. *The Women Who Flew for Hitler: The True Story of Hitler's Valkyries*. London, England: Pan MacMillan, 2017.

Myles, Bruce. *Night Witches: The Amazing Story of Russia's Women Pilots in World War II.* Chicago: Academy Chicago Publishers, 1997 edition.

Nathan, Amy, foreword by NASA Astronaut Eileen Collings. *Yankee Doodle Gals: Women Pilots of World War II.* Washington, DC: National Geographic Society, 2001.

Nelson, Sue. *Wally Funk's Race for Space: The Extraordinary Story of a Female Aviation Pioneer.* London: The Westbourne Press, 2019.

Nesch, Sonya. *WWII, Betrayal, Then Congressional Gold Medal: A Great Ride for WASP Jean Landis.* London: Trillium Press, 2019.

Nichols, Ruth, foreword by Richard E. Byrd, Dorothy Roe Lewis editor. *Wings for Life: The Life Story of the First Lady of the Air.* Philadelphia: J.D. Lippincott, 1957.

Noggle, Anne, introduction by Christine A. White. *A Dance with Death: Soviet Airwomen in World War II World's First Women Combat Fliers!* College Station, TX: Texas A & M University Press, 2001.

Nolen, Stephanie. *Promised The Moon: The Untold Story of the first Women in the Space Race.* New York: Thunder's Mouth Press, 2004.

Oakes, Claudia M. *United States Women in Aviation through World War I. Smithsonian Studies in Air and Space, vol. 2.* Washington, DC: Smithsonian Institution Press, 1978.

----- *United States Women in Aviation, 1930-1939.* Washington, DC; Smithsonian Institution Press, 1991.

O'Brien, Keith. *Fly Girls: How Five Daring Women Defied All Odds and Made Aviation History.* Boston, MA: Houghton Mifflin Harcourt, 2019.

O'Neill, Norah. *Flying Tigress: A Memoir.* Seattle, WA: Ascending Journey Press, 2005.

O'Shaughnessy, Tam. *Sally Ride: A Photobiography of America's Pioneering Woman in Space.* New York: Roaring Brook Press, 2017.

Owens, Lisa L. *Women Pilots of World War II.* Minneapolis, MN: Lerner Publishing Group, 2019.

Parrish, Nancy Allyson. *WASP: In Their Own Words: An Illustrated History.* Wings Across America Publications, 2010.

Pearson, Patricia O'Connell. *Fly Girls: The Daring American Women Pilots Who Helped Win WWII.* New York: Simon & Schuster Books for Young Readers, Reprint edition 2019.

Pellegreno, Ann Holtgreen. *World Flight: The Earhart Trail.* Ames, IO: Iowa State University Press, 1971.

Petrick, Neila Skinner, illustrated by Daggi Wallace. *Katherine Stinson Otero: High Flyer.* New Orleans, LA: Pelican Publishing Company, 2006.

Pimm, Nancy Roe and illustrator Alexandra Bye. *Fly, Girl, Fly! Shaesta Waiz Soars the World.* Minneapolis MN: Beaming Books, 2020.

Pimm, Nancy Roe. *The Jerrie Mock Story: The First Woman to Fly Solo Around the World.* Athens OH: Ohio University Press, 2016.

Polson, Shannon Huffman. *The Grit Factor: Courage, Resilience, and Leadership in the Most Male-Dominated Organization in the World.* Boston: Harvard Business Review Press, 2020.

Powell, Mary. *Queen of the Air: The Story of Katherine Stinson.* BookBaby, 2020.

Prince, Diana. *Women in Aviation.* Bloomington IN: Authorhouse, 2020.

Ramsey, Raquel and Tricia Aurand, foreword by Maj. Gen. Jeannie M. Leavitt. *Taking Flight: The Nadine Ramsey Story.* Lawrence, KS: University Press of Kansas, 2020.

Render, Shirley, foreword by Punch Dickins. *No Place For A Lady! The Story of Canadian Women Pilots, 1928-1992.* Winnipeg, Manitoba: Portage & Main Press, 1992.

Rich, Doris L. *Amelia Earhart: A Biography.* Washington, D.C. Smithsonian Books, 1996.

Rickman, Sarah Byrn. *BJ Erickson: WASP Pilot.* Palmer Lake, CO: Filter Press, LLC, 2018.

-----*The Originals: The Women's Auxiliary Ferrying Squadron of WWII.* Springboro, OH: Braughler Books LLC, 2017.

-----*Finding Dorothy Scott: Letters of a WASP*. Lubbock, TX: Texas Tech University Press, 2016.

-----*Nancy Love WASP Pilot*. Palmer Lake, CO: Filter Press LLC, 2019.

-----*Betty Gillies WAFS Pilot: The Days and Flights of a World War II Squadron Leade*r. Colorado Springs, CO: Flight to Destiny Press, 2020.

Rickman, Sarah Bryn with foreword by Deborah G. Douglas. *Nancy Love and the WASP Ferry Pilots of World War II*. Denton, TX: University of North Texas, 2008.

Rickman, Sarah Bryn with foreword by Deborah G. Douglas. *WASP of the Ferry Command: Women Pilots, Uncommon Deeds*. Denton, TX: University of North Texas Press, 2017.

Ride, Sally with Susan Okie. *To Space and Back*. New York: Lothrop, Lee & Shepard Books, 1989.

Ringenberg, Margaret J. with Jane L. Roth. *Girls Can't Be Pilots: An Aerobiography*. United Kingdom: Daedalus Press Books, 1998.

Russo, Carolyn. *Women and Flight: Portraits of Contemporary Women Pilots*. Washington, D.C.: National Air and Space Museum, 1997.

Ruzi, Jacqueline S. *Latinas in Aviation*. Naperville, IL: Fig Factor Media Publishing, 2020.

Seddon, Rhea. *Go For Orbit: One of America's First Women Astronauts Finds Her Space*. Your Space Press, 2015.

Seidemann, Erin. *Postcards from the Sky: Adventures of an Aviatrix*. Berkeley CA: She Writes Press, 2015.

Settles, Lauren Dalzell. *Could I be a Pilot? Evie's Journey to Becoming a Pilot*. Victoria BC (Canada): Friesen Press, 2020.

Sheinkin, Steve, illustrator Bijou Karman. *Born to Fly: The First Women's Air Race Across America*. New York: Roaring Brook Press, 2019.

Sherman, Janann. *Walking on Air: The Aerial Adventures of Phoebe Omlie*. Jackson MS: University Press of Mississippi, 2011.

Sherr, Lynn. *Sally Ride: America's First Woman in Space*. New York: Simon & Schuster, 2015.

Shipko, Mary Bush. *Aviatrix: First Woman Pilot for Hughes Airwest.* Seattle, WA: CreateSpace Publishing, 2015.

Shipko, Mary Bush, Kathy McCullough, Bonnie Tiburzi Caputo. *Women Who Fly: True Stories by Women Airline Pilots.* Las Vegas, NV: International Society of Women Airline Pilots, 2018.

Shults, Tammie Jo. *Nerves of Steel: How I Followed My Dreams, Earned My Wings, And Faced My Greatest Challenge.* Nashville, TN: Thomas Nelson, 2019.

Siegel, Rebecca. *To Fly Among The Stars: the Hidden Story of the Fight for Women Astronauts.* New York: Scholastic Focus, 2020.

Simons, Lisa M. Bolt. *The U.S. WASP: Trailblazing Women Pilots of World War II.* North Mankato, MN: Capstone Press, 2018.

Smith, Amber. *Danger Close: My Epic Journey as a Combat Helicopter Pilot in Iraq and Afghanistan.* New York: Atria Books, 2017.

Smith, Elinor. *Aviatrix.* New York: Harcourt Brace Jovanovich, 1981.

Smith-Daugherty, Rhonda. *Jacqueline Cochran: Biography of a Pioneer Aviator.* Jefferson, NC: McFarland Publishing, 2012.

Steadman, Bernice Trimble and Josephine M. Clark. *Tethered Mercury: A Pilot's Memoir: The Right Stuff—But the Wrong Sex.* Aviation Press, 2001.

Stone, Tanya Lee. *Almost Astronauts13 Women Who Dared to Dream.* Somerville, MA: Candlewick Press, 2009.

Stratford, Nancy Miller Livingston. *Contact! Britain! A Woman Ferry Pilot's Story during WWII in England.* Seattle WA: Createspace, 2011.

Strebe, Amy Goodpaster. *Flying for Her Country The American and Soviet Women Military Pilots of WW II.* Westport: Praeger Security International, 2007.

Sullivan, Kathryn D. *Handprints on Hubble: An Astronaut's Story of Invention.* Cambridge MA: MIT Press, 2019.

Teitel, Amy Shira. *Fighting For Space: Two Pilots and Their Historic Battle for Female Spaceflight.* New York: Grand Central Publishing, 2020.

Thaden, Louise, foreword by Patty Wagstaff. *High, Wide and Frightened.* Fayetteville AR: University of Arkansas Press, reprinted edition 2004.

Tiburzi, Bonnie. *Takeoff! The Story of America's First Woman Pilot for a Major Airline.* New York, NY: Crown Publishers, Inc., 1986.

Timofeyeva-Yegorova, Anna, Kim Green, editor, Margarita Ponomariova and Kim Green, translator. *Red Sky Black Death: A Soviet Woman Pilot's Memoir of the Eastern Front.* Bloomington IN: Slavica Publishers, 2009.

Tiscareno-Sato, Graciela, illustration by Linda Lens. *Captain Mama's Surprise/La Sorpresa de Capitan Mama.* Hayward, CA: Gracefully Global Group, LLC, 2016.

Turner, Lisa. *Dream Take Flight: An Unconventional Journey.* Hayesville NC: Turner Creek Publishing, 2019.

Turney, Mary Ann, editor. *Tapping Diverse Talent in Aviation: Culture, Gender, and Diversity.* Burlington, VT: Ashgate Publishing, 2004.

Vacher, Polly. *Wings Around the World: The Exhilarating Story of One Women's Epic Flight from the North Pole to Antarctica.* London: Grub Street Publishing, 2008.

Van Pelt, Lori. *Amelia Earhart: The Sky's No Limit.* New York: Forge Books, 2005.

Veca, Donna and Skip Mazzio. *Just Plane Crazy: Biography of Bobbi Trout.* Santa Clara, CA: Osborne Publisher, 1987.

Ventura, Marne. *12 Women in the Space Industry: Women Who Changed the World.* Mankato MN: 12-Story Library, 2020.

Verges, Marianne. *On Silver Wings: Women Airforce Service Pilots of World War II, 1942-1944.* New York: Ballantine Books, 1991.

Wagstaff, Patty with Ann L. Cooper. *Fire and Air: A Life on The Edge.* Chicago, IL: Chicago Review Press, Inc., 1997.

Walker, Diana Barnato. *Spreading My Wings.* London: Grub Street Publishing, 2008.

Wallace, Lane. *Unforgettable: My Ten Best Flights.* Batavia, OH: Sporty's Pilot Shop, 2009.

Wein, Elizabeth. *A Thousand Sisters: The heroic Airwomen of the Soviet Union in World War II*. New York: Balzer & Bray, 2019.

Weintraub, Beverly. *Wings of Gold: The First Women Naval Aviators*. Guilford CT: Lyons Press, 2021.

Weitekamp, Margaret A. *Right Stuff, Wrong Sex: America's First Women in Space Program*. Baltimore, MD: The Johns Hopkins University Press, 2005.

Welch, Rosanne. *Encyclopedia of Women in Aviation and Space*. Santa Barbara CA: ABC-CLIO, Inc., 1998.

Williams, Vera S. *WASPs: Women Airforce Service Pilots of World War II*. London: Motorbooks International, 1994.

Winegarten, Debra L. *Katherine Stinson: the Flying Schoolgirl*. Fort Worth, TX: Eakin Press, 2000.

Wright, Marsha J. *Maggie Ray WWII Air Force Pilot*. St. Louis, MO: Pen & Publish, Inc., 2007.

Wright, Sharon. *Balloonomania Belles: Daredevil Divas Who Took to the Sky*. Barnsley, England: Pen and Sword, 2018.

York, Beth Ruggiero. *Flying Alone: A Memoir*. Beth Ruggiero York Publisher, 2019.

(Picasa Microsoft photo library)

Films/Documentaries about Trailblazers

Pancho Barnes, an entertaining full-length television movie. Valerie Bertinelli portrays Florence "Pancho" Barnes. Born in 1901, she was a terrific aviator, setting and breaking world aviation records. Barnes was a founding member of Hollywood's first stunt pilots' union. She led a colorful life in the air and on the ground.

Fly Like a Girl directed by Katie McEntire Wiatt won a number of awards. Inspiring and educational about aviation's female pilots which encourages young girls to fly. Family-friendly and interesting now available on many video platforms. https://www.flylikeagirl.film/

Right footed is an award-winning documentary about Jessica Cox. Her inspiring life story is shared in a family-friendly format. Born without arms. Jessica Cox continues to live life with courage and tenacity.

Silver Wings Flying Dreams: The Complete Story of the Women Airforce Service Pilots is an interesting documentary by Bill Suchy Productions, LLC. Archival footage and contemporary interviews with World War II WASP in this award-winning and education film https://www.silverwings-flyingdreams.com/

She Wore Silver Wings, the true story of WWII ferrying pilot, Jean Landis, is informative. Also, the earlier PBS *American Experience Fly Girls* episode document true stories of our Women Airforce Service Pilots.

Skydancers is a television documentary about women aerobatic pilots which introduces viewers to dedicated sky women at the 27th World Aerobatic Championship.

Movies and documentaries about Amelia Earhart are abundant. Here are a few: PBS American Experience produced a well-researched documentary titled, *Amelia Earhart. Earhart's Electra: Eyewitness Account of What Happened to Amelia Earhart's Plane* and another, *The Mysteries of Amelia Earhart* are documentary-styled productions. The television film, *Finding Amelia Earhart: Mystery Solved?* and *The Final*

Hours: Amelia Earhart's Last Flight are other examples of how fascinating the life and disappearance of the world famous pilot is. In 2010, *The Extraordinary Life of Amelia Earhart* documentary was released. In 2009, Hilary Swank as Amelia hit television screens. Entertaining, it is worth enjoying the story of a woman who changed aviation forever. The 1994, Diane Keaton portrayed the legend in *Amelia Earhart: The Final Flight.*

Other documentary films are: Award-winning Heather Taylor's *Breaking through the Clouds* about the 1929 Air Derby. *Beyond the Powder: The Legacy of the First Women's Cross-County Air Race* documentary by Kara Martinelli White which is also packed with archival footage and important history.

Another documentary, *Pearl Carter Scott: On Top of the World*, and the earlier award-winning *Pearl The Movie-Pearl Carter Scott, the Youngest Pilot in History,* tell the incredible story of Chickasaw tribe member, Eula "Pearl" Carter Scott. Pearl was taught how to fly by the aviation legend, Wiley Post. On September 12, 1929, Pearl flew solo at age 13, making her our youngest Native American female pilot.

Another popular film is *Hidden Figures* about the talented Black women scientists of NASA. This gripping biographical drama chronicles their important contributions. Highly-acclaimed, earning three Academy Award nominations, this movie shared the lives of space engineer, Mary Jackson, mathematician, Katherine Johnson, and their NASA supervisor, Dorothy Vaughan. Their overlooked stories are important in understanding the many contributions of women in our race for space.

Netflix recently produced *Mercury 13* about the female volunteers who participated in tests similar to the male NASA Mercury 7 astronauts. NASA recently partnered with Public Broadcast System to produce episodes in the popular *Not Done: Women Remaking America* documentary series, "Women in Space" which touches on the Mercury 13 herstory with the major focus on the 1978 NASA astronaut class with six women.

Another episode in this PBS series features actress, Nichelle Nichols, who portrayed the strong Star Trek Enterprise Communications Officer in that popular television series. She served as a role model for many young Black women. Later, Nichols represented NASA around the county as a recruiter for the astronaut program and promoter of STEM education and careers.

NASA has a number of You Tube videos in their series *Aspire to Inspire* about the many contributions and opportunities for women at the National Aeronautics and Space Administration.

"If you don't face your fears, the only thing you'll ever see is what's in your comfort zone," NASA Astronaut, Anne McClain. (Photo Courtesy of NASA)

Online Resources & Organizations

Aircraft Owners & Pilots Association (AOPA) https://www.aopa.org/
Balloon Federation of America https://www.bfa.net/
Canadian Women in Aviation-CWIA https://www.cwia.ca/
Experimental Aircraft Association (EAA) Women Soar Society
　　https://www.eaawomensoarsociety.org/
Female Aviators Sticking Together-(F.A.S.T)
　　https://fastpilots.org/women-pilots/
Institute for Women of Aviation Worldwide (iWOAW)
　　https://www.iwoaw.org/
International Society of Women Airline Pilots (ISA+21)
　　https://isa21.org/
International Women's Air & Space Museum https://iwasm.org/
Latino Pilots Association https://www.latinopilot.org/
NASA-National Aeronautics and Space Administration Aspire to
　　Inspire https://women.nasa.gov
National Aviation Hall of Fame https://www.nationalaviation.org/
National Coalition for Aviation and Space Education (NCASE)
　　http://www.aviationeducation.org/
National Gay Pilots Association https://www.ngpa.org/
Ninety-Nines International Organization of Women Pilots
　　https://www.ninety-nines.org/
Organization of Black Aerospace Professionals https://obap.org/
Professional Asian Pilots Association https://www.asianpilots.org/
Sisters of the Skies (SOS) https://www.sistersoftheskies.org
The Amelia Earhart Memorial Scholarships & Awards
https://www.ninety-nines.org/scholarships.htm
Whirly-Girls-International Women Helicopter Pilots
　　https://whirlygirls.org/
Women in Aerospace (WIA) https://www.womeninaerospace.org/
Women in Aviation International (WAI) http://www.women-in-
　　aviation.com/Organizations/
Women Military Aviators https://www.womenmilitaryaviators.com/

Women Rock Wings http://womenrockwings.com
Women's Skydiving Network
   https://www.womensskydivingnetwork.org/
Women's Soaring Pilots Association https://womensoaring.org/
Women Who Drone https://www.womenwhodrone.co/

National Aviation Day is celebrated every August 19. (NASA Poster)

INDEX

ABOUT THE AUTHOR

In 1982, Dr. Penny Rafferty Hamilton began her newspaper and photography career. She continues to publish in many newspapers and periodicals on aviation and women's history topics. She has earned numerous national and state business, aviation, and writing awards, including recognition from the U.S. Small Business Administration, Federal Aviation Administration, National Association of State Aviation Officials, and Colorado Authors' League. She is a Laureate of the Colorado Aviation, Colorado Women's, and Colorado Authors' Halls of Fame. She is a graduate of Temple University, Columbia College (Distinguished Alumna Award Winner), and the University of Nebraska (Alumni Achievement Award Winner).

Hamilton is an active member of many aviation and writers organizations. As a General Aviation pilot, she co-holds a 1992 World's Aviation Speed Record set with her husband, William. With advanced degrees and extensive journalism experience, she is a prolific writer with a passion for promoting women and aviation history.

Other books by Penny Rafferty Hamilton, Ph.D.

Inspiring Words for Sky and Space Women: Advice from Historic and Contemporary Trailblazers (2020)

America's Amazing Airports: Connecting Communities to the World (2019)

A to Z: Your Grand County History Alphabet (2017)

Absent Aviators: Gender Issues in Aviation (chapter contributor) (2014, paperback 2020)

Around Granby::Arcadia Publishing Images of America (2013)

Granby, Then & Now: 1905-2005 (2005)

Country Woman's Christmas 2011 (contributor)
Capture My Colorado (contributor, 2008)

Visit her websites at:

http://www.PennyHamilton.com
http://www.TeachingWomentoFly.com

Dressed in an historic purple satin flying suit, aviator and author, Penny Rafferty Hamilton, pays homage to America's first licensed woman pilot, Harriet Quimby. (Photo Colorado Women's Hall of Fame/Kit Williams)

Made in the USA
Columbia, SC
01 November 2021